David Bottoms

ALSO BY WILLIAM WALSH
AND FROM MCFARLAND

*Speak So I Shall Know Thee:
Interviews with Southern Writers* (1990)

David Bottoms

Critical Essays and Interviews

Edited by WILLIAM WALSH

McFarland & Company, Inc., Publishers
Jefferson, North Carolina, and London

LIBRARY OF CONGRESS CATALOGUING-IN-PUBLICATION DATA

David Bottoms : critical essays and interviews / edited by William Walsh.
   p.   cm.
Includes bibliographical references and index.

ISBN 978-0-7864-4729-9
softcover : 50# alkaline paper ∞

1. Bottoms, David — Criticism and interpretation.   I. Walsh, William J., 1961–
PS3552.O819Z57   2010
811'.54 — dc22   2010030460

British Library cataloguing data are available

©2010 William Walsh. All rights reserved

No part of this book may be reproduced or transmitted in any form or by any means, electronic or mechanical, including photocopying or recording, or by any information storage and retrieval system, without permission in writing from the publisher.

Front cover: *The General Store, 1880* by Eduardo del Masso

Manufactured in the United States of America

McFarland & Company, Inc., Publishers
 Box 611, Jefferson, North Carolina 28640
  www.mcfarlandpub.com

... it's odd what the memory smuggles into the afterlife —
pocket charms against oblivion...
—"Easter Shoes Epistle"

Acknowledgments

Baker, David: "Signs from My Fathers." Parts of this essay originally appeared in *The Kenyon Review* and *The New England Review*. Reprinted with permission.

Bottoms, David: *Armored Hearts: Selected and New Poems*. ©1995 by Copper Canyon Press. Reprinted with permission. *In a U-Haul North of Damascus*. ©1983 by David Bottoms, originally published by William Morrow & Co. Reprinted with permission of the author. *Shooting Rats at the Bibb County Dump*. ©1980 by David Bottoms, originally published by William Morrow & Co. Reprinted with permission of the author. *Under the Vulture Tree*. ©1987 by David Bottoms, originally published by Quill/William Morrow & Co. Reprinted with permission of the author. *Vagrant Grace*. ©1999 by Copper Canyon Press. Reprinted with permission. *Waltzing Through the Endtime*. ©2004 by Copper Canyon Press. Reprinted with permission. *Easter Weekend*. ©1990 by David Bottoms. Reprinted with permission of Maria Carvainis Agency, Inc. All rights reserved.

Byrne, Edward: Revised and expanded from "The Rolling Circle: Memory and Maturity." *Valparaiso Poetry Review*, vol. 1, no. 2 (Spring/Summer 2000). Reprinted with permission.

Chappell, Fred: "David Bottoms and the Evolution of the GOB Aesthetic." First published in the *Sewanee Review*, vol. 117, no. 4 Fall 2009. Reprinted with permission of the editor and the author.

Friman, Alice, and Marshall Bruce Gentry: "Fishing from the Poetry Boat: A Conversation with David Bottoms." *The Southern Quarterly* 37, 3/4 (Spring/Summer 1999): 93–105. Reprinted with permission.

Hill, Jane: "To Own My Father's Name: Not Hiding the Masculine." Originally titled "To Own My Father's Name: Not Hiding the Masculine in the Poems of David Bottoms" and published in *Studies in the Literacy Imagination* 35.1 (Spring 2002): 25–59. Used by permission.

Hill, Robert W.: "Warbling with TV in the Background: David Bottoms in the Suburbs." *The Southern Quarterly* 37, 3/4 (Spring/Summer 1999): 80–84. © 1999 by The University of Southern Mississippi. Reprinted with permission.

Russ, Don: "'Up Toward Light': Resurrection, Transfiguration, Metamorphosis, and Evolution in David Bottoms' *Armored Hearts*." *The Southern Quarterly* 37, 3/4 (Spring/Summer 1999): 67–72. © 1999 by The University of Southern Mississippi. Reprinted with permission.

Suarez, Ernest: "Amazing Grace: The Aesthetics of a Spiritual Quest." Originally titled "A Deceptive Simplicity: The Poetry of David Bottoms." *The Southern Quarterly* 37, 3/4 (Spring/Summer 1999): 73–79. © 1999 by The University of Southern Mississippi. Reprinted with permission. "The Onion's Dark Core." Originally titled "David Bottoms" and published in *Southbound: Interviews with Southern Poets*, by Ernest Suarez. © 1999 by the University of Missouri Press. Reprinted with permission.

Walsh, William: "Logic of the Original Dream." Originally printed in *Five Points: A Journal of Art and Literature*.

Table of Contents

Acknowledgments — vi

Editor's Note — 1

Introduction: "At the Still Point"
W. A. SESSIONS — 7

1. The Vigilant Words of David Bottoms
   DAVE SMITH — 11

2. The Evolution of the GOB Aesthetic
   FRED CHAPPELL — 27

3. Amazing Grace: The Aesthetics of a Spiritual Quest
   ERNEST SUAREZ — 45

4. Fishing from the Poetry Boat: A Conversation
   ALICE FRIMAN *and* MARSHALL BRUCE GENTRY — 57

5. "If It Touches Us, It Touches Us": The White Southern Male Struggle with Race
   JANE HILL — 71

6. Warbling with TV in the Background
   ROBERT W. HILL — 87

7. A Real Mix: Rebirth and Gender in *Easter Weekend*
   MARSHALL BRUCE GENTRY — 94

8. Signs from My Fathers
   DAVID BAKER — 106

9. The Logic of the Original Dream
   WILLIAM WALSH — 120

10. The Rolling Circle: Memory and Maturity
    EDWARD BYRNE — 136

11. *Searching for the Kingdom of Heaven*: A Spiritual Journey
    MICHAEL SOWDER — 155

12. "Up Toward Light": Resurrection, Transfiguration, Metamorphosis, and Evolution in *Armored Hearts*
    DON RUSS — 176

13. The Onion's Dark Core
    ERNEST SUAREZ — 187

14. To Own My Father's Name: Not Hiding the Masculine
    JANE HILL — 204

15. Grueling Miracle: Faith in Middle Age
    LAURENCE LIEBERMAN — 240

Contributors — 269

Index — 273

Editor's Note

When *Waltzing Through the Endtime* was published in 2004, I was absolutely fascinated by David Bottoms' sixth collection of poems — it resonated unlike any collection I had read in years. By this time I had known Bottoms for twenty years and had read each of his books dozens of times, but over the course of several months, I read *Endtime* over and over, absorbing the expanded narrative, admiring the contemplative nature of the speaker on subjects such as religion, society, family, and memory. I began to dissect the poems as studiously as I had done in graduate school with the collected poems of such poets as Theodore Roethke and Richard Hugo, throwing myself into the text on multiple levels of poetic discourse. I was simply captivated by *Waltzing Through the Endtime*. This prompted a careful, scholarly reading once again of all of Bottoms' work from beginning to end, and thus began the idea, the long contemplation, of writing an essay to discuss the entire collection, desiring to express my thoughts about this compilation of poems, much in the vein of Laurence Lieberman with a 50- to 60-page tome or even a shorter Dana Gioia-esque essay; however, I soon realized that I could not.

First, the essay is not my stage — and, yes, I have written many essays over the years — but it is not the arena where I feel most comfortable. Second, and most importantly, I realized that, as I attempted to gather my thoughts, I suffered (if that is the right diagnosis) from a student/teacher relationship whereby I was muted by my relationship with Bottoms to such a degree that I was unable to clearly convey my thoughts regarding his poetry. Complimentary comments were even difficult to convey. I don't know if this happens to other poets, but for me, writing about Bottoms' work was troublesome — I had interpretations but it was difficult to be critical even in a praiseworthy manner.

Now, at this writing I've known David Bottoms for more than 25 years. I cut my teeth on his poetry and grew up, poetically, under his influence, reading his poems and novels, carefully studying the poets in the *The Morrow Anthology of Younger American Poets* (co-edited by Bottoms and Dave Smith), and continuing through an entire catalog of Southern writers, past and present, including James Dickey, Robert Penn Warren, Charles Wright, Betty Adcock, Fred Chappell, a long list indeed. I discovered Bottoms and the narrative poem the same way he discovered the narrative many years ago via James Seay's poetry, by accident. As an undergraduate, and like many students, a few student-friends and I were stumbling around Georgia State University's campus trying to jump on the writing train, but having no idea how to *become* poets. We wrote on our own, as lonely and isolated as one can be, having no understanding of the poetry machine that awaited us out in the world away from academia. But then I heard by what now seems like backroom banter, rumors almost, that there was a *real* poet on the faculty at GSU, not a scholar who wrote poems, but someone in the trenches who had won an award. Up until this time, I had met only one *writer* in my life, Harlan Ellison (known for his fiction and non-fiction). I realized that I needed to study with a *real* poet. I went to drop-add and dropped my entire schedule for the next semester and quickly arranged everything around Bottoms' class, even going so far as to lie to the registrar's office about having taken the needed prerequisites. And so, in 1984 I had my first poetry workshop with David Bottoms, and there I was sitting and listening, intimidated, not by Bottoms, but by the seemingly accomplished undergrad students who knew and understood more about writing poetry than I did. But there was hope that I could write a poem.

 In one of my first workshops, Bottoms opened up my poem like a heart surgeon, not with any meanness, just as an exercise to slice through the cancerous rubble. Essentially he said, "This does not work at all; however, I like the first line": 'I remember when you soaked corn seeds in a coffee can / and I walked with you through the till of the garden.'" He liked the imagery and the texture of the language. That's all I needed from him to believe I could write. I threw out the entire poem except that one line. For years I have repeated that line in my head. Then driving down the road, eighteen years later, and having repeated that one line a million times, the entire poem came to me. I drove home and wrote down the poem verbatim. In reality, I'd been working on that poem in my head for eighteen years because David Bottoms liked one line! It was aptly titled, "Germination." Bottoms' influence has followed me since. There I was twenty-five years ago sitting in his workshop trying to understand the DHM (deep hidden meaning he insisted we search for) and other poetic nuances he felt important to introduce to us — all those years ago, I was literally the most unlikely vehicle of grace to edit a book on his poetry.

Now, all these years later, what was I to do with my inability to adequately write an essay? I turned to my strength — the interview.

I have, over the years, interviewed hundreds of writers, including Nobel laureates Czeslaw Milosz and Joseph Brodsky, Fred Chappell, James Dickey, Ariel Dorfman, Rita Dove, and A.R. Ammons, as well as Bottoms in 1985 and 1986. This is the arena where I am most comfortable; hence, in 2004, I decided to interview Bottoms as a substitute for any essay I might have written. We met twice at his office at Georgia State University in August and November. An interesting and little known fact: it takes more effort to research and prepare for an interview than for an essay. One must be prepared to discuss all aspects of a book or a writer's life at a moment's notice without the luxury of time to gather and prepare one's thoughts as when writing and editing an essay. An interview can (and always does) navigate corridors you do not know exist; as W.H. Auden's speaker says in "As I Walked Out One Evening," "And the crack in the tea-cup opens / A lane to the land of the dead." An interviewer needs to be prepared for that journey, wherever it leads. Subsequently, the interview was published in *Five Points* in the tenth anniversary issue.

In 2008, I still had the urge to write an essay on *Waltzing Through the Endtime*. It was burning inside as though the embers of scholarship were reigniting every few weeks. However, I simply could not wrap my arms around what I wanted to say. Then one early morning while driving to the store, it dawned on me — *There was no way on earth I was ever going to write the kind of essay I wanted to write. It simply was not going to happen.* But it dawned on me soon after that I could edit a collection of essays and accomplish the same result. It was liberating. Immediately I knew what to do and how to accomplish this goal, so upon my return home, I drew up a tentative list of writers I would query. With a few telephone calls to some friends for encouragement, I was well on my way.

Although the current work primarily discusses Bottoms' poetry, I have included one essay regarding his fiction. Marshall Bruce Gentry discusses *Easter Weekend* and the issues of gender and rebirth, subjects prevalent in Bottoms' poetry. And of course the ideas of gender, masculinity, manhood, loss, rebirth are discussed in the poetry essays. Although Bottoms' fiction is not necessarily as comfortable a platform for him as his poetry, there are many similarities in regard to theme, characters, and plot running through the fiction and poetry. Has anyone ever noticed that Billy Parker, the main character in *Any Cold Jordan* (who I believe is Bottoms' alter ego — at least the argument can be made), is also mentioned in several of his poems? I like the idea of Bottoms' fiction and poetry feeding off and borrowing from each other, weaving in and out, and by taking a close look at *Easter Weekend*, we will also have a clearer understanding of the gender/rebirth in his poetry, a rebirth that expands with each new book under a different subject, be it waitresses with beehive hairdos, vultures roosting, or a father worried about his sick daughter.

What I have discovered as the editor of this collection is the seminal point in Bottoms' career as viewed by many critics, not just myself: it occurs in *Vagrant Grace* in "Country Store and Moment of Grace." Several writers discuss this poem, bringing to this book some similar thoughts, yet still profoundly different in their assessment. "Country Store" is the transitional point for Bottoms' poetic satori from a young up-and-coming highly competent poet (middle-aged at this point) to a mature poet solidifying himself as one of the finest voices of his generation. Where other poets of his generation have moved beyond the realm of being simply highly skilled poets, Bottoms has elevated himself into a class reserved for only a few. I suspect, as his growth continues, the next level for him will be among the elite of American letters, with Roethke, Warren, Wright, Hugo, Moore, Bishop, and others inspiring with such reverence. "Country Store" was the turning point in his career. Almost twenty pages in length, it is the prelude to the entire collection, *Waltzing Through the Endtime*. Upon reviewing my early notes from 2004 when I began to compare *Waltzing Through the Endtime* with *Vagrant Grace*, I wrote in the margins of "Country Store" the following:

> This is the prelude to "Endtime" and the idea about memory, especially with the long narrative structure.... This is truly the beginning of his structural change, as well as thematically with the idea of memory playing into religion and the after-life.

I believe, after reading the essays from these writers included in this book, I was spot-on. Yet, what good does that do if I cannot convey my thoughts to others? Hence, this collection of essays is a substitute for my own essay. And, of course, I know I could never have written as eloquently on Bottoms as the writers contained within these pages have done. With this in mind, I sought out those writers I knew to have a comprehensive knowledge of his work. I have assembled what I believe to be some of the finest writers in the country and I am pleased that they were willing to submit essays and interviews, bringing forth the first book on one of the finest poets of his generation.

In closing, I wish to thank the publishers for granting permission to reprint the material within (see page vi); my good friend John Williams for his assistance; and all the writers who contributed to this book.

William Walsh

Introduction: "At the Still Point"
W. A. SESSIONS

In the first of his Four Quartets, "Burnt Norton," T. S. Eliot has a line that sets up for Eliot the inherent contradiction of human reality: "At the still point of the turning world." As contradictory as it may seem to aficionados of the art of David Bottoms, I see Eliot's phrase as a way to understand that art. Finding in his novels and in his lyrics that "still point" in tension with a very "turning world," a reader can discover a source for Bottom's achievement: his recurring power of language and bullet-eye on the world around him with its special narratives and fictions, which he is constantly translating. In that antithesis, at its best in Bottoms' art, nothing is lost.

Driving down I-75 to teach in the heart of a city with the tenth largest economy and just about the worst traffic in the United States, Bottoms has always had to survive a daily world in order to find that "still point": negotiate departmental and university politics, endure as a father to a teenager, teach varying levels of students (with their phenomenal lack of literacy), buy groceries, pay bills, and deal with an aging body, to name the inevitable few. Every poet or writer has always had to have such courage in finding that "point" — and in no surprise, from Baudelaire to Faulkner, being "juiced" can be a help. For Bottoms, the entry into his "still point" appears to have been simpler. Singing and storytelling (and, for that matter, preaching) have been old Southern ways of surviving a very "turning world" in the late 20th century. For poets on I-75, these appear to be still functioning, although with new "turns" in the first decade of a new century that itself does not appear to be projecting Miranda's "brave new world."

Bottoms is, in fact, in a noble Southern tradition of poets and fiction-makers and artists who have remained in the South as it has made some very unattractive and even irrational turns. They have survived even the contemporary technological violence Flannery O'Connor had predicted — the remaking of the human being — and have recorded their own "still points" on the cultural battlefields: Faulkner, Welty, O'Connor, Dickey, all used the specific Southern landscapes to make universal landscapes. As a result, they have survived even themselves.

Eliot's line is a long way from the lavish Romantic landscapes of James Dickey, Bottoms' acknowledged master. Dickey deeply resented the Eliot influence, especially at Vanderbilt, where, after his war experience and earlier his football prowess (including at the high school he and Flannery O'Connor attended at the same time), the young poet felt humiliated. In a special irony, Dickey's last and very beautiful poem "Entering Scott's Night," and its riveting first line "Interweaving," develops a meditation not at all different from Eliot's contemplation that marks the Four Quartets.

Both deal with the presence of death — and more important, where memory leads, especially in the dying Dickey of 1996, beyond death. Memory opens imaginative forms of survival that are themselves continuing forms of life. Nothing explains better Dickey's radiant structure in "Entering Scott's Night" than Eliot's dialectic of two worlds. Using language deliberately echoing a medieval visionary poem (*Piers Plowman*), Dickey writes the greatest vision in the 20th century of the old human dream of purgatory — a space of preparation, penance, and ultimate transfiguration. As I have written elsewhere, Dickey's last poem offers an exquisite representation of what dying human beings, even young women and young men, think about.

"Entering Scott's Night" provides this perception of Bottoms' "still point" in its dialogue with time, and the way I see David Bottoms' whole canon. There is, in fact, a direct linguistic connection to Eliot and Bottoms amid Dickey's own self-perception in his own poem, as the speaker wanders like a ghost among ghosts dancing the Charleston (as his own parents did in the Buckhead of the 1920s, its Coca-Cola wealth that the scene recalls). The lines that evoke Eliot's are toward the end of the poem, just before the powerful coda: "It is Scott's / Moving in two times, among us / As we stand in fountain-raining, imperiled / In celebrant stillness" and then Dickey's final image of the "shadow of a woman / On serpent stone totally dancing."

In almost all of Bottoms' successful lyrics and narratives, what dominates is this same tension of "Moving in two times" and "celebrant stillness." For me, the best example reveals itself in Bottoms' memory-lyric,

"The Boy Shepherd's Simile." In his novels occur such moments, as in the actual moving into death in the final monologue in *Any Cold Jordan* and in the mad capering of *Easter Weekend* in an O'Connor moral landscape, a narrative that circles and circles the actual Rose Hill Cemetery. It is hardly necessary to point out in Bottoms' lyrics such concatenation of time and the still imaginative moment that subsumes time. These moments rise from U-Hauls, fishing boats, trees with vultures, and baseball bats to a kind of landscape beyond time but not quite eternity of any kind.

That larger space beyond time accessible to memory and the forms of language defines the reality of "The Boy Shepherd's Simile." It is the concern in this poem with formal elements of his lyric that distinguish this "still point" from others. The title announces it: the lyric operates on the fulcrum of a simile, a formal figure of speech using like or as to relate one world to another. The Greeks first codified these figures of speech to heighten the representation of their language and its own "still points" first in oratory and then in lyrics and drama. The point for the Greeks was not "feelings" or outburst per se — Wordsworth's Romantic "spontaneous overflow" — but the joyful structuring of these feelings into a palpable and accessible form that was both personal and universal. Bottoms' poem abounds in such formal concerns.

Bottoms begins his first stanza with a shocking reversal of common grammar. The first sentence (and sequence) has verbs that are intransitive but still very active and possessive. In common usage, these verbs do not take predicate adjectives, as here. "Wind rose cold under our robes, and straw blew loose / from the stable roof." In order to build the force of his verbs, Bottoms omits any modifier for the two nouns (no "the" that might be expected). The reversal gives power to "cold" — the crucial last line of the lyric — and its assonance with "robes" emphasizes the naked bodies underneath. The open vowels of "straw" and "blew" build to the liquid assonance and abrupt "st-"alliteration of "stable roof," the final word emphasizing the slant rhyme that ends the sequence.

Once the pattern of sounds are set, in the next sequence and four lines, Bottoms manipulates his lyric with the same formal musical devices: internal slant rhyme ("oak" and "goats"), the force and placement of the two key past participles ("tied" and "trucked"), and an interesting narrative device leading to the image that ends the stanza. The poet has begun with the boy-speaker identified as "We" and the "We" leads to what a boy would notice: "the gray dog shaking with age / and weather." The dog is "gray" in the "black air" and "cold" but unlike the boy, "shaking with age" as the poet-speaker may be. The next stanza builds on the artificiality of the pageant "scene": star with its electric light in the "bleached night," an outright metaphor, and then two brilliant uses of metonomy (the part for the whole, best known for the boy Bottoms in "Give us this day our daily bread" in the Lord's Prayer he early memorized): "overcoats" for people; "coat of black ice" for "the street."

Then the third stanza and the climax of the poem, where the narrator — the "We" already identified — declares his skepticism and disbelief. The boy shepherd knows what's "wrapped in the straw / and the ragged sheet" is a fake: "Mary Sosebee's Christmas doll of a year ago." Then in the midst of "flashbulbs" contrasted to the enchanting but fake "choir of angels" singing from the "risers" on "the wide front lawn / of the First Baptist Church," the boy for whom "believing was an easy thing" comes to a decision. He has his "still point" in the midst of his "turning world" from "shivering" dog to "flashbulb."

The boy could never lie that the art or artifice around him is natural truth — anything real. How can he resolve the boy's moment of nihilism and terrible loneliness without myth and its truth that can only be seen as a lie? The epiphany that follows, as powerful as in James Joyce's "Araby," forms the heart of the lyric. What Bottoms' boy knows and, in a far truer sense, sees, is that Mary Sosebee's doll "was like a child, a king who lived in the stories we were told." The imagination opened up by the "like" in the text — with its inevitable mixture with human myth and even history itself — provides living forms of survival for the human being: "who lived in the stories we were told."

Having a "story" where people and kings lived, the boy in the small Georgia town arms himself with his boy's "simile." He arrives "at the still point of the turning world." So the last lines of the lyric: "For this we shivered in adoration. We bore the cold." The "still point" — opened up by the "like" — has returned the speaker-man and the remembered boy-shepherd much more alive to their "turning world." They are ready to bear its "cold."

The Vigilant Words of David Bottoms
Dave Smith

Poetry is about identity. It assembles and references memory's matter. That this is so, the highly personal poetry of the 20th century makes perfectly obvious in the individual case, yet the collective memory of a people, whether regional or larger, expressing itself in history, legend, myth, type, even gossip, the totality of which may be loosely called culture, has an inevitable, if shadowy, presence in the work of any poet. The poetry of Seamus Heaney, for example, cannot be fully felt apart from its binding-up in the pervasive violence of the Irish experience any more than apart from the poet's obsessive tasting of Irish and English words, his personal existence in two languages. This issue of identity arises in T.S. Eliot's famous essay "Tradition and the Individual Talent" where Eliot considers the value of lineage, or culture, in a poet's development, a matter of great interest to the southern poet Allen Tate. Lineage, identity, and the permanent presence of nature are the central figurations in the eight books of poetry published by David Bottoms.

Tate argued that as late as the early part of the 20th century there was no literary culture in the American South. He could not point to the greatness of Faulkner or Welty, who did not yet possess public stature, nor to any lineage of poets whose accomplishment loomed as goal or obstacle. He was not unaware poets had existed in the South, even that they had here and there a sense of regional identity, but Tate, a young poet keen to the grandeur of internationally reputed Eliot, could see no cousin from Poe to Lanier as anything more than sketchy. Mr. Eliot had argued a new poet effects both past and future equally, altering perspective and, thus, possibility both ways. Mr. Tate was nagged by uncertainty that a regional poetry could matter without support of a lineage, and this may be said to be more or less the anxiety of any poet. Do my subjects, my interests, he asks, have any value beyond the limits of my kind? Perhaps for the poet emerging in the still vexatious southern arena, the pinch has seemed more intense and sustained. Bent or broken by this weight, numbers of poets from the South have fled, literally and metaphorically, in pursuit of what Tate called a culture. Such flights are commonly away from something even as they are toward something, and for poets both ends are manifested in the words *form* and *structure*, whose action is identity. Charles Wright, a poet important especially in the late work of David Bottoms, writes in "Sitting at Dusk in the Backyard After the Mondrian Retrospective," "Form imposes, structure allows —/ the slow destruction of form / So as to bring it back resheveled, reorganized, / Is the hard heart of the enterprise."

A native of Canton, Georgia, a man who has left the confines of his hometown on few occasions, and for no very long periods, David Bottoms is a third generation descendent of the poets Tate was at pains to generate, the so-called Vanderbilt Fugitives, or Agrarians. All of the commonly accepted signatures of southern style, in anecdotal matter and narrative structure, in attitude and vision, though I do not bother to adduce them as I think them well enough known, appear abundantly in Bottoms' poems. Doubtless, the source is somewhat environmental and equally so the legacy of those southern moderns. Even more specifically Bottoms looked to the local boy, James Lafayette Dickey. The second generation southern poets included Fred Chappell, Randall Jarrell, Donald Justice, Reynolds Price, Eleanor Ross Taylor, Miller Williams, Charles Wright, and others, but the giant seemed to be Dickey, a writer who would show David Bottoms it was possible to take leave of his southern subjects even as they remained the literal and transformative heart of his imagination.

Some, in the South, when sipping toddies, remark what a hole has been left among us by the death of Dickey, an absence that turned our world much duller, much less inspiring. Why did Dickey seem so compelling to Betty Adcock, to me, to David Bottoms? Anointed by Peter Davison in his 1965 essay in *The Atlantic Monthly* as the equal of poetry's scion Robert Lowell, and beknighted by frequent appearances in *The New Yorker*, Dickey said he wanted to write a poetry of "country surrealism." Whatever he meant by that, and it was not Donald Justice's delicate application of verse patterns, he pursued big narratives as volatile and immediate as his poetry readings. He intended to convince us he was the American poet born to lead us where no poets had yet gone, and he was equally determined to confuse the road taken with forays into the under-looked-at folk and places of the country, with tactics and strategies that tugged his lines as if they were made from stretch fabric, all of it shaping possible identities.

Who the southern man is/was has been a gritty head problem since Faulkner's Quenton at Harvard, and the southern poet was, well, more or less a derivative Mr. Eliot in bow tie. But after the big clash of World War II, and GI-Bill enfranchisement, all were invited to the literary dance where it was soon obvious some would quickly bag the red-neck boogie in favor of the dressage of verse. Justice and Miller Williams did that; James Applewhite and Kelly Cherry have followed suit. The early poems of Charles Wright show a European and Asian influence commingled with a verse shadow. But for Wright, as for James Dickey, two very different poets in whom the principle of amplitude is utterly common, the fundamental subject of poetry, identity, required passage through an evolving structure capable of looking at the self's experiences that are as strange as they may be familiar.

Dickey liked moving from one identity to another, lying as much as drawing on personal experience. I do not think he distinguished much, or thought the distinction mattered much, between what he did and what he imagined doing. His narrative skill, exuberant, colorful, fast-paced, and increasingly cinematic was based on a remarkable descriptive talent that united with a fine sense of cadence built of short, phrase-based lines. He could slow down or speed up a reader at will and his control of pace, with his unusually visual imagination, drove readers into and out of experience surprising in its mythical and personal resonance. I am thinking of fox hunters, life guards, quilt makers, combat fliers, voyeurs, stewardesses falling from airplanes, and even more particularly poems employing what H.L. Weatherby called "the way of exchange" wherein Dickey's narrator and an animal enacted (seriously, one might say) exchanges of being. These stories look, now, more ordinary than I once thought them and it is startling to see how much they are stubbornly, strangely written, as if he had always been pursuing language, not idea. He came to places, to anecdotes and their people only to find in that idiom of country surrealism, or angularity that opens perception, they were all him in disguise. Yet the one thing which never changes in Dickey's poem is the world of nature, fecund, joyful, supportive, occasionally dangerous, ever the emblem of meaning. If, as he writes in "The Lupanar at Pompeii," it is true that "We can never really tell/ Whether nature condemns us or loves us...," it is to nature's place he goes nevertheless to test a self, to make a durable identity.

Given adequate allowances, I think we may say Dickey's is a pastoral poetry. The pastoral poem is often defined by the presence of praise for natural phenomena and the protest of abuse of nature by the various encroachments upon and diminutions of the "wildness" once commonly around us, standing in that function as the core of an Agrarian argument against displacement of stewardship that is, in effect, a violation of a religious, or ordained, order. Put that way, the pastoral is also the poem Charles Wright has been writing for the last several decades. No good reader, however, would confuse Dickey's dramatic perambulations with Wright's brooding, cerebral, inner-dramatizing narration of poems that read more like Socratic dialogues, self-interviews, and lectures, all of them occasions which tersely establish by something like water colorist efficiency a limed landscape that is always occasion for the upleap of an idea, with a subsequent return to the trout-cool water, then yet another spring of the mind. With Dickey one feels play in the fields and wilds is a sensuous activity from which at ephanic moments comes an ancillary insight; with Wright one feels the flow of insight rides along like a vacuuming thought which periodically touches ground or tree or fluttering thing. Wright says *Description's an element, like air or water.* One of the pleasures in Wright is the painterly vista he describes in these last lines from *Black Zodiac's* "Disjecta Membra," "I think of landscape incessantly, / mountains and rivers, lost lakes / Where sunsets festoon and override, / The scald of summer wheat fields, light-licked and poppy-smeared. / Sunlight surrounds me and winter birds/ doodle and peck in the dead grass."

What dominates Wright is the hieratic, spuming, prophetic, often epigrammatic voice of an ordinary man, and Wright is always at pains to show he is one of us, if given to sophisticated thinking in which nature is text. At least he is the sort of ordinary man who *might* say "The unexamined life's no different from/the examined life" and "Destruction takes place so order might exist...." He is not so ordinary, perhaps, in the long Asian influence that survives in his tendency to think in koans — "Sacrifice is the cause of ruin./ The absence of sacrifice is the cause of ruin." But Charles Wright long ago understood that poetry whose only action is thought, even given the most intense hydraulics and roundabouts and switchbacks, all characteristic of his thinking, would bore the reader. Setting nature as Bible, like the rock that turns thought to white water rapids, Wright has made his poetry a continual weave of nature and pronouncement, a literal networking of consciousness. In "Lives of the Saints" he quotes Gertrude Stein as having advised writers to "face the facts" and Wright agrees, making his way that of

> Pretending there's nothing but description, hoping emotion shows;
> That's why description's there:
> The subject was never smoke,
>   there's always been a fire.

What the facts of our identity may be seemed text to Mr. Tate but the problem, he well knew, was the struggle of the religious imagination that deals in the visible as gateway to the invisible. David Bottoms has that kind of imagination and, consequently, his poems chronicle the struggle of the soul as much as the struggle of the ordinary bloke. Bottoms looked to Dickey to learn to understand and accept the strangeness of his local experience, to seek his own country surrealism, which Seamus Heaney, on his turf, has called "making strange." Wright seems to have shown Bottoms, in his later work and especially in *Waltzing Through the Endtime*, which I think is his most unified, coherent, symphonic of books, a way to push language toward inclusive form, a structure with a greater "carry," and there to find the resources for framing, if not answering, identity's questions. For David Bottoms, Dickey and Wright have represented, with an occasional nod to Robert Penn Warren, the possible ways to entertain and embody the world his poems travel in. This way was and mostly remains, for David Bottoms, the Agrarian pastoral, its complaint the entrapped and mortal soul which looks to nature for ontological answers. Like others, he started in abstraction and had to learn. His early poem "Coasting Toward Midnight at the Southeastern Fair" shows us where he began:

> We all want to break our orbits,
> float like a satellite gone wild in space,
> run the risk of disintegration.
> We want to take our lives in our hands
> and hurl them out among the stars.

Well, it *is* early work, void of real image, its statements bald, three parts cliché, and hardly compelling. It has the argument, however, that aligns Bottoms with those against the fettered, diminished life, his central theme. It doesn't offer an identity except in the glancing and metaphoric hero of spaceman, but it rejects a limp identity. Bottoms will learn to frame his concern in two ways: the poem as the rhetorical description of imprisonment in a static nature or as the celebration of the soul moving freely upon and embracing natural environment such as pond or lake. He took from Dickey immediacy of texture and detail; from Wright, later on, he took a persuasive pace of rhetoric, the work in a narrator's mouth of cumulative power. His control of such skills showed in "Under the Boathouse" where he describes a man who has dived into a lake and somehow impaled his hand on a fish hook whose line remains tethered to the murky bottom. Threatened by drowning the narrator says he:

> knew the shock of all
> things caught by the unknown
> as I kicked off the bottom like a frog,
> my limbs doing fearfully strange strokes,
> lungs collapsed in a confusion of bubbles,
> all air rising back to its element.

Here the poet lets image do the work of discourse, gaining both dramatic intensity and lucidity of lyric expression. Yet rhetoric surrounds and qualifies the simile of the hooked man and we are probably most won over by work we recognize as foredone, somewhat, by Dickey. He, as much as Bottoms, gives us that "shock of all/ things caught by the unknown...." One hears Dickey in gesture, line, rhythm, even in the adverb "fearfully," and almost certainly in the transformative resurrection image.

This sort of influence detection may be a pedant's delight, but more interesting is the approach to nature and the shifting poetic form that Bottoms begins to show. His drowning man is image of the trouble; here the pastoral voice is stopped by nature, gateway to redemption, and this invokes the problem of identity. In the historic male and rural vision of the South, a man fishes, hunts, knows the creatures, farms, acclimates himself to what is beyond the momentary and even the cyclical; he seeks to know and acknowledge what is permanent, a divinity more Calvinist than redemptive. This is core Agrarian thinking, evident today in Wendell Berry and Fred Chappell. But when the Agrarian man's sense of nature's meaning falls deficient or corrupt, the natural environment rises up as threatening as may be imagined. A nature truly alive is dangerous. The signs are everywhere in Bottoms from snakes to malevolent alligators to children falling through ice to disembodied voices, animal spirits, wasting soldiers, vermin, buzzards, drunks, evangelists, would-be angels, miasmic fog that blinds. I am reminded of Mr. Tate's remark that Edgar Allan Poe's world was dead and we are, living our own deadness, therefore his cousins. Tate did not mean the ordinary presence of algae-ridden dead zones or oil spills or benzene in our vegetables; he meant the world that lacks a supernatural underpinning to its cause-and-effect, if it has that, lacks redemptive purpose. And consequence. This worried the same issue raised in Mr. Robert Frost's poem "Design." The Agrarian imagination locates that purpose in natural scenes which it reads as parable, as fable, as sometime exemplar.

In fact there is little distinction between fable and parable. *Fable*, says the *The Princeton Encyclopedia of Poetics*, is "a brief verse or prose narrative, whose characters may be animals or inanimate objects acting like humans..." and adds that all "fables are didactic in purpose...." No entry is offered for *parable*, but the OED reveals that beyond being simply "a comparison; a similitude" parable is a "fictitious narrative or allegory (usually something that might naturally occur) by which moral or spiritual relations are typically figured." Arising in the murk of ancient days, as literary types, these developments of creation myths often work by chronicling journeys.

Bottoms is unusually attracted to portraits and transformational journeys, some of them imitative of the Jesus Journey. A man travels through a wilderness where he is exposed to and defined by "death" he assimilates well enough to bring back its particulars. In "The Drowned" the narrator, out motorboating, finds a floating corpse and tells us "my stomach jumped like something caught" thereby enacting the parable moment we can see without the poem's dramatic build-up. Here's the whole anecdote:

> I ease the paddle out and touched his heel.
> He didn't turn or move, only gazed straight down
> into the deepest part of the Etowah
> as though fascinated by something I couldn't see.

Again and again, this poet intuits, pursues, and celebrates what he calls "...something unknowable/ curling under roots, the thing lost" that in the world still wild might yet be recovered, a kind of secret to how things work essentially. Against all the mysteries, all a man has is consciousness, the great Romantic talent, which to the imagination that covets the sacred, Bottoms' kind of imagination, means juxtaposing present action and subsequent introspection by what he calls "the fanatical ministry/ of the brain" which holds potential for faith and salvation. The wilderness may be time; the travel may be ritual. Among the most compelling of Bottoms' poems are chronicles of travel that urge recognition of what composes a timeless and choiceless order of being where dangers, or threats that give the poem consequence, are heralds of ethical and moral awareness. There, the narrator experiences glimpses of a shadowy, but almost always inevitable religious system. This traveler is most often in a boat riding a slow current or a car whose pace is long-distance. Animals that appear are conventionally rather than unusually symbolic and rarely come evil, but are often aggressive. Communities, nourishing, male, and fractal, are celebrated, as in "The Light of the Sacred Harp" where a campfire gathering is a communion "in the good new warmth of God's old house/ the warmth of the bottle carried through the woods...." Drinking with comrades, exchanging fishing anecdotes, the narrator in the woods learns what to fear and why, what life holds and where.

Ordinarily a parable journey reveals character, the unshaped "stuff" of a man's good, his potential. Bottoms employs this structure in "Sign For My Father, Who Stressed the Bunt." Baseball, the most pastoral and ritualized of American games, has since before the Civil War been called the "great American" game in recognition of its mysterious incarnation of something in our identity. I take it that something is the Agrarian and rural sense of self, though it was long ago transplanted where few fields and tranquil vistas for learning exist. The object of baseball is, of course, to win by scoring more runs than the other team. But of nearly equal value is the way one wins, which means the way one manages choices. The uninitiated observer imagines that baseball is a game of powerful swings against powerful pitches, a contest of muscle and luck in which the better star carries his team to success, or dooms it. Baseball insiders tend to reify another strategy, what one-time New York Yankee player and manager Billy Martin called "small ball." Its way is to advance runners by controlled, deceptive, contact-disciplined hits such as the bunt or the coordinated hit-and-run which surprise defending players and catch them unprepared to stop a runner's move base by base, an offensive strategy communicated from a single consciousness by camouflaged signals. "Small ball" is cerebral and cooperative; the "sacrifice bunt" characterizes a willingness to yield self in favor of community. It resists greed and free-lancing; its play is patient, statistical, cautionary, the parallel of fatherly wisdom, predicated on a history of situation and response, not much different from a poem's action.

Sign for My Father, Who Stressed the Bunt

On the rough diamond,
the hand-cut field below the dog-lot and barn,

> we rehearsed the strict technique
> of bunting. I watched from the infield,
> the mound, the backstop
> as your left hand climbed the bat, your legs
> and shoulders squared toward the pitcher.
> You could drop it like a seed
> down either base line. I admired your style,
> but not enough to take my eyes off the bank
> that served as our center-field fence.
>
> Years passed, three leagues of organized ball,
> no few lives. I could homer
> into the garden beyond the bank,
> into the left-field lot of Carmichael Motors,
> and still you stressed the same technique,
> the crouch and spring, the lead arm absorbing
> just enough impact. That whole tiresome pitch
> about basics never changing,
> and I never learned what you were laying down.
>
> Like a hand brushed across the bill of a cap,
> let this be the sign
> I'm getting a grip on the sacrifice.

What a sly, truthful little confession it is. A strategy of conservative odds stands juxtaposed to individual desire for instant, big success. The boy looks to his father's demonstration and sees, through the lens of time, personal growth. Lyric form depends on this conventional here/there, now/then dichotomy which Bottoms stages as movement to wisdom: Dad was right.

Does it matter that we knew that? Homiletic wisdom is only as interesting as the language that bears it. Quality, in poetry, lies not in merit of idea but in word choice, textures, rhythmic compulsion, oscillations and parallels, compressions, all those little steps made to establish emotional assent. This poem reminds me of Robert Hayden's "Those Winter Sundays" where the aging narrator recalls his father's habit of waking early "in the blueblack cold" to make a fire for the house and to polish his boy's shoes that he might attend church. The narrator also remembers, now with regret, the "chronic angers of that house" as he slowly comes to ask "What did I know, what did I know/ of Love's austere and lonely offices?"

Brief, complex in emotion, all memory and little act, the lyric poem makes luminous what we had not remembered well enough and had not acted. Both poems, Bottoms' and Haydens, are emblematic rites of passage, a lyric mainstay, which work only in good word choices. Three examples from Bottoms will suffice: *sign* depicts action and heralds change; *rough* signals the field's essential nature and the boy's unpolished state, alluding to a diamond; *hand-cut* tells us the power of human action as it simultaneously locates the wilderness from which the civil place is never distant. How clever the student remarks.

Cleverness in poetry is no great virtue. It is merely one part of the building to judgment which discovers the value of field work, or play. Play is part of how things work, or fail to work, perhaps the central question, in Bottoms' world. In civilizing, assimilating, integrating, and ordering the self, play is fundamentally *loving*. Loving leads to production. That's why the father can drop a baseball "like a seed," something that cannot be contravened. The narrator, who cannot "take my eyes off the bank...," is gambling on power ball and he must learn the economic and reproductive power of the *seed*. This little parable, Bottoms knows, echoes the struggle of the South's Agrarian economies which habitually leave both farmers and their seed in the grip of bankers, those money-lenders in the temples, a story embedded here in image. That's another example of the lineage the poet calls upon. It sets up the salute of homage in the emphatic last word that ends the poem:

> Like a hand brushed across the bill of a cap,
> let this be the sign
> I'm getting a grip on the sacrifice.

I do not know the precise point at which David Bottoms recognized his way was not Dickey's, but signs of change that increase with each book become manifest in "Country Store and Moment of Grace" from *Vagrant Grace* (1999), and change dominates the fifteen poems of *Waltzing Through the Endtime* (2004). What was less a radical change in structure than a shift in emphasis from narration to speculation is couched in a new line arrangement, a visual stepping, that affirms purpose. It is, of course, not unusual for poets to change their way of saying; indeed, that is the characteristic pattern of contemporary American poetries. Dickey's shift from short, unrhymed, nine-syllable free verse lines to what he described as "wall to wall" lines in his middle books and then, later, to the evocations of what he called "states of being" poems reveals the pattern. For many poets formal evolution is accompanied by the influence of another poet, usually a variant of the lineage. David Bottoms turned to the rhetorical strategy of Charles Wright.

Wright, by education, experience, aesthetic orientation, and temperament, seems hardly at all regional. Yet he explicitly defines himself as southern while practicing a poetics of abstract modernism. Often called a mystic poet because his work is speculative in the latent and philosophic concepts he finds manifested by natural scenes, Wright is as deeply connected to the Agrarian and pastoral tradition as Dickey or Bottoms. His habitual balance of image and rhetorical gloss is far more parable-like and openly symbolizing than Dickey, a strategy that may have turned Bottoms toward Wright's phrase making in clusters and tiers of short lines that function like terraces in a mountainside, creating a palpable motion of the eye and the mind. Wright has long contended he does not make stories in his poems, but the patient narration of the mind's struggle to *know* is not only among the greatest of narratives, it is the reason for his description-and-thought-sequence form. The poems in *The Other Side of the River* are, of course, overt narratives, and few of his books are without a scheme of chronology sufficient to guide the reader. Still, one feels the brilliance of Wright's poems lies in lyric evocations of mood, feeling, sensibility, in the contest of nature's matter put to the doubting intellect. His early poems come in short, terse, highly imagistic form; middle poems move to expanded line lengths, sequence compositions, and more overt story shapes; the later poems employ multiple tones, dictions, the whimsical and sober voice braiding, the poem functioning openly as the run-on of an intensely religious spirit faced with a physical world whose abundance is as marked as absence of the sacred. The God-haunted despair in Wright, the bite of theodicy, seems to have encouraged a bittersweet residual faith, if it is faith, in Bottoms' *Waltzing Through the Endtime* something like junction boxes through which passes voltage ramped up and down by each poem's dramatic action, these are, though extended and expanded, fables of would-be enlightenment, the voices of their speakers humming more than speaking, the book itself a choral performance in which old-fashioned call and response underlies the elliptically segmented narratives, a book that begins with "Easter Shoes Epistle" and loves the burgeoning world even as the poet notices "Everything struggling, yes/ toward severance...." In *Waltzing Through the Endtime* Bottoms enacts a structure of crisis, building poems in sections or panels, these made of hovering, broken off fragments of lines whose effect is a stuttering rhythm of momentum. The poems are ambitious, learned and allusive, uncommonly familiar as tools in a barn we feel easy to the hand but whose performing actions we no longer know. They are growth tales.

"Vigilance," the fifteenth poem in the book's sequence, questions resilience, courage, the ability to push back, one of the virtues of poetry, concludes Bottoms' formal quest, or journey and, I think, tips hat to Wright as conductor. The poet begins with a description of morning, the first of numerous elliptical segments that nurse the poem forward not as chronological account but as zig-zagging thought:

> All morning in the secret place
> among the jays and finches biding their time at the feeders,
> the cardinals, the towhees,
> the stray mosquito and the sweat bee,
> the pacified Lab with her beef joint
> and the long caravan of ants
> trekking the wilderness of needles and dry grass.

Detailed as a Seurat, he summarizes the scene, irregular and offset lines we by now expect to break into idea declared, intercepted, interrogated. Six lines later, Bottoms announces his point:

> Days I've pondered
> what my mother-in-law calls the Endtime, and the limp millennium,
> which has simply rolled over....

Like Hardy writing "The Darkling Thrush" in 1899, Bottoms is anxious about the advent of the 21st century, portent of the end of world to some, a mere date to others. He thinks about meteor showers he has recently seen, sounds of children at play, and "what I need to know," whether it's in a flower, a bumper sticker, or "the old truths [that] are never old-fashioned...." John Barth once wrote that self-knowledge is bad news-if it may be the ultimate source of vigilance.

Bottoms interrupts his musing to remember meeting the southern fiction writer Barry Hannah, a man renowned not only for outrageous behavior but also for fiction that has had little resort to the supernatural.

The Vigilant Words of David Bottoms (Dave Smith)

> One night in a cancer ward
> in Oxford, Mississippi,
> > Jesus appeared to my friend Barry Hannah.
>
> *I've neglected you,* Barry said, and Jesus,
> a tall man, barrel-chested, nodded quietly, or simply stared—
> I've forgotten the whole story.

Once again Bottoms shifts his narration, remembers his father-in-law "Suddenly in the headlights of his truck/ Jesus standing on the shoulder of the road." This moment of brusque recognition—"These are the blessed, yes"—Bottoms uses to bring Flannery O'Connor and her story "A Good Man Is Hard to Find" into the mix. O'Connor, master of the grotesque and the exaggerated fable, permits Bottoms to adduce the multiple ways in which contemporaries have seen Jesus appear—in clouds, shadows, flowers, soup, tortillas, on walls—which invites onto the poem's stage William Blake and great Emerson for whom Nature is the visible body of God.

Among such incongruent absurdities, Bottoms appears to ask, acknowledging the loved and maybe strange members of one's own family, what is one to make of signs before "these centuries of slowly accruing misery?" This is the core of the pastoral, the nudge to spirit quests, and, doubtless, the urgent cause of much that has put poets to paper. Absent any real answers, Bottoms says "Vigilance, I say. Vigilance and virtue, or what we can muster..." which seems spinally desperate, a caveat whose dullness might offer the poem no purchase at all, if Bottoms had not taken, smartly, one more step. My grandmother used to say, responding to if/then constructions of events I offered in self-defense, "If a bullfrog had wings it would fly." Parables like such enigmatic wisdom. Bottoms summons the narrator's mother-in-law, as skeptic to stand not as end to the ramble of this consciousness but as a Mercutio who knows truths may be never be logicked to revelation. Her advice, and it is that, is:

> *Yes*, says the old woman, stirring her cocoa,
> *If the owner of the outhouse*
> > *had known when the river would flood....*

Why, boys, then he wouldn't have needed faith, would he? Or vigilance? Or the measure and words of a poem, which as Saint William Faulkner told us exist to give the human heart courage, which we need. And, if we are lucky, a poem gives its dollops of fun, too. Bottoms' poems do.

I have known poet Bottoms for almost thirty years. I have had the pleasure of reading his books in manuscript, his moves often surprising me. An exceedingly patient and thoughtful poet, his as-yet unpublished manuscript, *Working the Heavy Bag*, shows shortened, compacted, more anecdotal poems than one expects. Vignettes of grandfather, father, mother, wife, and daughter, they possess a liquid quality, as of water running from a marsh, clean, austere. The world of nature, fished in, walked over, still alive with a spooky essence that "skulked/ through tree line and subdivided shadows, static of crickets/ and trembling leaves, following blood/ and scent of meat/ to leap my backyard fence…," has nevertheless receded in favor of a domestic interest. Bottoms, as a man in his fifties will, has turned villager, burgher, his tone autumnal, death being on his mind. I think it too simple to say he writes merely tales of a diminishing family life, yet the poems portray generations untying like boot knots, and reveal, in lyric snapshots, moments we see how much each of us was kept, secured, buoyed by the other, until the unraveling. We are, after all, only nature's tolerated visitors, adrift in time that offers us no endgame. More pointed, a kind of courage, is Bottoms' sardonic humor in "Adios, Horses," a tale of the boy with a pony that doesn't want the boy; in "My Father's Garbage Can," where the father calls the son to drive fifty miles and put away the garbage can that has, as if malignantly, appeared "empty beside the road"; and in two bar poems, "Walking the Floor Over You" and "Love at the Sunshine Club," in which our hero, remembering how he was sucker-punched by a jealous dude, concludes "how could I ever stop/ believing in love?"

Loneliness and pity and sorrow are the drying-out mortar of a world so exquisitely felt in Bottoms' newest poems that love seems as real as bricks, damaged but omnipresent. There is, finally, a resigned acceptance in which a mature poet comes to reside, his skills not so amenable to elaborate fictions and baroque webs of words as when younger, but the compensation begins lines and phrases tuned perfectly exact. Charles Wright says in his "Still Life on a Matchbox Lid" that "The heart is colder than the eye is./ The watchers, the holy ones, know this, there is no shortcut to the sky." *Description*, as Wright says. But a little more, as Ms. O'Connor shows when in "The Artificial Nigger," Nelson, the grandson, fails to recognize certain people boarding the train as "niggers," and tells his grandfather, Mr. Head, "You never said they were tan. How do you expect me to know anything when you don't tell me right?" Getting it right is all we want of a poet, or ought to want anyway. In "My Old Man Loves My

Truck" the senior Bottoms is visited by the son, come ostensibly to make a repair or fill the elder's pantry, but the occasion draws the old one out to the driveway:

> my old man leans on his walker in the doorway of the kitchen
> and gazes across the carport at my truck.
>
> And sometimes when the trembling is too much,
> he edges his walker over the stoop and inches onto the driveway.
>
> My old man loves my truck. It has all the right dents and scratches,
> just the proper amount of rust.

And though he catalogs and touches and rattles keys, not once does he take the driver's seat, for that is long gone to him, as gone, really, as the son who now merely waits. To go? To know? To become, himself, one of the old ones?

I began by saying poetry is about identity, who we are, but also who we become in the vortices of imagination, in what death takes, in what nature and culture give. Elegy is one way of claiming what we need; prayer is another. The poems of *Working the Heavy Bag* are relentlessly personal watchers, rememberers. They have a newly stark rendering of the actual, the power of the documenting image, really, not merely a good eye but a shaping eye such as one finds in photographers such as Steiglitz or Weston or, in the South, Dorothy Lang. Bottoms now reaches something like the faces of 19th century daguerreotypes where amazement, awe, and refusal to buckle shines like bone through the skin. The most astonishing thing is that Bottoms has gone from the strategies of amplitude so successful in *Waltzing Through the Endtime* to a strategy of restraint, a minimalism so efficient in *Working the Heavy Bag* casual readers may not realize the lineage of poets from whom he descends. Just as Mr. Eliot indicated the new poet would do. It is with precisely such a backward-forward double perspective that he ends the book, his poem "Heron on the Oconee" offering an iconic moment in which identity, the old man's and the poet son's, is not the thing known but the process of knowing, a fable of what being is:

> Near the end, the way my old man stared into the distance,
>
> the way he leaned from his armchair
> toward a window, elbow quivering on his walker,

and gazed through oak branches into a broken sky,
is the way this heron, ruffled, muddy,

stares downriver as the water rippling into the trees.

And what is vigilance, we may say, but not having to, mind, if not words in our heads ringing as we, too, watch the water going away? Or coming forth.

Works Cited

Bottoms, David. *Armored Hearts: Selected and New Poems*. Port Townsend, WA: Copper Canyon Press, 1995.
_____. *Vagrant Grace*. Port Townsend, WA: Copper Canyon Press, 1999.
_____. *Waltzing Through the Endtime*. Port Townsend, WA: Copper Canyon Press, 2004.
Davison, Peter. "The Difficulties of Being Major: The Poetry of Robert Lowell and James Dickey." *The Atlantic Monthly*, 220 (October 1967): 116–121.
Dickey, James. *Poems: 1957–1967*. Middletown, CT: Wesleyan University Press, 1967.
_____. *Sorties*. New York: Doubleday, 1971.
Eliot, T.S. "Tradition and the Individual Talent." *Selected Essays: 1917–1922*. New York: Harcourt, Brace, 1932.
Frost, Robert. *Frost: Collected Poems, Prose, & Plays*. New York: Library of America, 1995.
Hardy, Thomas. *Selected Poems*. Ed. Robert Mezey. New York: Penguin, 1998.
Hayden, Robert. *Collected Poems*. Ed. Frederick Glaysher. New York: Liveright, 1985.
O'Connor, Flannery. *O'Connor: Collected Works*. New York: Library of America, 1988.
Wright, Charles. *Appalachia*. New York: Farrar, Straus and Giroux, 1998.
_____. *Black Zodiac*. New York: Farrar, Straus and Giroux, 1997.
_____. *The Other Side of the River*. New York: Random House, 1995.

The Evolution of the GOB Aesthetic
FRED CHAPPELL

Robinson Jeffers' first book of poems was titled *Flagons and Apples*, Wallace Stevens' was *Harmonium*, Edith Sitwell's *Facade*, A. R. Ammons' *Ommateum* and Robert Bly's *Silence in the Snowy Fields*. David Bottoms' first full-length collection was called *Shooting Rats at the Bibb County Dump*. It was preceded by a slightly less funky title, a chapbook, *Jamming with the Band at the VFW.*

The aggressive reactionary nature of his early program is hard to miss. Here was a poetry that announced its subjects and also announced what its subjects were not. Bottoms was not going to experience another statue with Howard Nemerov or contemplate a minor Renaissance painting alongside John Ashbery; he was not going to set up a fragile curio shop next door to Marianne Moore. He was going to hang out at the garbage dumps, the rancid beer joints, and the sluggish, snaky rivers of the deep south.

Shooting Rats was an intriguing title and the volume contained poems that worked hard to live up to its promise. I once tried one of them as a blindfold test on one of my bright graduate students when the book was new, handing her a Xeroxed copy of "Watching Gators at Ray Boone's Reptile Farm."

"Whatcha think?"

She regarded it attentively then gave me a serious smile. "It's pretty good," she said. "A strong example of the GOB style."

"Gob? You mean, like a sailor might write?"

GOB = Good Old Boy, she informed me. "You know, like James Dickey, Dave Smith, Richard Hugo sometimes. Good Old Boys going hunting and fishing and playing sports and sitting around long-faced in bars."

"That's kinda dismissive," I said.

"You're supposed to say *snobbish*. These poets like to think if you take issue with their subject matter, you're a cultural snob."

"Well, I don't know about that."

She nodded. "No," she said, "you wouldn't."

I was forced to consider her remarks at length. She was a well read person, a poet of bright promise, and a feminist, though not of the standardized Ms. Krankypants persuasion. When she spoke critically of poetry, she never tried merely to score points.

One of the qualities that had attracted me to this kind of work by Dickey, Smith, Hugo, Rodney Jones, James Seay, James Whitehead, Sidney Lea, and others was the feeling of liberation it triggered. It was solid stuff for the most part, not requiring for its composition Ezra Pound's encyclopedic historical knowledge, T. S. Eliot's accurate but sniffish acumen, Wallace Stevens' vocalic arpeggios, or Kenneth Koch's coterie urban blab. The incidents GOB poetry addressed did not take place in museums, cathedrals, and lecture rooms, and rarely in Europe. They took place in the American outdoors. The poems were not about things that stood still to be gazed at but about things that went *bang, woof, slither, plop,* and *whoopee,* things that lay within the purview of my provincial, not to say parochial, experience.

It would take time and broader experience — and more ethical openness — for me to realize that my predilections were snobbish too, in a reverse way. My uninformed guess is that David Bottoms came to something like this same realization but has proceeded to a very different resting place.

That happens — if indeed it does happen — later. First let us try to enumerate some characteristics of Bottoms' early aesthetic.

Here is the poem I tossed at my well prepared grad student:

Watching Gators at Ray Boone's Reptile Farm

While we stand behind the concrete railing
and yellow cockatoos cry through mosquito heat,
the gators never move,
but look like floating logs almost ready to sink,
wait as though long patience had taught them something
about humans,
an old voice crying up from the swamps of our brain.

Once that cry called a small boy
over the railing and the logs came alive.
A black man in a Bush hat salvaged the legs.
On the bottom of the pool
Ray Boone found a shrunken white hand clutching a stone.

Our hands clutch concrete as we lean against the railing
as though leaning might bring us closer
to that voice crying now through our common memory,
the answer to all the animal inside us [39].

First we are aware of the easy, informal diction as *gators* drops off its *alli-*. Then the gerunds —*crying, clutching, leaning, crying*— thrust at us their kinetic energies. Bottoms' poems are filled with gerunds; motion is continual. Violence is delivered in understatement that would do Hemingway proud: "A black man in a Bush hat salvaged the legs," and the melodramatic shock of "a shrunken hand clutching a stone" would warm James Dickey's heart.

Most important is the identification with the primal mind which Bottoms asseverates twice. In the first stanza, the floating gators summon forth "an old voice crying up from the swamps of our brain." That motif also ends the poem, "That voice crying now through our common memory, / the answer to all the animal inside us."

In Bottoms' early to-mid–career poems, primordial animalism is almost sacralized and his customary image, so customary that it becomes symbolic, for this holy impulse is the reptile. Where Nemerov will adore a Henry Moore and Ashbery a Pontormo, Bottoms will appreciate a cottonmouth moccasin. In *Rats*, the hallowed reptile or primitive animal shows up in "The Catfish," "Hunting on Sweetwater Creek," "The Copperhead," as well as in "Watching Gators."

In a U-Haul North of Damascus (1983) offers these examples: "Wakulla: Chasing the Gator's Eye" ("the reptile that moves beneath you"), "In a Jon Boat During a Florida Dawn," "Sleeping in the Jon Boat," and a reprint of "The Copperhead." *Under the Vulture-Tree* (1987) gives us "Gar," "Rats at Allatoona," the title poem, and "On the Willow Branch." *Armored Hearts* (1995) presents the title poem, "Snake on the Etowah," "In a Kitchen, Late" and....

Well, the catalogue can be extended as far as 2004 with "Little Drop of Wickedness" in *Waltzing Through the End Time*. By this time, however, the theme has lessened in force and frequency of appearance and the meanings attendant to it have changed. The copperhead in "Wickedness" serves as a symbol for the evil within human beings, like that within the blackguard who deceives "a lonely woman and middle-aged" to obtain gifts from her, then spits upon her in an airport terminal and tells her "she's fat and ugly / and disgusting to see naked on his bed." This is not the same kind of copperhead lauded earlier for being "quiet and dangerous and unafraid, / all spine and nerve." This is the Eden serpent of Genesis with no redeeming qualities.

Another GOB staple is alcohol, either beer or whiskey — and never wine. In *Rats* it is a necessary accoutrement for the title poem, for "Below Freezing on Pinewood Mountain," "Smoking in an Open Grave," "Writing on Napkins at the Sunshine Club," "In Jimmy's Grill," and "Crawling Out at Parties," where the first line joins the theme to the reptilian motif: "My old reptile loves the scotch." A strong example from *U-Haul* is "Drunks in the Bass Boat"; the strongest from *Vulture-Tree* is "Arcana Mundi":

> sometimes, then, over a last drink
>
> of Gordon's, I get so entranced by the stars swelling
> in the black sky, I believe they're busting
> to tell me something [23].

Armored Hearts gives us "Sleepless Nights"; *Vagrant Grace*, "Steve Belew Plays the National Steel." In these latter two collections references to alcohol become less frequent and only incidental. *Endtime* shows up as a near teetotaler.

The same is true of the blood-sport theme. It is most frequent in *U-Haul*, in poems such as "The Christmas Rifle," "Gigging on Allatoona," and "Kinship." This theme too appears less frequently in the later volumes, but in *Hearts* "Elegy for a Trapper" gives us a melancholy variation.

Often blood-sport and alcohol are linked. *Rats* opens with "The Drunk Hunter" and the title poems begins, "Loaded on beer and whiskey, we ride / to the dump in carloads...." The figure of the hard-drinking hunter is also a favorite with southern fiction writers and is drawn, as a number have told me, from personal experience. With so many Good Old Boys out sloshing through Nature, armed and tipsy, it's a wonder that one of them didn't pot Mary Oliver.

The Evolution of the GOB Aesthetic (Fred Chappell)

Of course, David Bottoms and the other writers who pursue this strain can plead the interests of verisimilitude. "This is how it is where I come from," they might say. "I have done the same things myself, in accordance with southern male custom. For poetry, one reality is as genuine as another."

Such justification will probably be accurate, but it does not exclude the possibility that the choice of the subject is literary reaction as well as reportage. This will be a reaction not only against the citified, sophisticated culture chat of James Merrill and Richard Howard but also against the southern literary predecessors of this generation of writers. They turned their backs on the gentility, the intellectualism, the ironic paradoxes, the stringent wit of Fugitive poets like Allen Tate and John Crowe Ransom. Those figures appeared as mandarins to them and they determined to explore the contemporary folk culture they knew as an antidote to the Metaphysical sensibility of their elders.

A glance at one final familiar GOB theme is in order because it is so steadily and passionately a preoccupation. "Jamming with the Band at the VFW" introduces us to Bottoms' love of country music and his experiences as a performer. Here is the first stanza:

> I played old Country and Western
> then sat alone at a table near the bandstand,
> smug in the purple light
> that seemed like a bruised sun
> going down over Roswell, Georgia.

The lines go on to describe others present, a short bald man in a string tie dancing with "a woman with a red beehive." The speaker, who is clearly Bottoms himself, drinks beer, listens to the "tear-jerking" music and thinks of English classes, poetry workshops, his graduate degree, and "the arty sophisticates / who attend readings in Atlanta." He opposes the "arty" bunch to all the men "turning gray who dream of having died / at Anzio, Midway, Guadalcanal." Too predictably, perhaps, he casts his lot with the beer-joint denizens and rises to dance with "the woman with platinum hair / and rhinestone earrings."

This poem can have effect only within a contrived framework. One used to meet World War II veterans at poetry readings, as well as at grungy beer joints. Many poets were themselves veterans, James Dickey prominent among them. And it is a poor honky-tonk that cannot list at least a couple of arty sophisticates in its roster of regulars. Where else can a TA or freshman English instructor afford to drink?

In short, "Jamming" is a poetic manifesto of a frankly southern cast. It appeals to anti-intellectual bias and class division. It is a real-men-don't-eat-quiche statement and sounds the drone string of country music's insistent descant. Its message is identical with that of Popeye in the animated cartoons: "I yam what I yam." Push the attitude another centimeter in its forward direction and it becomes truculence.

These are some of the objections that might be brought against "Jamming," but they finally make little difference. The poem is still effective. It succeeds in the way that a politician succeeds who appeals to his base electorate. At the time of composition, it would have been fresh and even a little daring and its appeal can reach beyond its imputed audience. In Atlanta, a roomful of arty sophisticates would understand and applaud. Whether a roomful of African Americans, or other largely minority groups, would do so is an interesting question.

It does not disserve Bottoms' work to note that the subject matter of much of his early poetry is identical with that of country music. Huntin' and fishin,' Whiskey River, musical heroes like Lester Flatt and the Allman Brothers — what is in the stockpile of the music that is missing from the poetry?

Well, Mother, of course, because contemporary poets consider Mother a subject too sentimental for graceful treatment. Father is permissible; there are lots of GOB poems about Father because of implicit masculine competitiveness and approved male bonding. Country music has no such prissy reservations and will laud Mother to tearful excess. ("Mama Tried.")

And romantic heart-woe is a staple, a favorite theme of the beer-soaked jukebox and the chickenwire-caged bandstand. ("D-I-V-O-R-C-E") *U-Haul* first broaches this theme with "In a Pasture Under a Cradled Moon," a heart-wrenching effort about the aftermath of a miscarriage. The title poem, "In a U-Haul North of Damascus," treats the subject more thoroughly, speaking of the bitter conflicts between man and wife that ensued the miscarriage. It also brings forth a moving prayer for a change in the speaker's life, one that would result in changes in his outlook and his poetry:

> Somewhere behind me,
> miles behind me on a two-lane that streaks across
> west Georgia, light is falling

through the windows of my half-empty house.
Lord, why am I thinking about this? And why should I care
so long after everything has fallen
to pain that the woman sleeping there should be sleeping alone?
Could I be just another sinner who needs to be blinded
before he can see? Could I be moved
to believe in new beginnings? Could I be moved? [60]

It required courage to write this poem with its frank confession of personal shortcoming and helplessness. It took another measure of the same stern stuff to choose it as the title for the collection and to make its inconclusive ending serve as the dominant tone for the book. Placing it as the penultimate piece, Bottoms indicates, whether purposely or not, that *U-Haul* is a transitional volume.

The subject matter may be similar, but there is a world of difference between "In a U-Haul" and some example of canned, overly orchestrated, whining Nashville lost-love lament. The note of tentative resolve—"Could I be moved?"—with which the poem ends underlines its seriousness.

Can we be moved?

In Protestant religious tradition strong, radical motion of the spirit can begin only after the spirit itself is transformed. At the tent revival meeting, in the drowsy white clapboard church, on the slimy river bank, the sinner is saved, his old personality shucked off so that he may be born anew.

The first poem in *Under the Vulture-Tree*, the volume that follows *U-Haul*, is titled "In the Ice Pasture." It is a lyric narrative that tells of a horse that escapes his pasture in freezing weather and wanders "fifty yards onto the pond / to fall neck-deep through the ice." The narrator hurries to procure an ax from his basement, then goes out upon the pond to rescue the animal, "half a white statue in a fountain of ice."

He eases across the frozen sheet, testing the ice with the ax handle, until it gives way and he drops into the water, clutching the horse's mane as he sinks "chest-deep / in the shock of the cold."

It is a perilous episode:

> How long did I hang there, numb,
> bodiless, before the body of the horse rose under me
> and what we were lunged hard, broke
> to the air, to the wind turning us scaly
> with water? [12]

The commotion they make together rouses the world around them, the dogs and cattle, everything, "till the night / cracked like an egg shattered in the storm / of two beasts becoming one, / or one beast being born."

The poem does not say whether the pair escaped drowning by their own efforts or whether the tumult summoned human aid. The closure focus is on the rebirth metaphor.

The identification of speaker with animal is a familiar trope in Bottoms' poetry at this point. His speakers have identified themselves, closely or tentatively, with all animals within eyeshot, not excluding cockroaches. The usual means of identification has been that the animal in question, gar or copperhead or alligator, calls from the dark background of the speaker's mind his "old reptile." But in "Ice Pasture" speaker and horse conjoin to form a new spiritual hybrid.

This could only take place if the animal itself possessed some sort of higher spiritual capacity or harbored some kind of transcendent ambition. It is possible that Bottoms proposes this premise, for the second stanza of "Ice Pasture" sets this rhetorical question:

> What was he trying to become out there,
> thrashing to get a hoof up
> like an old beast cracking his shell? [11]

In *Rats*, "Calling Across Water at Lion Country Safari" prefigures this concept in different terms. This earlier poem describes a visit to a large zoo compound with its zebras, ostriches, giraffes, and reptiles. The narrator is photographing the sights as his tour car rolls along and the reflection off his lens attracts the attentive gaze of a silverback gorilla stationed on an island surrounded by a moat. As the gorilla stands in the mouth of a cave, the camera's shutter "catches his eye" and he seems to beckon to the photographer to come to him, "the long talking arm circling in and out, calling me / across water, the only thing he believes is really between us." In "Ice Pasture," that water had frozen to form a bridge between animal and man, but the disintegration of that bridge made them one. This poem signals a different tone in Bottoms' treatment of the relations between animals and humankind.

In his title poem, "Under the Vulture-Tree," the poet reports or imagines ("as I passed under their dream") drifting in a jon boat beneath the limbs of a dead oak filled with vultures, "hundreds," and describes them as looking like elderly men "who have grown to empathize with everything." Contemplating this sight, he concludes that they are like "dwarfed transfiguring angels" that as scavengers "pray over the leaf-graves of the anonymous lost, / with mercy enough to consume us all and give us wings."

As noted, Bottoms has always been at pains to ennoble in poetry such generally less well regarded animals as rats, copperheads, and cockroaches, and here vultures go into his holy menagerie. In bald terms the poem says only that upon death our bodies return their constituent elements to the elements of the universe from which they came and that vultures may act as agents of that reversion. But the language of the closing rises above Lucretian atomism with *transfiguring angels, pray, mercy,* and *give us wings.* The poet has something further in view than attempting to weaken our prejudice against certain kinds of animals. He desires to raise these animals to a sacred level.

But this ambition is paradoxical because he never really lets go of that D. H. Lawrence blood-knowledge, reptilian-brain mysticism until much later in his career. The poem that follows "Vulture-Tree" in the volume by that name is "On the Willow Branch" which recounts another mysterious near encounter by night with an unidentified red-eyed creature in a willow tree and brings back his familiar frisson as "the old brain clings to the spine." His vision is two-tiered: There are "higher" animals that represent the transcendent, highly spiritual side of the human makeup, while "lower" animals link us to the muck of primordial swamps.

As if David Bottoms had planned for it to happen on schedule, the tenor of his verse and the thrust of his impulse changed in *Armored Hearts*, a book of selected and new poems. It is perhaps too tempting to say that the first set of poems in the New selection reprises his customary themes. "Armored Hearts," "Snake on the Etowah," "In a Kitchen, Late" and "American Mystic" undertake the primitive animal-kinship concept again, enlisting, in order, snapping turtles, another copperhead, cockroaches, wasps, and a possum. The following poem, "Sierra Bear," does not recount a personal experience, however, but an episode lifted from the writings of the naturalist John Muir.

Muir, all unaware, hiked smack into his first "Sierra bear" and, not knowing how to behave in this situation, threw his arms into the air and rushed at the bear while shouting. The encounter ended with a mannered exchange almost Henry Jamesian in its cultural ambiguities:

> Confused bear cocked back on a haunch,
> artist's blundering arms frozen toward embrace —
> what pardon these moments become
> when the bear wades off through lilies and grass. [118]

"Sierra Bear" is notable for its distancing from its subject animal. Not only does the incident happen to John Muir instead of to Bottoms, the closure is not a realization of mystical brotherhood; it is a flash of amused social commentary.

The more personal pieces that follow "Sierra Bear" are of a new sort. "Home Maintenance" expresses not only the anger and pain of divorce, it also hints at some of the guilty feelings involved. The animals in the ironic "Elegy for a Trapper" impart no mystical revelation to the speaker. The man who made his living by capturing wildlife has died and his family has disappeared except for three abandoned hounds. The remains of his trapped animals are mere images that only symbolize a way of life forever gone: "the hide of a coyote / draped on a tailgate, / a skinned bobcat, glassy, pink, / frozen upright on a stump."

"Elegy for a Trapper" might stand as a farewell to Bottoms' earlier pantheistic mode. The wilderness that called him to worship with all its primal violence and stark, factual beauty is beginning to recede in the world about him and in his interior world. Another value system is struggling to take its place and the change is evidenced in such poems as "Last Supper in Montana," "The Pentecostal," "The Blue Mountains," "Free Grace at Rose Hill," and "Zion Hill" in *Armored Hearts*.

The GOB narrator that is Bottoms' accustomed persona follows in the tracks of many a Good Old Boy before him as he embraces the traditional church religion to be saved. The Good Old Boy is a rebel at heart, of course, and though he has been surrounded by this particular religious milieu since birth, he has either rejected it or avoided thinking about it at any length while he cultivated his own soul and pursued his strongly individualistic desires. But at last he joins the long line of sinners who file down the main aisle of the expectant church or the sweaty revival tent toward the bright altar. His eyes are bloodshot, his head throbs, and his mind is weary unto numbness. Here at last, though, is rest and salvation.

Wait ... Not so fast. It's none so easy as all that.

"Last Nickel Ranch: Plains, Montana" describes the evening prayer ritual at his in-law's house trailer. There his wife's father "calls the family into a huddle" for silent prayer and the nature sounds from outdoors grow louder. The speaker thinks of prayer and "the humility necessary for prayer." But as he is gathered into the group hug, he sees outside "the eagle's shadow // sliding down the ridge, one dark / blade of muscle / beautiful for its simplicity." He thinks of his past life: "I know what I've valued"; he remembers how the night before he heard a coyote howling and went to the window:

> In the darkness behind the glass
> I saw myself, and behind my eyes the stars flew
> into the pines [124].

The difficulties are not merely that old habits die hard, that a Good Old Boy finds humility tiresome, or that the white robe of Christianity is a burdensome mantle. The problem is a more ancient one, the clash of religions and cultures. For most of his life the speaker has put his faith in a semi-pagan, mystical, totemic pantheism. For him, the call of the wild has been as powerful as was the call of the Cross for Saints Paul and Augustine. The eagle's shadow does not distract him from prayer, it tugs him toward another system of beliefs. That shadow manifests the power of the old religion and for him to break away from that primitive faith, a new revelation is required.

In "Last Supper in Montana" we get a partial glimpse of the process of conversion. During one of his father-in-law's prayer rituals, the speaker recalls how he tried to recover his life after a disastrous divorce. He attempted at that time to renounce the temptations of the world by listing them down on paper and then burying the list in the earth.

Did that ceremony of primitive magic work? He cannot say for sure, but there was a forceful revelation, the feeling

> that something
> left me, and the wind knocked me down.
> I don't remember what I felt like—
> something small in the violence—
> but I sprawled on my back
> across that grave, clutching the wet grass.... [128–29]

The four poems on the pages following "Last Supper" in *Armored Hearts* address the subject of revelation, though they are not all autobiographical. "The Pentecostal" tells the story of the father-in-law's vision of

Christ "walking / along the shoulder of the road." In "The Blue Mountains" the speaker's wife's niece and her husband are persuaded by religious motives to flee the "Sodom-and-Gomorrah" of Portland, Oregon, before God destroys it. That destruction never takes place, but the fearful couple is rewarded with a revelation from the natural world, the owls they saw, "great horned and gray," that became emblems of the glory of the afterworld. In "Free Grace at Rose Hill" religious revelation takes the form of wind traveling through a graveyard. The narrator has seen in Pentecostal churches other people experiencing moments of exaltation, though perhaps not the real, true thing:

> No, that wasn't grace either,
> though grace had been there —
> Isn't it like this cemetery where the roses
> quaking in their terraces are not the wind?
> It swirls where it wants to swirl.
> If it touches us,
> it touches us [132].

"Zion Hill," however, questions motive, wondering if the desire for the peace of salvation is "less out of devotion / than despair." Even so, the speaker imagines achieving grace and thinks of it as receiving a letter announcing a sudden munificent inheritance.

A handful of poems in the early volumes and particularly in *Armored Hearts* are so anticipatory of personal religious salvation that a reader going through Bottoms' work chronologically might expect that *Vagrant Grace* (1999) would be a bright record of happy fulfillment. It is not — or not completely so.

More overtly traditional religious poems are placed here than in earlier volumes, but this is not a book of unambiguous triumph of grace over the skeptical, or at least laggard, soul. "On Methodist Hill," "A Family Parade," "Our Presbyterian Christmas," "A Morning from the Gospel of John," "In the Wilderness," and "Occurrence in the Big Sky" all treat of recognizable religious themes, but there are other poems in which former positions and attitudes still evince themselves.

I am sorely tempted to classify as "backslid" poems the elegy for James Dickey called "A Canoe," the whiskey-music tribute, "Steve Belew Plays the National Steel" and "A Walk to Carter's Lake," in which ev'ry Prospect pleases and only Man is vile:

I'm glad I've stopped pretending
to love people
and the cities where people can't love themselves.
This is what the quiet accomplishes,
and the water trusting
the shadows to eventually peel back from the trees [59].

My adjective, "baokalid," is too judgmental. The poet whose first work showed such affinities to that of James Dickey, Richard Hugo, and the troubadour, Hank Williams, Sr., was not going to turn into George Herbert overnight. Or ever. The former habits of thought and feeling are not only ingrained, they still command a reluctant, or regretful, allegiance; the natural world still offers objects to contemplate, incidents replete with mystery — as when a traveler peering from a hotel window in a lonesome western town sees a great blue heron flying over the square below. The shadow of that flight reminds him of his visit to a Florida aquarium where he was startled by a huge ray whose presence troubled his sleep. Upon waking, he seemed to glimpse the shadow of that ray swing over the town and pondered "the talent the world shows for mystery, / sending these glimpses on wings."

The noun that is missing from this poem, "Heron Blues," is "angel." The word might have been too sentimental in context even for Hank Williams. But it does show up in "Occurrence in the Big Sky," a piece that serves as entryway, as it were, for the religious themes of *Waltzing through the Endtime*.

I think that "Occurrence" is an important poem in the development of Bottoms' beliefs and of his aesthetic. That does not mean that I understand it; I don't. I can only make conjectures.

"Occurrence" is structured in three parts. The first describes a house still under construction, fresh and raw. A woman, a widow I must suppose, lives there in the confusion. She dreads to inventory the things she must bring here from her former dwelling. The second part offers a change of voice, more impersonal, as it speaks of the soul of a human being trying to come to terms with its own eternity. The soul is like a carpenter who must quit his work before the job is finished, who must

walk through an untrimmed doorway
into a windy field, nothing
on the horizon but the signal fires of angels [89].

Bottoms' metaphor for this individual eternity is a life pursued in a lonely farmhouse, where the soul tries to adjust to bewildering circumstances, "the first violent gust of timelessness," "gust of past and future dovetailing."

Part three introduces an "I," an observer who has seen two eagles aloft, "high against a white ridge of clouds," fighting over prey of some sort. The scene was "in the sky like a page from Revelation." Then the prey was dropped; it was a snake and it fell, coiling and twisting, through the air until one eagle swooped and caught it, "rose and broke the clouds."

I cannot for the life of me join the three parts of this poem in any fashion, lyrical, narrative, or thematic. It stands for me as a triptych in which the three depictions are unrelated. Even so, it possesses an emotional force and it ends with a thunderclap of wonderment disclosed in its final image. The whole of it is like a chapter of Revelation, powerful without being really comprehensible. The closing picture is perhaps this poet's best use of a natural image ascending to visionary mode.

"Occurrence in the Big Sky" falls at the end of *Vagrant Grace*, so it would seem to be of importance to Bottoms and I think we shall not be badly mistaken if we take it as a sort of introduction to *Waltzing through the Endtime*, the most openly religious, in traditional Protestant terms, of the poet's six full-length books of verse.

The title of the volume is taken from its end-poem, "Three-quarter Moon and Moment of Grace," which serves as a coda, a fugato summing-up and variation upon the dominant themes of memory, mystery, regret, and conversion.

It opens with a middle-aged narrator pacing "barefoot through his yard"; he plucks a mandolin as he strolls and counts his worries, musing the story of his life: "*Waltzing through the Endtime*, my mother-in-law calls it, / wringing out my spirit/ like a dirty dishrag..." His memories burden him and give rise to fears about the afterlife. He thinks of this burden as a totesack: "And what are we dragging in that heavy sack / if not the cornerstones of Heaven, / or the charcoals of Hell?"

Then he pauses and listens to the silence of the night and comes to a moment of measurable comfort in the fact that God must remain unknowable, "this opulent millennial stillness —/ as though the Great Mind / after long concern lingered on the edge of a thought, / which in its complexity / may seem to us only more drifting, everything washing away / in a current of light..." He then experiences a sensation of "your hand rising with mine / on the same gust of wind..."

We may conjecture that this wind is identified with, or related to, the Pentecostal wind that shed grace upon Christ's apostles, as in Acts 2:2. We may conjecture also that the other hand belongs to his wife, daughter to the speaker's highly religious in-laws.

"Three-quarter Moon" may not be felt by all readers as a poem complete in itself, but as an end-poem to the whole book, it serves usefully. I have chosen as dominant themes of *Endtime* memory, mystery, regret and conversion, and if I list one representative example of the treatment of each, I would point toward these:

Memory: "Easter Shoes Epistle";
Mystery: "Vigilance";
Regret: "Homage to Buck Cline";
Conversion (or Salvation): "Andalusia Visit."

A book of poetry is not, however, a checklist of themes that have been snugly compartmentalized into separate lyrics. *Endtime* is demonstrably designed as a whole fabric in which topics, images, themes, and approaches appear, submerge, reappear, and interlace. "Homage to Buck Cline" voices regret for the speaker's teenage rebellious disrespect for a law officer whose war wounds have debilitated his body and whose duties have soured his disposition. Buck Cline is a middle-aged cop, "making / his poor living / out-toughing the tough." He could have arrested and jailed the speaker for traffic violations, but he let him off with a warning: "'Reckon your daddy'd like to get you out of jail?'"

"Buck Cline" is also about memory, not only the grateful memory the speaker still holds of the lawman, but the painful memories that made the poet's father ("daddy") the man he was, with the shrapnel that was gnawing into the small of his back, the bone splinter "the Japanese navy left in his leg, / that memory always alive and violent, though never spoken, / having in its pain too much of the divine, / the unapproachable..."

"Buck Cline" is the central poem in *Endtime*, one of its longest and most complex, though there are others close to it in spirit, method, and theme. "In the Big House of the Allman Brothers My Heart Gets Tuned" stands as one companion; "Shooting Rats in the Afterlife" may stand as another. "O Mandolin, *O Magnum Mysterium*" is a rhapsody on the entwined themes of memory, regret, and mystery brought together — harmonized — under the rubric of music. "Black Hawk Rag" is about forgetting how to finger the bridge of the rag tune of that title and the regret that forgetting entails.

Because *Endtime* is more complexly organized than Bottoms' preceding volumes and more ambitious in the design for the whole, the poet found it fitting to make some changes in technique. "Easter Shoes Epistle," "O Mandolin," "Allatoona Storm," and others employ longer lines than are customary for Bottoms. The language is more discursive, the descriptions more detailed, and the musicality deliberately recalls that of Whitman, whose familiar lines, "Darest thou now, O soul, / Walk with me toward the unknown region…?" serve as epigraph for the book. The whole collection, including its shorter poems, is couched in this new idiom, as if Bottoms is exhibiting himself as a reborn poet, as well as a reborn soul. The other epigraph, from Flannery O'Connor, avows the central theme: "…the greatest dramas naturally involve the salvation or loss of the soul." That concept of drama would mean nothing to Aeschylus, but its sentiment underscores the background and milieu in which almost all of Bottoms' poems take place.

As if to demonstrate the change that has overtaken him, the poet returns to the central notion of one of his earliest poems to display broad differences. "Shooting Rats in the Afterlife" recalls "Shooting Rats at the Bibb County Dump" only with title and autobiographical incident. Where "County Dump" is bitterly fatalistic, a plaint against mortality, "Afterlife" is a less certain statement, more concerned with the nature of memory and its ambiguities than with death itself. In "County Dump," wounded rats crawl "into the darkness we're all headed for." "Afterlife" speculates on what eternity may offer human beings, the possibility

> that somewhere down the pike these landscapes are waiting again,
> or are, perhaps, the only things we take with us —
> our psychic terrain —
> as though through memory we create our own afterlives —
> which can't be the entire breadth of it all,
>   but in some way a homeland,
> a landscape out of which we might ramble into the afterlives, yes,
> the memories, of one another… [20]

One memory Bottoms takes into this imagined afterlife is of the Bibb County dump and the cruelties perpetrated there, recalled in "Afterlife" with more detail than in the earlier poem:

> Patience then, and the heavy breath of silence…
> three minutes, five, until finally

that small scratching —
>softly at first, around the low edges, then louder
as it seeped toward the center and up... [23].

It is going way yonder too far to say that "Afterlife" is an act of repentance, a sort of palinode to "County Dump." But there is no doubt in the poem that the speaker would like to replace that too-vivid memory with a happier one. The scene he would like to recapture is of "preaching" one morning as a child standing on a wooden crate in a yard:

I don't recall the congregation — a couple of guineas, a laying hen or
two — only the essence of my trance,
>and the slats of the apple crate
swaying up and down, threatening to crack... [21]

The memory of the dump and the guns will not go away; the poem ends with another glimpse of one of those episodes; even so, "what I'd like to get back is that sermon to the guineas, that fire / unleashed in words."

"Andalusia Visit" is unclear in parts because the poet leaves out so much background information (to be supplied, no doubt, at public readings), but the train of the narrative seems to be that the speaker has a nightmare about an old woman in a house during a thunderstorm. When the speaker enters, she is upset: "*You're not Billy,* / she said, jerking around twice, / rolling her neck like a peacock..."

The speaker she addresses is not Bottoms the poet, and not his persona as narrator:

Somehow in the dream I had stumbled
>into another man's afternoon,
another man's storm, but had come back startled and blessed,
the way someone leaving confession might slip
into the wrong raincoat
>and find himself walking an unfamiliar street,
the clouds departed, the stars
above the brownstones more passionate than neon,
his head clearing,
>his deep pockets bulging with possibility [49–50].

That is an odd concept, the receiving of grace by proxy, as it were, and I cannot picture how a sacrament — the taking of the Host, for example — might work in such a situation. But maybe the poet conjectures that this method might be as close as a former, mild reprobate of the Good Ole Boy breed can come to true salvation.

The fact of the matter is, David Bottoms has accepted the words of the New Testament and of some of his churches, and has been accepted by them, but still walks in a mist of doubts and nagging speculations.

In "Vigilance" he returns to his old theme of finding transcendent religious signs and symbols in the natural, circumstantial world. He recalls how others — Barry Hannah, for instance, and his father- and mother-in-law — have received signs and seen visions. He recalls, too, all the news accounts of the revelatory images turning up in odd places — "on an outside wall of a Tim Hortons restaurant," "a tortilla scorched with the face of Christ," "the Virgin swimming / in a bowl of vegetable soup."

Most interesting to him was a dream his mother-in-law recounted. "She was floating down the river on an outhouse." In the darkness ahead she heard the sounds of a waterfall. She attached great significance to this dream, but the poet, whose vaunted wayward past is always with him, withheld assent and refused judgment, " *It was not the Jordan*, she says, but claims it still as a sign./ Who knows?"

Maybe nobody knows. David Bottoms testifies that he does not. For him the pilgrimage continues.

Works Cited

Bottoms, David. *Armored Hearts: Selected and New Poems*. Port Townsend, WA: Copper Canyon Press, 1995.
_____. *In a U-Haul North of Damascus*. New York: William Morrow, 1983.
_____. *Shooting Rats at the Bibb County Dump*. New York: William Morrow, 1980.
_____. *Under the Vulture-Tree*. New York: William Morrow, 1987.
_____. *Vagrant Grace*. Port Townsend, WA: Copper Canyon Press, 1999.
_____. *Waltzing through the Endtime*. Port Townsend, WA: Copper Canyon Press, 2004.

Amazing Grace: The Aesthetics of a Spiritual Quest

ERNEST SUAREZ

In *Vagrant Grace* (1999), the book that followed his fifth collection, *Armored Hearts: New and Selected Poems* (1995), David Bottoms unveiled a new aesthetic. The fifty-year-old Bottoms veered away from compressed narratives and figurative language, and towards seemingly looser poems with a more conversational tone. Examining the changes in Bottoms' verse within the context of his career shows how variations in his creative practice are linked to his shifting conception of the relationship between memory and the present, particularly in relation to the metaphysical.

Bottoms has long been associated with the post–Robert Penn Warren/James Dickey generation of narrative southern poets, which includes Dave Smith, Fred Chappell, Andrew Hudgins, Rodney Jones, Betty Adcock, T.R. Hummer, and others. Warren presented Bottoms with the Walt Whitman Award for his first book, *Shooting Rats at the Bibb County Dump* (1979), but critics have most closely identified him with Dickey, with whom Bottoms shared a friendship for sixteen years. Like many of his peers, Bottoms has had to negotiate the Dickey legacy. Bottoms has observed that "it's not uncommon to hear southern poets say that they've always felt like they were standing in Dickey's shadow" (*Southbound* 90). Indeed, the parallels between Bottoms and Dickey are so evident that it's difficult to find an article — or even a book review — on Bottoms in which Dickey isn't mentioned. They are both natives of Atlanta, distinctly southern, and storytellers-in-verse. Both poets' early work is characterized by tightly controlled, accessible narratives, which often emphasize the instinctual and the transcendental. Later in their careers they each turned to writing longer, seemingly looser poems. However, the differences between them are substantial. Formally, Dickey's early poetry is heavily cadenced, largely composed in dactyls, anapests and trochees, which he uses to create an almost hypnotic rhythm that plunges the reader into his characters' experiences. Thematically, he explored the relationship between naturalism and romanticism. Dickey believed no moral force governed the universe, and claimed the "real god is what causes everything to exist, like the laws of motion" (*Southbound* 9). The transcendental transformations his characters undergo are what he called "creative lies," a willed romanticism that forges an illusion of meaning in a naturalistic universe.

"For the Last Wolverine" (1966) can be viewed as Dickey's *ars poetica*. The poem opens by acknowledging that wolverines are threatened with extinction ("They will soon be down/ To one") and stresses the species' predatory nature. But the narrator insists "that is not enough/ For me," and that he "would have it all" his "way." As the narrator describes the wolverine mating with the "New World's last eagle," the poem's emphasis shifts towards the imaginative, "Dear God of the wildness of poetry, let them mate/ To the death in the rotten branches,/ Let the tree sway and burst into flame// And mingle them, crackling with feathers,// In crownfire. Let something come/ Of it something gigantic legendary...."

The narrator's invocation of the "God of the wildness of poetry" suggests the animal's survival is more than a matter of the species' continuation; it links the wolverine and the eagle's existence to imaginative acts vital to art. The narrator's vision is an illusion — a romantic transformation of nature — but one seen as necessary to the human imagination. He declares that the "timid poem/ needs the midless explosion" of the wolverine's "rage," and ties it to creativity, "I take you as you are// And make of you what I will,/ Skunk-bear, carcajoy, bloodthirsty// Non-survivor.// *Lord, let me die but not die// Out.*"

In contrast to Dickey's cadenced "creative lies," Bottoms' early poetry is cast in free verse and doesn't tend to emphasize romanticism or a post–Darwinian, secular universe. For Bottoms, unlike Dickey, the imaginative act isn't a necessary illusion or an existential undertaking; it's a means of tapping into the world's underlying design. Bottoms' uses various devices — metaphors, similes, archetypes, myth — to "spring the poem into the figurative," and "reveal something about the hidden things of the world, the vague or shadowy relationships and connections that exist just below the surface of our daily lives" (90–91).

The title poem of *Shooting Rats at the Bibb County Dump* plays with light and dark imagery to suggest the drunken and violent characters are destined for eternal darkness. The final stanza begins by referring to rats, but concludes by referring to people:

> It's the light they believe that kills.
> We drink and load again, let them crawl
> for all they're worth into the darkness we're headed for.

The "vague or shadowy" relationship the poem reveals is the tie between the characters' motivations for shooting rats and their own empty destiny, the "darkness *we're* headed for" (my emphasis). Like "Shooting Rats at the Bibb County Dump," other poems in the book — "Wrestling Angels" and "Smoking in an Open Grave" — describe people engaging in destructive behavior resulting from their fear of death, and implicitly, from lack of a spiritual touchstone. Many poems — "The Lame," "Faith Healer Comes to Rabun County," "Learning to Let the Water Heal," "Rubbing the Faces of Angels" "The Orchid" — are underpinned by a tension between mortality and faith. The book's final offering, "Speaking into Darkness," provides two epithets, a phrase from Galway Kinnell, "O corpse-to-be," and one from Dickey, "this night mortality wails out." The poem opens by using a biblical allusion to explore the relationship between birth and death:

> First it was the apple
> in grandma's bowel,
> the way it grew to grapefruit size,
> bulged beneath the hospital sheet,
> like a giant rotten egg,
> flexed and swelled into death's pregnancy.

Bottoms' use of figurative language and Christian imagery typifies much of the poetry in his first five collections. "First it was the apple" suggests the taint of original sin, resulting in God's curse of hard labor, pain in childbirth, and being cut off from immortality, while calling the tumor a "giant rotten egg," and the phrase "death's pregnancy," link birth and death, and stress the cycle of life.

The subsequent two stanzas reflect the tightly plotted quality of Bottoms' early work. The poem depicts the narrator's increasing sense of death's encroachment as he recalls his family's reaction to his grandmother and grandfather dying. The narrator describes various occasions — 4th of Julys, moon flights, baseball seasons, Christmases — but an increasing awareness of mortality tempers the joy associated with these moments. The sensation tugs at him:

> melting into one night,
> no brighter than the grain of the door
> I have closed behind me,
> the room in which I sit alone tonight
> studying the way my life has flexed and grown;
> in the oval mirror on the wall
> the texture and coloring of my beard,
> the hooked, bent nose,
> the muddy eyes probing
> the wrinkled flesh around their lids.
> Grandfather, tonight I want to be that face
> moving backwards into the mirror,
> want to shrink back up my mother's pink tube.

The description of the door closing behind him echoes the end of the second stanza, when the narrator recalls his mother sitting alone, grieving her mother's death. But in contrast to the poem's first three stanzas, in which the narrator studies the death of others, the narrator turns his powers of observation on himself, as he peers into a mirror and contemplates his aging countenance. The line "Studying the way my life has flexed and grown" closely parallels the end of the first stanza, when the narrator contemplates how his grandmother's tumor "Flexed and swelled into death's pregnancy," and sets up the end of the stanza. The link between death and birth created at the conclusion of the first stanza melds into a desire to reverse time and "shrink back up my mother's pink tube."

The concerns and techniques displayed in *Shooting Rats at the Bibb County Dump* are evident in Bottoms next two books, *In a U-Haul North of Damascus* (1983) and *Under the Vulture-Tree* (1987), as well the new material in *Armored Hearts*. But, as several reviewers noted, in *Vagrant Grace* (1999) and *Waltzing Through the Endtime* (2004), Bottoms' verse changed from a style influenced by Dickey to one more akin to Charles Wright's. For instance, David Baker has observed that *Vagrant Grace* reminded him "more of the recent work of Charles Wright than of the natural dramatics of Dickey or the grandeur of Warren" (153). Similarly, Ilya Kaminsky has claimed that in *Waltzing Through the Endtime*, "Bottoms' line sometimes reminds one" of "Charles Wright" (134). But like previous critics' association of Bottoms with Dickey, such assertions need qualification.

In *Vagrant Grace* and *Waltzing Through the Endtime* Bottoms moves from a more traditional line to a balanced or split line reminiscent of Wright's, but there are significant formal differences between the two poets. Wright is a life-long admirer and disciple of Donald Justice, the Florida-born minimalist who taught Wright at the University of Iowa. Wright composes in unaccentual syllabics and relies on alliterative sonics; from book to book his lines vary between eight to fifteen syllables, sometimes leaning towards compression or towards greater amplification. Philosophically, he is essentially a late romantic whose narrative perspective is consistently informed by the subject/object split, the fluid dynamic between individual perception and the world outside the self. Whether Wright draws on the landscapes of California or Appalachia, or western or eastern mystical traditions, he is a spiritual yearner who never quite achieves belief. A passage from *The World of the Ten Thousand Things* (1990) typifies how his narrators engage the landscape in search of metaphysical meaning but butt up against nothingness. The narrator watches stormy "fast-running clouds" sunder in the November sky, "...then break to a backdrop of Venetian Blue./ Wind spills from the trees./ How much, thrums Expiation, half/ Asleep in the wings, how much will it add up to?/ Always the same answer out of the clouds,/ always the same sigh."

Wright's narrator hopes to discover something beyond the world of naturalistic fact, but the "sigh" he attributes to the clouds is a projection of his inability to find it. Wright's mystic yearning differs from Dickey's illusory romanticism, but both poets' assumptions are ultimately secular. In contrast, Bottoms readily embraces the metaphysical. In "Allatoona Storm," from *Waltzing Through the Endtime*, Bottoms' narrator sits by a lake reading a book of ancient history, and like Wright's, contemplates the sky:

And in Egypt, it said, no historical evidence for the presence of the Jews.
No plagues then, no exodus, no forty years kicking around
in the wilderness —
                    so forget about the walls of the parted Red Sea
crushing Pharaoh's chariots, startling as it was in Technicolor.

Sure, they had the facts. It was history, archaeology.
And from there I might've quibbled with plenty of lovely pictures
in my illustrated Old Testament —
                          the ostrich following the elephant
into the clumsy ark, the bolting prophet in the belly of the fish —

> but the sun over the lake was slicing through the clouds
> in such a miraculously thin veil,
>   and the rose trellis lifted to the thunderbolts
> the waxy face of penitents, and all evening
> the stooped magnolia, leaves gray as sackcloth, trembled…

In sharp contrast to Wright's narrator, who searches the heavens for meaning and finds "Always the same sigh," Bottoms' narrator observes a thunderstorm, and affirms his belief in the transcendental. The choice of the word "quibbled" is telling. Historical and archeological findings may conflict with biblical passages, such as the parting of the Red Sea, but discrepancies between secular evidence and biblical accounts are viewed as little more than nitpicking. The narrator locates the metaphysical in the everyday. Nature is personified through Christian imagery, as the sun parts the stormy heavens in a "miraculously thin veil." Roses are likened to "penitents," and magnolias stoop and tremble in awe of what unfolds above, imagery that projects the narrator's reverence.

However, Bottoms turn from compressed narratives like Dickey's to meditative, balanced lines à la Wright is more than a stylistic change. While neither Dickey nor Wright share Bottoms' metaphysical assumptions, the move from tightly plotted poems to looser, more conversational verse reflects an ontological shift in Bottoms' work. Much of Bottoms' early poetry centers on epiphanies, moments of sudden revelations and declarations. In "Under the Vulture-Tree," the narrator drifts down a river on a boat, and passes a tree full of vultures perched on branches, resulting in a flash of insight:

> And I drifted away from them, slow, on the pull of the river,
> reluctant, looking back at their roost,
> calling them what I'd never called them, what they are,
> those dwarfed transfiguring angels,
> who flock to the side of the poisoned fox, the mud turtle
> crushed on the shoulder of the road,
> who pray over the leaf-graves of the anonymous lost,
> with mercy enough to consume us all and give us wings.

Many early poems that don't stress the metaphysical or use Christian imagery follow similar patterns. "Sign for My Father, Who Stressed the Bunt" plays off a series of puns, metaphors and similes, leading to the last three lines, when the narrator, who had "never learned what" his father "was laying down," declares:

> Like a hand brushed across the bill of a cap,
> Let this be the sign
> I'm getting a grip on the sacrifice.

While some poems in *Vagrant* Grace, a book which Bottoms' calls "transitional," resemble those in his previous collections, other poems are longer and contain non-linear story lines (in conversation). The collection's centerpiece, "Country Store and Moment of Grace," consists of eighteen un-numbered sections that shift between the present and the past. Unlike the tightly wrought narratives of Bottoms' first five books, the action unfolds through a series of often apparently unrelated scenes in a manner that resembles Wright's "undernarrative," a technique which Wright describes as "the story line that's underneath the imagistic line on top.... You come out to the landscape and you see where you are and then you go back in the tunnel, then back out to the landscape again," allowing him to move between the speculative and the concrete (*Southbound* 49). Bottoms tends to be less concerned with using the landscape as a touchstone for the philosophical, and more concerned with the social, but the way in which the poem winds and wanders from section to section is clearly indebted to Wright, who, like Dickey, is a poet Bottoms has long admired.

The seemingly loose structure also reflects the book's title, *Vagrant Grace*, and Bottoms' conception of grace. The poem presents the narrator's attempts to paste into "memory/these little scraps of consequence" at a time in life when "memory becomes portentous,/ like some new found gospel/ promising, finally, the whole fantastic story/ and unscrolling into fragments." The narrator, a contemporary white suburbanite, recalls sundry childhood incidents from the 1950s and 1960s, when racial strife racked his rural community. Remorse pricks and jolts his memory, leading to greater comprehension of grace, a revelation that extends beyond ordinary perception. The narrator comes to understand that the relationship between various memories, present and past, and grace is "vagrant," not cohering to a readily definable cause/effect structure.

Bottoms' suggests his approach relatively early in the poem, when the narrator watches his twelve year old daughter attempt to rake leaves into piles:

> Rachel rakes a few into a pile the wind disperses,
> And again I'm drawing parallels
> to the memory...
>   gusts behind the eyelids,
>   mulch of cosmic swirl...

In contrast to his previous emphasis on figurative language and archetype, Bottoms begins the poem in a prosaic, conversational manner. The narrator recalls his grandfather relaxing in a rocking chair by a pot-bellied stove. The older man is "wanting no trouble, pondering/ in his afternoon daze the promised serenities/ of the afterlife." He's comfortably lodged in the general store he owns, surrounded by the familiar sensations of "wood sizzle,/ and the raw smell of bologna and cheese, rack/ of Slim Jim and jerky, Tom's Snacks." But, as we discover in the next section, the world around him is hardly serene; it's engulfed by "wallowing clouds of discontent ... / ... rising from the Ralph Bunche School...," the local black high school where African-Americans are gathered, clamoring for civil rights.

The narrator remembers working "one afternoon"

>   when the store's jammed up around the stove,
>   I zip my jacket to pump a tank of gas—
>   rusted-out pickup, sagging
>   on its springs,
>   and looped around the rearview
>   a stiff noose
>   hanging like a pair of dice.

The theme of lynching resurfaces at several points in the poem, but the next section abruptly turns from the thread of racism and violence to the theme of storytelling. The narrator informs us that, "All through my childhood/ I hardly heard a story unfold around that stove.... Where were the storytellers I'd grown up/ to hear about?" These remarks seem unrelated to the issue of racial unrest, but, as becomes clear later in the poem, Bottoms is addressing the tendency to mistakenly stereotype. Rural southerners hanging around a woodstove in a country store are supposed to be storytellers. But the narrator can only recall poor, uneducated, ill, and tired working people, not cracker-barrel wits. He remembers "mostly grunts/ or nothing at all...":

>   Brooding or tongue-tied,
> worn-out in their walked-down boots and overalls shabby
> with clay and tobacco juice,
> or crippled, or sick,
>   coming straight
> from the mill where they'd retched out their lungs
> into smoking-booth peach cans,
>   weak
> and lint-crowned, wanting to get home.

These men are maimed spiritually as well as physically. As the narrator later points out, some of them are members of the Ku Klux Klan, the "Empire." He remembers being "eleven or twelve," and hearing the men joke about "*Nigger knocking*" while his grandfather silently rings the cash register. He considers his own complicity, and wonders if he joined in on the mirth, asking "who am I here/ pushing through the screen and into the air?"

The moment is an example of the "little self-judgments, needle jabs of regret" that motivate the narrator to make sense of the past and recognize grace. When the narrative switches back to the present, his suburban surroundings remind him of the past:

> And late into the night
> those prickly fingers of moonlight
> pointing from the bedroom wall, those sweaty sheets,
> that black noose of fuchsia
>   dangling from the planter.

Like the "prickly fingers of moonlight" that accusingly point at him, later in the poem the words "black," "noose," and "dangling" lead to additional recollections of lynching. But Bottoms uses these scenes to do more than describe guilt-ridden memories; they serve as catalysts for understanding others' suffering and bringing the narrator closer to God. However, Bottoms doesn't unravel the narrator's development in a linear manner. Past and present form a tapestry of apparently loosely connected incidents that move him towards the prospect of comprehending grace.

Bottoms raises the possibility of grace in the section that follows through an episode that once again seems unrelated to other moments in the poem. He recalls his grandmother's grief at the news that her son —

the narrator's father—had been killed in the Pacific Theatre during World War II:

> Fifteen months she thought him dead
>   and fell every evening
> at the alter of Oakdale
> until a woman in the church dreamed him wounded
> but face up,
>   alive in burning water...
>
> Tears and worn-out prayer bones
> and everything else is gravy—

Like the issue of stereotyping, Bottoms will later link the concept of grace to the theme of racism. But first the poem devotes sections to the narrator's memories of the Klan driving by his childhood home, of a black woman whose husband was lynched, and of corrupt local politics, until the penultimate section, which returns to the cold December day recalled in the poem's opening section.

Once again, several Klan members are in the store, gathered around the stove, discussing a violent racial incident in the news, when a cotton-haired black woman unexpectedly enters to buy a Coke. They are poised for confrontation, but the moment transpires without conflict:

> and the black hand digging
>   into the pocket of her coat
> brings out a coin purse, read and blue and beaded,
> like something you might buy
> on a reservation.
>
> Wood crackles
> as the door cries low on cold hinges...
>
> Cheated again, they see,
>   and a glassy angularity hardens
> on those faces
> as though each has seen history for what it is
> and not for what he's imagined.

The moment emphasizes the contrast between the characters' expectations and the reality of the situation. Rather than a politically charged confrontation, the characters only encounter an elderly lady who purchases a soda. The poem doesn't claim the Klan members, who feel "cheated," or his grandfather were instantly transformed, but the next section returns to the present, and the narrator recognizes the episode was a "moment of grace." The poem turns into prayer of witness:

> We go on now
> building on what they were obliged to build on,
> pasting into memory
>   these little scraps of consequence
> and self-acquittal,
>
> so that it's Amen finally to what can't be changed,
> to the noise of headline and newscast, feint
> and bluff of history,
> while the real thing
>   plays out quietly somewhere else...
>
> like my grandfather rocking up
> out of his chair,
>   not gauging their faces,
> not glancing at me watching, stunned, from the feed room
> as the woman fingered coins
> and lifted from the drink box a bottle of Coca-Cola,
> so that suddenly at the scripted moment
> the script fell away,
>   his hand simply opening,
> his head nodding slowly
> as she dropped two nickels and faded
> in the drizzle....

Unlike Bottoms' early verse, which stresses a moment of revelation, insight stems from the way in which memories accrue and give shape and form to the past. The importance of the grandfather's actions only become clear after decades of "pasting into memory/ these little scraps of consequence." The poem's form reflects the narrator's comprehension of the relation between past and present, and the "vagrant" manner in which memory cobbles together meaning. The narrator ends with homage to memory and the passage of time, as a series of Amens punctuate how the past is continually transformed into the present ("Amen even to the K-Mart where his grocery stood").

The techniques and concerns Bottoms explores in *Vagrant Grace* and *Waltzing Through the Endtime* suggest his desire to continue growing artistically. In essence, *Armored Hearts: New and Selected Poems* serves a signpost between one phase of his career and another. Near the conclusion of "Country Store and Moment of Grace" the narrator asks,

> What's left in these last moments but memory?
> And what is memory
> but the mirror image of hope?
>
> So Amen also to hope....

These sentiments reflect a noteworthy marker in Bottoms' poetic and metaphysical journey. Bottoms has increasingly emphasized the significance of memory and its impact on the present and the spiritual, a dynamic that continues to inspire aesthetic changes in an important poet's evolving quest to "reveal something about the hidden things of the world."

Works Cited

Baker, David. "Story's Story." *The Kenyon Review*, New Series, Vol. 24, No. 2 (Spring 2002), pp. 150–167.
Bottoms, David. *Armored Hearts: New and Selected Poems*. Port Townsend, WA: Copper Canyon Press, 1995.
———. *In a U-Haul North of Damascus*. New York: William Morrow, 1983.
———. *Shooting Rats at the Bibb County Dump*. New York: William Morrow, 1980.
———. *Under the Vulture-Tree*. New York: William Morrow, 1987.
———. *Vagrant Grace*. Port Townsend, WA: Copper Canyon Press, 1999.
———. *Waltzing Through the Endtime*. Port Townsend, WA: Copper Canyon Press, 2004.
Dickey, James. *Poems 1956–1967*. New York: Macmillan, 1968.
Ilya Kaminsky. Untitled review. *Library Journal*. Feb. 15, 2005, Vol. 130, No. 3, p. 134.
Suarez, Ernest. *Southbound: Interviews with Southern Poets*, Columbia: University of Missouri Press, 1999.
Wright, Charles. *World of the Ten-Thousand Things*. New York: Farrar, Straus and Giroux, 1991.

Fishing from the Poetry Boat: A Conversation

ALICE FRIMAN *and*
MARSHALL BRUCE GENTRY

This interview was conducted in 1995 following David Bottoms' reading in the Allen and Helen Kellogg Writers Series at the University of Indianapolis shortly after the release of *Armored Hearts: Selected and New Poems* from Copper Canyon Press, and again in 1997 at the South Central Modern Language Association meeting in Dallas. Friman composed the poetry questions — Gentry, the fiction questions.

Friman and Gentry: One of the things that comes through strongly in Under the Vulture-Tree *is the character of the "I" as hero, one who saves. How is the person who wrote the new poems in* Armored Hearts *different from the "I" who wrote* Vulture-Tree?

Bottoms: That's not a difficult distinction. *Vulture-Tree* was written when I lived in east Cobb County on a little pond. I was married to my first wife then, and things were relatively calm in my life. I spent a lot of time fishing and playing guitar. I was teaching at Georgia State. I was in a pretty good place in my life. Or so it seemed. Yes, I remember "White Shrouds" came out of that house and "In the Ice Pasture" and "Ice" and "Red Swan" and "The Voice of Wives Dreaming." It was a period of relative peace and ease just before I went to the University of Montana to be the Hugo Poet-in-Residence. Living in Montana was a turning point, personally and professionally, because it opened up a whole new landscape. I went out there to teach and my wife stayed home in Georgia. Our relationship had been growing more and more distant. We didn't really have much in common, although there was no animosity. We'd gotten married when we were very young, and when I came back from Montana, we decided to split.

How long were you in Montana?
　　I was only there for one term that time. Then I came home to Georgia and went through the divorce. I'd met my present wife, Kelly, up there. She was in law school at the University of Montana, and so we had a long-distance relationship for about a year. I got several grants that year, and I think I spent most of the money on airline tickets. After the divorce and a year of living the long-distance relationship, I took a year off from Georgia State and moved to Billings to finish *Easter Weekend*. Kelly had moved there to start a law practice. Consequently, the novel has all that Montana stuff in it.

You said Vulture-Tree *is from that time of relative peace before everything sort of shredded apart.*
　　Peter Davison told me once — he had stayed with us in that house — that he was very sorry I'd lost that place because he knew it was really important to my poems. It hadn't really occurred to me how many of the poems came out of that house and pond, but a lot of them did. Fortunately, Montana was a good place, too. It was so open. It was a totally new landscape. The poems, when I got to Montana, opened up a little bit too, so that many of them ceased to have the hard closure that characterizes most of my other poems. That vastness of landscape, I think, was very good for me.

In the Shooting Rats *poems, especially "Watching Gators at Ray Boone's Reptile Farm," there are themes that run through the complete* Armored Hearts. *One is the idea of a common memory — what you call the "breathable past." Would you discuss that?*
　　I think we're talking about two different things here. I talk a lot in my classes about archetypes, about this notion of racial memory which I find fascinating. But those particular poems are interesting because they came out of an idea I got from Carl Sagan — I forget who actually pioneered all this research, but Sagan distilled it in his *Dragons of Eden*. It was the notion of the triune brain, that the brain actually developed as three different brains, all of which are still there. The first is that little mass of tissue at the top of the spine, the R Complex or the reptile brain, which supposedly controls eating, sex, and ritual, and then on top of that formed

the limbic or mammal brain, which controls emotion, and finally on top of that the neo-cortex, huge in comparison, which supposedly accounts for abstract thought and differentiates us from other creatures, which I guess isn't quite thought to be true anymore. Aren't they figuring out that apes actually abstract in some small way? Anyway, that's where those things come from — the notion of the reptile brain. Okay, here's an odd thing. The first time I met James Merrill, I was really pretty intimidated. We were going out to lunch with all these hoity-toity people in New York, and the first thing he said to me was a line from my poem "Crawling Out at Parties": "My old reptile loves the scotch." It was very nice of him to do that. It put me at ease, gave us something to talk about. Anyway, he had also felt that strain running through the poems, and he was genuinely interested — something I found strange for a man whose poems are so polished and urbane. Well, the triune brain, that's where it comes from. I suppose I've always been drawn toward the primitive aspects of the psyche. It runs through *U-Haul, Vulture-Tree, Armored Hearts,* all the animal poems.... I think I still have the same notions about how that affects us in our relationships. The most important aspect, of course, is how it connects us with the world, the wilderness. It's our last remnant of wildness, of the primordial.

And for you the animal world is what?

The animal world is the real world. To me the world out there in the woods is the real world, the world the way it was made, and everything else is something of an aberration, much less significant. Nature is always right. The very best poets have always understood this. It's a notion, of course, that's fundamental to the Romantic movement. Actually, it's just plain fundamental. What I really want to do now is move to the woods. That's my big dream. Very often in our lives, if we give it the chance, the old reptile brain will recognize something, remember, and sway out toward it. I often catch it trying to make connections. Like that old poem "The Copperhead" where a fascination or an affinity in the persona is pulling him down into the water and toward the snake.

Would you talk about the technique you use to evoke the past? In poems like "The Voice of Wives Dreaming," "The Desk," "The Anniversary," and "In Louisiana," the past seems to be called up into a vivid present without your ever resorting to a rhetorical device like saying "I remember." How do you do that?

I don't think about that. It may all be related in some peripheral way to the act of narrative itself. Narration is often the past made immediate — it's just storytelling, of course — and the importance of detail is to make the world alive again on the page. It's a matter of being convincing. I really believe that all readers are basically skeptics, and your first obligation as a writer is to overcome that skepticism. You can only do that with convincing detail, to make readers willingly fling away that disbelief, at least for the period of the poem. That's Coleridge's phrase, isn't it? The "willing suspension of disbelief." Anyway, verb tense for the sake of immediacy or anything else is only a narrative technique, one of many things you use to convince the reader of your veracity.

In the poem "In a Kitchen, Late," you speak of "making yourself no presence in the room." Would you talk about the importance of passivity or negative capability?

That poem is essentially about making yourself no human presence. In the poem it has to do with trying to re-enter the wilderness; the roaches are bringing a little bit of it back to you. Still, it's impossible for you really to do that — face it, you like your nice house in the suburbs. And more to the point, you're self-conscious, you rationalize. Any creature that is self-conscious can't ever totally regain the instinctive impulse that governs the life of animals. James Dickey probably has the best poem in the language about this whole question. It's called "The Sheep Child." Jim told me once that he didn't care what anybody said about that poem, he didn't think it could be faulted for originality of point of view. Well, that's what the poem's all about, right? It has some great lines: "I saw for a blazing moment/ The great grassy world from both sides,/ Man and beast in the round of their need,/ And the hill wind stirred in my wool,/ My hoof and my hand clasped each other." Here's one of the fundamental questions of human existence, this great feeling we have of being displaced from the natural world by virtue of our own self-consciousness. This is the whole story of the Fall, isn't it? And here he unites these two aspects again — the rational and the instinctive — in the point-of-view of this sheep-child, and of course the irony is that this is so horribly unnatural the sheep-child dies immediately. What a great line, "My hoof and my hand clasped each other." Anyway, I think that's the whole notion of making yourself "no presence in the room." It's an attempt — feeble as it might be — to experience that reunification to whatever degree you can accomplish, which probably isn't very much.

In light of that, how do the jon boat and water fit in?

Water is a medium into the natural world, that's all. The boat is a mode of transportation. The act of fishing itself is really fascinating to me, emotionally and psychologically. I talk about poetry a lot in terms of fishing.

Like Thoreau?

Well, fishing is a great metaphor for poetry, if you think about it, at least the way I look at poetry. My kind of poetry is this constant dredging up of things out of the psyche. I like what Seamus Heaney says in a very nice essay called "Feeling into Words." The first time he ever wrote what he thought was a good poem, he says, he felt like he'd let down a shaft into himself. Poetry, the act of creation, also had become an act of self-discovery. I feel the same way, and fishing is an interesting metaphor for the process. You're out there alone in the little poetry boat, throwing out your lure — a wonderful word here — and you're casting down into the depths, the psychic depths. Of course, you're going for the creative impulse, the stuff of the great poem, you're going for the seven-pound bass, but you don't know what's down there. You just have to be willing to cast out that Rooster-tail or that Jelly Worm and take whatever hits the line. Carl Jung had an interesting notion about creativity. Ironically, the seeds of creativity are mixed into what he calls the "slime from the depth," that psychic slime, the ugliest and most animalistic aspects of our personality. These are all those fearful things we've confined, repressed into our subconscious. But if you're after the creative impulse, you have to be willing to wallow around in that a little bit. Or coming back to the fishing metaphor, you have to be willing to drag up whatever hits your lure — gar, loggerhead, water moccasin, alligator. All of this for me — the water, the jon boat, the fishing — is metaphor for the creative act. It's also a literal part of my life and I enjoy it.

Why call the entire new and selected poems Armored Hearts?

"Armored Hearts" is a poem that I've read a lot over the last few years. It's one of the earlier poems in the last section of that book, the new poems, and it just sort of kept coming up at readings. People kept saying they liked the name. And it suggests several interesting things to me. Of course, it refers to turtles and that armament they have, but it also refers to a kind of a defensive mechanism I think that we all learn to build early on in our lives. In some ways, living in our culture requires an armored heart. I talk a lot to my students about the creative act, about where ideas come from, and all I've ever figured out is that the writer must simply be as sensitive to the world as he or she can stand, hoping that an idea hits. But sensitivity is a dangerous thing too. The world can be overwhelming. All hearts have kind of an armament, I think, that we learn to build up as self-defense. Otherwise, the grief would squash us. The trick is finding that fine line, absorbing every impulse you can from the world without overburdening yourself, without getting squashed.

In "Armored Hearts," the two human characters seem like the two sides of yourself — the one who saves things (going back to David Bottoms as hero here), and the other one, a darker one, like the turtles themselves, clinging to solitude.

Actually both men in the poem are saving things. One is trying to save the ducks, the other the turtles. I guess I'm drawn more to the turtles. They're that sort of submerged aspect of the personality, the secretive — I might even say the mysterious, the almost mystical aspect of the personality, the psyche, much more primitive than the ducks. The ducks fly, they're airy. Yes, I'd side with the turtles. So the persona goes out at the end of the poem and strips the bait off the hooks of the guy who's trying to catch them.

I want to ask the question again. Isn't there some of you in the guy with the pistol? I say that because of the way you introduce the poem at readings, making the guy trying to save the ducks sound so sympathetic. Everybody in the room who hasn't read the poem expects you to side with the saviour of ducks — then they are shocked when you read the end of the poem.

Maybe that's the social aspect of the personality — getting along with our neighbors, socializing — oh, the turtles are killing the ducks, how horrible, of course you've got to go get those turtles. But then the other aspect emerges and becomes dominant. And essentially it becomes dominant at night, doesn't it? In secret. He goes out at night and strips away the bait.

The "I" in your newer poems seems different from the rest of the book, much darker.

I might agree. As I said, I went through a divorce when I was 37 or 38. That was a terrible thing, though it was not a messy legal business as some divorces are. I'd been married for 15 years and gotten very comfortable, then suddenly I had nothing. I think I left that marriage with about

$1000 and a truck. I just gave it all away, house, bank account, everything. So I was asking a lot of questions about my life and where I was going, and frankly, the next few years were quite a struggle.

So all of these new poems came from those years?
    Yes, and then on top of all that, every word I'd ever written went out of print. All those books that Morrow published sold pretty well for poetry — about five thousand copies each, the editions all sold out — but they didn't reprint them. It was disheartening. But this isn't uncommon for American poets.

You've said you couldn't get your editor on the phone.
    That's right. I couldn't get a phone call returned by my editor at Morrow. So I'm spending my whole life writing poems and I'm wondering — why am I doing this? Why am I beating my brains out doing this? Obviously, the only good reason to write poems is because you enjoy it. You certainly don't do it for the money or the fame. Young writers often have silly ideas about this. I see it all the time. That's why I talk about the dangers of false ambition. The only good ambition, of course, is to write something you like. But, yes, it was a difficult time in many ways, having worked so hard for so long and not even to have a book in print, not a novel or a book of poems, and about the only way to deal with that in the poetry was to write a poem like "Allatoona Evening." But my vision has always been pretty bleak. Then again, there's hope out there, too. My life has changed dramatically for the better with the new marriage and the birth of our daughter. Surprisingly enough, people have said that since we've had this little girl, I must be writing tons of nice poems about being a father, and it hasn't really happened. I mean, I love her with all my heart, but I guess artistically my personality isn't geared toward writing sunny poems. Dave Smith said one time in an essay that all poems are about two things — life and death. I wrote a little piece a few years later and said that he was at least half right — all poems are really about death. One book I like to point out to students is Ernest Becker's *The Denial of Death*, a great book that won the Pulitzer for non-fiction in 1995. The premise is, of course, that there is only one real truth in our lives and that's our death. Becker says that all the other aspects of our personality are geared to deny it. They're all lies. Of course, they're very healthy and necessary lies, otherwise we'd just walk out in front of a truck. One of the best metaphors Becker uses is an onion. You take an onion, put it down on a table, and

slice it in half. The core of the onion is your death, and all the layers built up around it are the layers of your personality, all of your interests, the things you involve yourself in — I'm going to be a great poet, I'm going to be a great pianist, I'm going to be a great painter. Well, these things are only distractions, denials, lies, they won't save us. Where are Whitman and Yeats? Where's Vladimir Horowitz? Where are Gauguin, Matisse, Picasso? But here's the point. These things, even though they are lies, are the material of art. This is the stuff out of which we make poems and stories, so in that sense all poems are about death. At the heart, at the core, there is always that fundamental truth. Even the sunniest poem has this kind of death shadow, this dark spot at the core of it. "Why are we reading all these sad poems in class?" Because all poems are about death. Everything is, in its own way.

You've talked about the poet as an FM receiver.

Yes, that's one of my cornier metaphors for the poet. I think I was talking about creativity in general, the whole process. And I was talking again about that Heaney essay, "Feeling into Words," the way he speaks of creativity as two separate stages. I like that. The first is that sort of initial idea or inspiration, that first impulse that a poem needs to be written, and then the second stage is the going to the word processor, the typewriter, the number 2 pencil, and fleshing out the original impulse, applying all that you've learned about craft. Of course, this second stage can actually be facilitated. This is what we try to do in writing classes when we teach folks about figurative language, sound devices, narrative, diction, myth. But the first stage — the initial impulse — which to me is the real creative act, is slightly more mysterious. There really doesn't seem to be very much you can teach anyone about that. Either it happens or it doesn't, the idea comes or it doesn't. The only thing anyone can do, I think, is to make himself or herself more available to the world, more receptive to things going on, and so the analogy of the radio receiver. The world is trying to send us these signals and we have to be tuned in.

What are the differences between writing poetry and fiction?

Well, for me about the only similarity is that I write them both in English. Fiction writing is much more like a job. Novelists always have something to do — you get an idea for a piece of fiction, you sit down for a couple of weeks and you plot it all out, and you have something to work on from nine to five for the next two or three years. You feel like you're accomplishing something. "Oh, I got my ten pages today," and you can sleep well at night. The process of poetry is nothing like that. Poetry is much more a product of the inspired moment. You get your idea and you flesh it out, you work through it, then you need another one. Don't get the notion this is something that takes place in fifteen or twenty minutes, or even an hour or two. Maybe a draft might take that long, but then the real work of revision comes. Still, the process rarely takes two or three years. And very often I'll nurse along several poems at a time. Soon enough, though, you're faced with the problem of the next idea. And most days, quite frankly, you won't have one. A lot of young poets sit down at their typewriters every morning and face that blank page without the foggiest idea propelling them. They just have this need to create, this need to write. I empathize with them, but I think that's one of the worst forms of self-abuse a poet can practice. I never go to the typewriter unless I have a pretty clear grasp of some propelling idea, unless the world actually has suggested something interesting to me. And this is the problem with so many poems these days — they just don't have any sense of necessity about them. The real poem, the necessary poem, doesn't come often, and patience is something young writers usually have to learn the hard way. I think I said somewhere that writing a poem is like getting a short-term contract from God. You get this one done and if you do a good job, then maybe another contract will come along.

In "Sign for My Father, Who Stressed the Bunt," are you talking about sacrifice in terms of what's required to be a poet?

No, I think that's reading too much into the poem. You can certainly extend the notion of sacrifice to any of the arts, nothing worthy is accomplished without sacrifice and all that, but I don't think that poem was ever intended to be metaphor for art. The poem is about my father and about baseball. The sacrifice in its figurative sense is the sacrifice of one generation for the next.

"Under the Boathouse" seems like another poem very much about writing. You don't think so, even with a naked man jumping head first into the lake he knows nothing about?

I don't know. I suppose you might read that as a metaphor for the creative act, the willingness to dive in. But I didn't think about that. We were talking about fishing as a metaphor for poetry and that's the same sort of thing. One thing that I find interesting about "Under the Boathouse" is the way it works figuratively. I spend a lot of time with students talking about narrative, but I'm pretty careful to warn them that narrative isn't all you need to make a good poem — not nearly enough. For me, at least, much of the art of poetry is the way it works figuratively, the way it suggests something beyond itself. The poem needs to spring from that concrete situation or narrative context into what we call the Deep Hidden Meaning, the DHM. Usually this happens through language, but oddly enough, there is at least one other way this can happen. That's when the narrative itself becomes figurative, when it touches archetypal pattern and myth. This is what I was going for in "Under the Boathouse." In the elements of the narrative it touches what Jung calls the "myth of the night journey," the submersion, the symbolic death, ascension and rebirth illustrated in the Old Testament story of Jonah and the whale. Students are also pretty quick to recognize the elements of baptism here, and they're right. The poem is literally about a man diving into a lake, but the narrative pattern resonates in the reader in ways that he or she may not immediately recognize. If you look at the language in that poem, you'll see when the persona of the poem is surfacing, ascending, he looks up and he sees the shadow of his wife on top of the water, like an angel in a dead man's float. And he makes references to heavenly litter, things like that. So the language in the poem tries to bear out the archetypal pattern.

Any Cold Jordan connects music and crime. Any connection to the poetry? You say your writing is autobiographical, and both novels head toward crime with a lot of energy.

    That's a pretty interesting question. I haven't really thought about that at all, but the poem "The Desk" comes immediately to mind. Also "In the Black Camaro," "Rendezvous: Belle Glade," and "Light of the Sacred Harp." And "Wrestling Angels," an even older poem, which is about a graveyard vandal. It probably has more to do with the notion of authority, and the notion that we all have these impulses in our lives, these notions that we as individuals are really more significant than any imposed authority. I mean, that we feel we have more moral authority — that our needs account for more moral authority — than the Cherokee County Board of Education or the Indianapolis City Council, or the Police Department, or the Constitution of the United States. Who are these people who keep forcing us to live by their rules? Well, in art we can explore these things. My agent, Maria Carvainis, has a good line. She handles a lot of commercial fiction, of course, and she's sort of condensed the art of fiction into one sentence: "All good fiction is about the right to sin." There's a lot in that — the whole conflict between legal authority and moral authority, which can lead to a kind of justifiable sin and justifiable rebellion.

That's certainly true in the poem "The Desk."

Yes. The persona just says to himself, "This desk really belongs to me. I'm just going to go on up there and get it." And he goes up to the old school building at one o'clock or so in the morning with a crowbar and a hammer, and he breaks in.

In Any Cold Jordan, *Jerry Lamberti symbolizes the danger of being ruined by artistic integrity, the refusal to sell out. Do you think in terms of high and low, integrity and selling out?*

I don't know. If I had a talent to write a really popular novel and knew that I could write this book and it would sell like *The Bridges of Madison County*, I might be tempted to do that. Just one. But I feel like whatever flaws my two novels have, they were both written primarily from an artistic impulse. I really feel like *Easter Weekend* has an interesting sort of mythic underpinning, with the open grave and the Easter business. The book came to me the same way that poems tend to come — with that sort of initial flash of an idea. And it was all there, as a whole. I don't feel as if I compromised very much. I didn't write it for the popular taste, I wrote it the way I wanted it. Two screenplays have been done, and both give it a happy-ever-after ending. That's what you expect from Hollywood, and I've never been very interested in Hollywood. The only thing those guys care about is what sells. But I am interested in talking about Jerry Lamberti. He's based on a friend of mine who's an incredible blues musician but mostly a kind of acoustic Delta blues guitarist, a Josh White-type. He's spent thirty years of his life living in real poverty in Macon, Georgia, because there's just no commercial market for that kind of music. I think I have a lot of respect for that. And that's really the same question that Billy Parker has to deal with. He's happiest with his music when he's playing what he enjoys, when he feels he has some sort of artistic integrity. His problem is simple, at this point in his life he needs some commercial success. But in order to achieve that kind of success he has to compromise, he has to sing the hokey country stuff the drunks want.

So what about the jon boat business, what about Billy's passivity? Is this a copout, a sign of his failure?

Well, there are different kinds of success. When he's out there fishing, just floating alone on the water, just trying to become a part of it all out in the wilderness, or when he's playing his own music, he's very close to the voice in many of my poems, to the aesthetic of something like "Allatoona Evening." This is a different sort of ambition. And really the only one that counts. It's that sort of personal integrity and peace that he has accomplished there that accounts for so little in the real world, the world of the American economy, but accounts for so much on a personal level.

Who is your audience, and is it different for poetry than for fiction?

I don't really visualize any particular audience. I think I just try to say things as best I can, as though I were writing for any literate and intelligent person. I remember reading somewhere that someone, maybe Peter Stitt, asked Robert Penn Warren "How do you read a poem?" and Warren thought for a minute and said, "Slowly." And I think that says what I really feel about audience. Anyone who will take the time and really give the poem the consideration it deserves is my audience.

Do you have people you show your poems to?

Yes, but I don't show them to many people. I only have one person I show them to regularly, and that's a friend whose name is Bob Hill. He wrote that Twayne book on Dickey. I'll work on a poem for a few days until I've done about all I can do for a while, then I'll pick up the phone and say, "Bob, I'm going to fax something over to you." If he has any problems with it, I'll just go back to work. The benefit of this is enormous because I know that I've gotten a very intelligent and thoughtful reading.

Whenever you talk about Easter Weekend *you say something about religion. Would you compare how religion comes into that novel with how religion comes into the poetry?*

Religion in *Easter Weekend* is only kind of an underpinning that acts as background and gives the book some mythic depth. We see these characters moving across a landscape and we recognize certain archetypes operating, and this opens up possibilities for irony. Will Connie be resurrected? Questions like that. In the poems, religion is much more personal and substantial, important in a more direct way. The poems draw on it and wrestle with it in ways the fiction has yet to attempt. It's fundamental to the poems, but peripheral to the fiction.

Would you talk about the St. Augustine epigraph to Armored Hearts? *What does it do? What does it say about you?*

Why did I put that in there? I was reading St. Augustine's *Confessions* and that passage just jumped out at me. And when I was putting *Armored Hearts* together, I remembered it. Then I looked at three or four different translations. The one I used is by far the least literal, but the most beautiful. "My soul is like a house," Augustine says. Maybe I meant to suggest that the book is also like a house, a place where the soul expresses itself. The book reflects what's working in the soul, and it's not all nice stuff. All is not sunlight and flowers. There are dark thoughts. "It is in ruins," he says. And I think that's particularly apt to the latter part of the book. And then he says, "but I ask you to remake it." St. Augustine was talking to God. Only God can put some order there.

Are you religious then?

Yes, though for a long time I felt odd about discussing it. In these days of the religious right, if you say you believe in God, many folks are apt to think you're unsophisticated, if not a little simple. This attitude seems very arrogant to me. There's an intelligence of the head and an intelligence of the heart. But to answer your question, I was raised Southern Baptist, and though it's meant less to me at various times, I think that over the last ten or so years Christianity has become very important. I don't go to church every Sunday, and I think the Christian church as we know it today is a far cry from the early church Paul founded, nevertheless I call myself a Christian. I'll point you to a good book I just read —*Jesus: A Life*, by A.N. Wilson. Wilson is not a theologican, but a historian, the biographer of Tolstoy and C.S. Lewis. He spends about two hundred and fifty pages stripping away the various Biblical myths concerning Jesus's life, looking for the historical person. When he gets through, not much is really left of our assumptions. He rationalizes the resurrection as a case of mistaken identity, a point on which we disagree, and chips in other ways at Jesus's divinity. Nevertheless, the book is a fascinating look at the Jewish culture and Jesus's role in it, especially the politics of the region, and it was for me, ironically, a real medicine for my own faith. But the St. Augustine epigraph is essentially a prayer, and I find it meaningful. He talks about perfection as being a kind of evolution, of God helping him to remake his life, not instantaneously, but gradually. What the poems are trying to do, especially in the last half of *Armored Hearts*, is find a gradual working toward resignation and peace. Christianity provides that through a shedding of false ambition, which just creates in us anger and frustration. "Allatoona Evening," the last poem in the book, is very important for me in a number of ways. It's a poem that came out of many frustrations — writing and teaching and a lot of other things — and I think the key lines of the poem are about this equating of anger and ambition, where the bats and the whippoorwills and the copperheads and everything out there by the lake say "lay it down … your ambition,/ which is only anger,/ which sated could bring you to no better place." Even if all our ambitions were sated, they could bring us to no better spiritual place than this one moment here beside this lake with "these three stars soaking up twilight." I really like the ending of that poem.

So what would you say is a healthy kind of ambition?

For a poet, the healthiest kind is to want to write the best poem you can write and leave it at that, regardless of what happens to be the current taste of *The New Yorker*, or whatever they're thinking at *American Poetry Review* or *The Georgia Review*. Who could care less? What you're trying to do is write the best poem you can write, and figure out how that illuminates and helps you in your own life. I tell people in my classes, "Whatever else happens, you'll always have your poems. Your relationship to your own words. Keep that as a joy. You can always have that, and it doesn't depend on anybody else."

"If It Touches Us, It Touches Us": The White Southern Male Struggle with Race[1]

Jane Hill

A native of Canton, Georgia, in Cherokee County, David Bottoms, born in 1949, grew up during the 1950s and 60s. Since he began publishing poems in the early 1970s, Bottoms has often used Canton and his experiences there in his exploration of male identity. Juxtaposing the gender conceptions of his father's and grandfather's eras with those of his baby-boomer generation, Bottoms has, over the span of a quarter-century, articulated a revised version of the southern male. From his model we can draw valuable conclusions about the place of gender and family in the region in the current moment.[2] But his poetry also provides an insightful portrait of how southern males of Bottoms' generation have both incorporated and transformed the racial attitudes of their fathers and grandfathers. Although race has not been a major subject matter for Bottoms, *Vagrant Grace* (1999) includes his longest published poem to date, "Country Store and Moment of Grace," an eighteen-page work that first appeared in *Poetry* magazine. In that poem, Bottoms weaves a tapestry from his cultural legacy regarding race, the dramatic alterations in attitudes toward race that have occurred during his lifetime, and his present life in a fashionable suburban community north of Atlanta. From that tapestry, we can read a story in which race becomes an additional gauge by which to measure the ways that baby-boomer males born and reared in Appalachia see themselves, their heritage, and their present-day reality.

In reading Bottoms' poetry, I assume that he has relied primarily upon a single poetic persona throughout his career and that we can trace the evolution of that persona, the first-person speaker of so many of his poems, from the early work of the 1970s up to *Vagrant Grace*. In watching the shifts in that character's conception of his role as a man living within the specific current of history that delineates him from men of other times and places, including his male forebears, we begin to see the poet's gradual yet steady (re)alignment with the traditional image of southern maleness even as we also note how he modifies and expands that image. What are the particular gifts that the masculinity that ultimately presents itself within the context of his work offers its readers?[3]

In his first collection, *Shooting Rats at the Bibb County Dump*, Bottoms addresses the issue of race in this environment in "Stumptown Attends the Picture Show" (AH 14), a poem that he locates specifically with an epigraph: "on the first attempt at desegregation in Canton, Georgia." Writing with uncharacteristic detachment in third-person, the poet remembers how his community responded to the rumor that local blacks were planning to integrate the Canton Theater. While clearly of the white community there, the speaker is also beyond them in both time and place. He looks backward in time, remembers with the hindsight of someone who has lived through integration and, perhaps, in places other than Canton. Absent from the poem, except as they are implied in the word *desegregation*, are the town's African-American citizens; thus, those familiar with the body of the poet's work can infer from the idiosyncratic point of view he adopts here that he is consciously or unconsciously situating himself in sympathy with the minority in this plot. Like them, he is only an implied presence. The poem's focus is white reaction to an implied threat.

That reaction involves "[canning] Vivien Leigh" in favor of "the real show" taking place outside on the sidewalk in front of the theater. Having abandoned the reels of film scheduled to project images of what readers will probably conclude is the South gone with the wind in Leigh's most famous movie, the projectionist uses "folding chairs against the theater doors" to protect his space, behavior Bottoms compares to that of heroes in the westerns that play in that space. On the other side of the doors, "good old boys line the sidewalk, / string chain between parking meters / ... / dig in like Rebels in a Kennesaw trench." This set of images accomplishes many things for our detached speaker. He invokes the popular culture version of the Old South myth, as constructed by the film adaptation of *Gone with the Wind*, underscoring the illusory nature of that particular vision of the region. He also suggests that the efforts to preserve and protect that legacy are at once fragile — folding chairs in front of glass doors, chains looped between parking meters — and comic, but also perhaps noble in their connection to those in the trenches on Kennesaw Mountain. As the ticket girl Martha watches from her glass booth, the Canton moon and the flickering streetlights transform her vision much as a "magic lantern" (or a film projector) might. Martha is, according to the speaker, unable to "follow the plot," a failure that her co-worker, the projectionist, shares. Thus, Bottoms tells us that ordinary Canton folks find themselves involved in a narrative beyond their comprehension; in addition, they seem bound to process the real history unfolding before their eyes as if it were an artifact manufactured by Cecil B. DeMille or David Lean.

The proud southern whites, descendents of men who fought a war in the name of states' rights, also find themselves at the mercy of "the State Boys" who have been summoned by radio, local control having been deemed inadequate to the task presented by an emerging new world order. The poem ends before any actual confrontation takes place. Like the African-American citizens and the speaker himself, the actual confrontation is missing. The community's anticipation is Bottoms' concern here. Like the poem's characters in the sixties, we readers are forced to wait while "the State Boys [wind] down some county road, / moving in a cloud of dust toward the theater marquee." Bottoms freezes a moment in time. The citizens of Stumptown, Canton's black neighborhood, are ready to make a move. Despite incomprehension, their white neighbors are ready to resist that move. In 1980, when *Shooting Rats* first appeared in book form, the speaker consciously leaves himself and his readers frozen in a moment significant because "Only one thing is certain: / elements from different worlds are converging, / spinning toward confrontation."

Not until nineteen years later, when *Vagrant Grace* appeared in 1999, does Bottoms resolve, in print, his feelings about that key moment in his hometown's and his region's history. "Country Store and Moment of Grace" (VG 37–55) is set literally in the speaker's grandfather's store and figuratively in a world that no longer exists.[4] The poet is conscientious in recreating the lost world; his techniques are those of local color, the sense of nostalgia similar to that in Sarah Orne Jewett's evocation of a Maine fishing village in her regionalist classic *The Country of the Pointed Firs*. The poem opens with the grandfather performing yo-yo tricks in the store, "...wanting no trouble, pondering / in his afternoon daze the promised serenities / of the afterlife" (37). Using his trademark first-person narrator in this poem, Bottoms lovingly catalogs the items that he remembers and, at the same time, establishes the cultural identity which has shaped him:

> Pot-gut stove and wood sizzle,
> and the raw smell of bologna and cheese, rack
> of Slim Jim and jerky, Tom's Snacks,
> peppermint, drift of kerosene from a paint can,
> and from where he sits,
> glazed sweetness
> of stacked tobacco… [37].

Gospel music plays on the radio; the wood floor has been carefully oiled for many years; the light inside comes from naked bulbs suspended from the ceiling.

This nostalgic portrait is disturbed by the same rumors of change that set Canton on edge in "Stumptown Attends the Picture Show." This time the poet calls to our attention "…those wallowing clouds / of discontent…" generated by "the Ralph Bunche School" (38). The speaker remembers going to pump gas for a customer during this period of threat. The vehicle, a "rusted-out pickup, sagging / on its springs," features, looped around its rearview mirror, "a stiff noose" (38), a sign of resistance even more ominous than the chains between the parking meters in the earlier poem. The aura of resistance within the world of the store seems almost "natural," as if this is the developmental stage to which the region has evolved at this moment in its history. The speaker remembers no conversation out of which a planned response emerges — instead, he recalls a silent, masculine world in which communication occurs through "…mostly grunts / or nothing at all" (38). Yet the feeling is definitely one of a united community, a group of like-minded thinkers bound by tradition and history. In retrospect, the poet concludes that these men were silent, rather than the lively storytellers of regional legend, largely because they were "…crippled, or sick," victims of mill work that leaves them "[retching] out their lungs / into smoking-booth peach cans," "weak / and lint-crowned, wanting to get home" (39).

The context established here provides the possibility that the resistance to change signaled in the stiff noose looped round the pickup's mirror is not merely or even primarily a resistance to integration per se so much as it is a symbol of a broader resistance to change. The men who congregate in and shop at the grandfather's store, the grandfather himself even, become representatives of that generation of southern men who see their agrarian past forever eclipsed by industrialization — here, specifically textile mills — and they know in their very bodies the destruction inherent in that shift.

Knowing that they will never again get home to the world they long for, they — from their perspective at least — understandably seek to preserve whatever shreds of the familiar that remain. If one of those happens to be segregation, so be it. Resistance to change is resistance to change. The face of that change is less material than the impetus that propels it.

In his present-day suburban reality, where the only evidence that his grandfather's world ever existed seems to be his own memories, the middle-aged speaker sees these events at the store as "...portentous, / like some newfound gospel" (39). Presiding over the barbecue grill as his young daughter plays in the safety of their upscale subdivision, the poet struggles to reconcile his memories with the world he now inhabits. The men he remembers bear — again in their very bodies — evidence of the sacrifices their world has exacted: one left a hand in Italy during the war; another has been crippled in a logging accident. They lack the sophistication so pervasive as to be ironic in the speaker's present reality. In his neighborhood no one would manicure himself with a pocket knife, as one of the men at the store was prone to doing. Nor would anyone in East Cobb openly use the expression "Nigger knocking" (41), to which his grandfather makes no response when it is voiced aloud in his store. Instead, he goes on doing his work, ringing up items on the cash register, as if the words themselves and the actions they evoke were insignificant. While his grandfather seems unaffected, the speaker remembers his reaction as child: "Blood rush and the white haze / of laughter...," but looking back he also has questions: "Whose laughter? And who am I here / pushing through the screen and into the air?" (41).

As in the earlier poem, the speaker seems intent on separating himself from the context of his white world. He must leave the store — in general, a site of great security and comfort for him — in order to breathe, and it is, according to the narrative he reconstructs in middle-age, the racist language and intolerant attitude of his grandfather's friends that make him flee. His sense of alienation from the dominant male culture of his childhood years is further reinforced as he remembers a turkey shoot sponsored by the Canton Little League. In this world guns are "...cherished / blue steel cradled in the plush / of unzipped cases" (42), but in his room at night he sees "that black noose of fuchsia / dangling from the planter" (42), and internally he feels threatened, scared, not brave, not ready to raise one of the cherished weapons from its plush case and bag a turkey, even within the secure confines of a Little League fundraiser. By feeling — in his own body — the threat of the imagined noose, the younger version of the speaker aligns himself with those implied victims of the noose on the pickup that he pumps the gas for, and in that alignment he inevitably separates himself from the prevalent white male culture of Canton.

But the speaker's relationship to that culture and to the men who create and sustain it is more complicated than a simple baby-boomer's rebellion against injustice. By moving directly from his fear of the fuchsia noose dangling from his bedroom planter to memories of his father's experience in the Pacific during World War II, Bottoms succinctly captures the dilemma of the sensitive baby-boomer. His patriarchal legacy is not only racism but also great heroism. Bottoms has written in several poems of his father's war experience.[5] But in this long poem he tries to imagine that experience from his grandparents' perspective:

> Whenever I think I know about grief,
> I imagine an only son lost
> in the Pacific,
>   an ear to the Philco for sketchy news...
> Coral Sea, Midway, Guadalcanal...
> and picture my grandmother collapsing one
>   morning
> by the mailbox,
> crushed letter like a rock in her hand.
>
> Fifteen months she thought him dead [43].

Again, Bottoms seeks to paint a precise picture of the world his grandparents inhabit at this point in time by lovingly cataloging images from almost a decade before his birth. He imagines their sense that everything about their world is "gravy" once their prayers are answered and their son resurrected from what to them had been his certain death. That gravy includes items common to many Canton homes in the forties and defines the world from which the speaker springs:

>   King James Bible,
>   ragged paperback *Gone With the Wind*,
>   green stamps, soda caps,
>   a few mail orders collecting around Christmas...
>   pans of Dr. Pepper
>   heating on the stove...

> rags for quilts, a box of buttons,
> thimbles and needles,
> and unraveling off-key in the kitchen
> the scratchy thread of one old song,
>   *when the shadows*
> *of this life have grown*... [43–44].

As much as he now reverences this world that predates him, the speaker also must acknowledge the ways in which he took that world for granted during his childhood. To make that acknowledgment, he recalls his grandmother's spring Montgomery Ward catalog, which he steals from her mailbox and then thoughtlessly leaves out in the rain. The catalog is, for him, access to a world of imagined maleness: "the spinners and lures, / those willowy rods that thrashed the riffles / of northern rivers" (44), but he cannot extend his imagination to include what the catalog might mean to his grandmother. Thus, he remembers that he is

> ...not stunned
> to find it like something hurt
>   wrapped in towels
>
> on the kitchen porch,
> nor stunned now to glimpse again her
> face that only time I saw her weep
>   [44–45].

By juxtaposing the hypersensitivity of his metaphoric identification with those threatened by the noose with his complete inability to imagine his grandmother's sense of loss about the catalog, the speaker indirectly suggests that he is limited in his capacity to understand his grandparents' suffering during their only son's time in the Pacific and also reveals his present-day ironic awareness of the extremely fragile link he can claim to true understanding of the complex pain of racism — for both racist and victim — during the era of his childhood.

The structure of "Country Store and Moment of Grace" involves complex shifts in time and place, but those shifts — fault-lines in the poet's moral character perhaps — reveal the complexity of his effort to reconcile his personal story and his adult identity with the master narrative of his region. Thus, when he moves out of his belated recognition of his inadvertent cruelty toward his grandmother into a present-day scene in which his neighbor, a stockbroker, blows leaves to maintain his "tidy suburban driveway" (45), Bottoms finds himself thinking of another line from that old hymn that he remembers from his grandparents' kitchen, "like a bird from prison bars has flown" (45), and feels moved to embrace both the noisy stockbroker sending his "oily cloud [sifting] through the trees" (45) and his flawed self: "[S]o be it," he thinks, "Yes, so be it. Amen to the tidy suburban driveway, / to all souls sweeping up loose scraps" (45). By granting this blessing to himself as a soul seeking to make sense of the scraps of his cultural past, the speaker reaches a turning point in his exploration of race and male identity in the post–World War II South.

Having turned a corner in his spiritual quest, having freed himself from the prison of his expectation that he can make perfect order from memories of a past littered with the scraps of competing moral demands, the speaker is free to evoke Jesus — the Jesus of his childhood, of his grandparents' world, a Jesus captured in the stained-glass windows of their churches. This is the Jesus that the speaker will ask to guide him, to "shepherd these sheep / across the hills of remorse" (45).

Bottoms' next juxtaposition establishes the particular focus of the poet's remorse in this text. He moves back again to his childhood, to a Sunday evening when the family's routine — Arthur Godfrey, Ed Sullivan, and corn and barbecued chicken for supper — is disturbed. The speaker leaps to the window to see what is causing a commotion of horns, "a legion of noise" (46), but his father jerks him back, his

> ...fist on my belt, holding,
> his head shaking, a look on his face.
>
> My mother walks in from the kitchen, dishrag wringing
> a water glass. Her eyebrows wrinkle... [46].

Although sheltered by his parents, the speaker remembers years later familiar names — "Lipscomb, Lusk, Dilworth, Pope" — images that enter his memory "like familiar smells," men "tough as ax handles, blunt / as the pistol butts hanging from their pockets" (47).

These familiar figures are the source of the commotion from which his parents seek to shield him, but one of them is also the "tall man in his eternal bibs" who buys ice cream every Saturday at the store for a "small girl in coat-rags" (47). The young girl is deaf, but when she enters the store, "all rough talk [ceases]," and she moves through these tough, blunt men, the air transformed into "an aisle of grace" (47). Another man gives her a Hershey bar; yet another, peanuts. Her face, even amidst smoke and shadow, becomes luminous. How is the sheltered boy who witnesses both the commotion and the generosity to reconcile these scraps of his culture?[6]

One of these men, Dilworth, speaks of his reaction to the federal government's threats regarding desegregation. He says he would "Close it down ... / fore [he] let Lyndon Johnson run it" (48), a sentiment to which Lipscomb and Lusk nod their agreement. The speaker may be confused by the complex world in which he finds himself, its images an intricate mass of benevolent and threatening messages, but he is sure of one thing at the moment of Dilworth's proclamation: "And what is more frightening / than a room of quiet men?" (48). That quiet, the communal acquiescence, signals the cultural solidarity here. These men may find themselves in a changing world, but they are sure of their reaction: they will close that world down before they will allow it to be changed from outside.

The next shift in the poem takes us into the world of Stumptown, Canton's African-American section, and Bottoms directly represents those citizens absent, except by implication, in the earlier poem about the theater's integration. Evoking the most familiar of Christian narratives, the Christmas story, the speaker de-familiarizes it by portraying Christmas in Stumptown and further by making the climate uncharacteristic for North Georgia in December — the possibility of snow hangs in the air on this remembered Christmas. A woman — an African-American woman — anticipates her man's return, imagines the decorations they'll put on the tree he'll bring. She imagines stars, the star of advent, but in her story that image becomes the gold star on the door of a Canton police car that drives up the road toward her house. She feels this "dull yellow star ... / ... down her nerves" (49) and experiences — in her body —"...a shiver / against terrible weather" (50). Using a technique of intercutting almost filmic, Bottoms shifts to a scene of the Canton judicial system, pre–Civil Rights era, its outlandish corruption the perfect punctuation to his sympathetic engagement with the black woman's Christmas fear. The corruption in his memory is pervasive: "Dead are the corrupt / and no less dead are the less corrupt..." (51), and the present-day speaker ponders his desolate winter backyard, where "...The hummingbird feeder drops / like a Japanese lantern" (51).

Then he quick-cuts to the scene he has been building toward for fourteen of the poem's eighteen pages: "December 1960" (51). The speaker is eleven. The weather is bad, storms blowing in from Alabama, and the rumors about racial unrest are equally threatening. Cars have been burned in front of the Canton Theater that the poet left frozen on the edge of confrontation nineteen years earlier in his poetic career. "Then," into this atmosphere comes, "that familiar crunch / of gravel as a car rolls up to his gasoline pumps" (51). The grandfather's store. Its atmosphere unchanged: "Brooding men and veil of blue smoke / and the hot belly of the stove" (51). Into this sacrosanct male haven, where the phrase "nigger knocking" coexists with the gentleness that treats the deaf girl in the ragged coat to a moment of grace, walks a black woman. This is the much anticipated test of Dilworth's determination not to allow Lyndon Johnson and the feds to reshape his reality further than it already has been. This is the test of the speaker's relationship to his patriarchal legacy that has been in the making throughout Bottoms' poetic career.

The woman fishes out her coin purse "like something you might buy / on a reservation" (52), an image that allows the poet a shorthand connection between this woman and others that America's male-dominated reality has oppressed. This black woman with her coin purse off a reservation is about to commit a radical act: she is about to buy a Coca-Cola in a white man's store. The men around the stove have been awaiting just such a moment, but the speaker's grandfather denies them the confrontation they imagine themselves desiring:

> ...suddenly at the scripted moment
> the script fell away,
>   his hand simply opening,
> his head nodding slowly
> as she dropped the two nickels and faded
> into the drizzle, in the shiver and groan of muffler,
> the crunch of tires on gravel [53].

The woman does the most deceptively simple of things: she buys a soft drink. The speaker, in the present day, does a thing equally deceptive in its simplicity: he endorses his grandfather's behavior:

> And Amen now to that failure of nerve
> or heart, or among those hardening glares, that victory
> of nerve or heart.

> Amen to its passing into memory
> and Amen to its passing again out of memory... [53–54].

The men's "hardening glares" convey what the dominant male culture thinks of the grandfather's "failure," which the speaker remembers as a failure precisely because he is a product of that culture. But the poet, the adult that cultural product becomes, uses the term *failure* ironically, for the adult descendent of this grandfather embraces his ancestor's violation of the male code, celebrates the failure that he has clearly internalized, registered as memory, and then let go so that he might remember the grandfather as a traditional southern male, a conventional hero, so that he might grow from eleven to adulthood without understanding that he, like his grandfather and his father, whose firm hand on his belt he remembers from the night that racial unrest in Canton interfered with Ed Sullivan, will have, to borrow a phrase from William Stafford, to revise his life. These men — three generations of Canton men — will have to transform themselves and their connection to their culture's code for masculinity. But the eleven-year-old speaker is not ready to piece these varied scraps of his heritage regarding race into a quilt — however crazy its design — that will sustain him in his adult world. He must, even now, say amen to whatever trick of memory allows him the time and space necessary to claim the totality of his heritage.

The male circle that defines the grandfather's story reacts according to tradition in that they feel "Cheated again," "a glassy angularity [hardening] / on those faces" (52), and Bottoms names their reaction at this moment in time — December 1960 — the moment in which each recognizes that he has "...seen history for what it is / and not for what he's imagined" (52). A generation of men who feel that history has, in many ways, already cheated them of far more than is their fair share of sacrifice, must now confront the bitter reality that history will again have its way with them. In wrestling with this peculiar legacy as a southern male, Bottoms speaks for his generation — as evidenced by the poem's inscription to three fellow strugglers (Richard Bausch, Joe Hendricks, and Tom Trimble) — and names directly their position in regard to the legacy they have inherited:

> We go on now
> building on what they were obliged to build on,
> pasting into the memory
>   these little scraps of consequence
> and self-acquittal... [53].

The construction of memory so that one may acquit oneself is, of course, an ironic position, an irony that Bottoms openly accepts: "so that it's Amen finally to what can't be changed" (53), but he also contrasts the headlines and newscasts of the time with what his remembered experience suggests is their incomplete, even false, and inflammatory version of truth, what he labels the "…feint / and bluff of history" (53), with "the real thing" that "plays out quietly somewhere else" (53), in the smoky atmosphere of a store in Canton in 1960, in the hearts and minds of its owner, his son, and his grandson.[7]

As the poet writes in the 1990s, a K-mart has replaced his grandfather's store, a change that embodies the myriad ways in which the world of childhood no longer exists, except in his memory. Even to that radical change, this adult speaker is able to say "Amen to the leaving behind of places / that might have been less lovely and often are…" (54). This mature recognition of the dangers of nostalgia is no less complicated, however, than is anything else about being a southern male of Bottoms' s generation. As the mature poet says, "What's left in these last moments but memory? / And what is memory / but the mirror image of hope?" (55).

Amen is a word used to express solemn ratification or hearty approval, so when the poet ends this longest poem of his career, he ends by saying "Amen" to hope, to the belief that his specific memories of his cultural past do provide space for the conviction that hope is possible, even when what we talk about when we talk about the South is race. If we reassemble the fragments of the old spiritual that Bottoms scatters throughout this poem, we can hear in those words passed down to him from his grandparents, but also from the presence in his culture of the African-Americans whose spiritual it is, the ultimate statement of this southern male. The words of the spiritual convey that he has escaped the prison of the limited vision of southern masculinity too easily embraced by many of his forebears and peers: "when the shadows / of this life have grown…" (44), "like a bird from prison bars has flown" (45), "Like a bird / from prison bars" (51).

If race is the shadow under which southern identity is formed, when Bottoms proclaims here that

> *when the shadows of this life . .*
> yes,
> lengthen into the shadow of memory,
>
> and finally
> to that shadow, [he will say] Amen [55],

he establishes that he can face "that shadow," the ultimate judgment that will come at death, with a clear conscience on this issue and that, furthermore, he believes that those generations of southern men who precede him in death can also enjoy a clear conscience. He doesn't deny what has happened; he asserts his solemn ratification of the overall pattern of the southern (hu)man experience. His conscience, perhaps dressed by the broader culture in rags of shame, like the coat of the deaf child in the store, has been granted an aisle of grace by his grandfather's quiet acceptance of two nickels for a Coca-Cola, nickels drawn from the purse of and conveyed by the hand of a black woman. Down that aisle of grace he is willing to proceed.

Bottoms is the man to speak Georgia's truth not because he has written poems that celebrate the hyper-masculinity of certain aspects of his region's culture, but because he is a man who has claimed that tradition and deconstructed it in poems such as "Stumphouse Attends the Picture Show," from the same era in his career as the poems that then-Governor Roy Barnes cited in naming him to his laureateship, and "Country Store and Moment of Grace." Out of his long project of deconstructing southern masculinity, in Bottoms' later work a new masculinity emerges. In it, he claims his complicity in the darker side of his gender and regional heritage, but he makes that claim in the constructive voice of a new masculinity. Not for this Bottoms the ominous silence of his grandfather's generation, a silence shared by his father and his peers as well, as Bottoms makes clear in "A Sunday Dinner" (VG 84–87).

Bottoms, using race as an instrument, has forged such a desirable middle ground for himself and other southern men of his generation. As he returns the catch deemed too small by a careless fisherman in "The Catfish" (AH 23) to the water, Bottoms returns southerners to a relationship with their heritage that might be labeled as he labels the fish's natural environment: "the current of our breathable past." For men, Bottoms acknowledges, that past includes violence and injustice. "Night Strategies," another poem from *Vagrant Grace* (27–28), figures those negative elements in terms of the rape of a young girl during the war in Sarajevo. But whether the subject is gender or race, Bottoms, like his famous predecessor in the struggle with the morality of race, Huckleberry Finn, may ultimately be harder on himself than he should be. In "Night Strategies," overcome, like Huck, by the tightness of the place he occupies morally, the speaker, who is bathing his young daughter, realizes that the only answer to the world's mad injustice "is this nervous / exaggeration of tenderness" (28) that he has learned to practice. He goes on to say that "...every ministry of my hand, clumsy / and apologetic, asks her [the daughter] / to practice such a radical faith" (28).

We might read the quarter-century of Bottoms' poetic career as another version of this hand fumbling with exaggerated tenderness, clumsy and apologetic, as the man who owns that hand continues to come to terms with the wisdom he has learned from Homer: "Like the generations of leaves, / ... the lives of mortal men" ("Homage to Buck Cline" 6). And, as he must ask his daughter, he must ask us to practice a radical faith in the possibilities inherent in the emerging male.

In "Homage to Buck Cline" (*Waltzing through the Endtime* 27–34), Bottoms' speaker, standing on line in his suburban world to buy tickets to a movie, runs into an old man from his hometown. As he and the man recognize each other, "the bells of the First Baptist [chime] / an old hymn, far off" (4); the old man leans in to give the speaker his version of truth: "'Your old man,' he said, 'you should've seen him / play football,' meaning Canton High, 1941 / the fall before the war" (4). Having established his context, the old man prepares to convey truth in a single word:

> and that word he edged toward, the way
> he uttered it with such reverence over the church bells,
> as if he'd tasted its weight
> on his tongue for years, careful for the perfect usage,
> that true word that said it all — "Tough" [31].

Bottoms' poetic voice says amen to the man's sentiment, but the toughness that he embraces is not the toughness of the football field or even the battlefield, so much as it the toughness required to be an awkwardly tender male in a world that seeks to produce a somewhat different version of masculinity. Toughness — "victory" — is taking the black woman's nickels, holding your son back from the forces within your world that might destroy forever his ability to become the man that you are shaping him to be.[8]

Notes

1. The quote in my title is taken from "Free Grace at Rose Hill" (AH 132).
2 In his book *The Company We Keep: An Ethics of Fiction*, Wayne C. Booth calls for a return to ethical criticism, a practice that he defines, in part, by a call to revive an ancient metaphor for

our relationship with written texts. He suggests that we think of those works as friends, of their authors' gifts to us as friendship offerings. He says, "Perhaps most obviously, this metaphor spontaneously revives a kind of talk, once almost universal, about the types of friendship or companionship a book provides as it is read" (170). He then goes on to acknowledge the reader's role in this metaphorical exchange: "We judge ourselves as we judge the offer. Here is circularity with a vengeance. But we need not fear it as a vicious circle, so long as we do not pursue hard final judgments of 'wicked' or 'blessed' but rather ways of testing and improving our re-creations" (178). For Booth, and for me as I approach the emerging representation of masculinity in Bottoms' work, "ethical criticism [is] any effort to show how the virtues of narratives relate to the virtues of selves and societies, or how the ethos of any story affects or is affected by the ethos — the collection of virtues — of any given reader" (11). I believe Bottoms offers his readers, through his account of his personal evolution as a man, a chance to reconsider masculinity (including masculinity as it is revealed through the lens of race) in the late twentieth century, to test and improve our initial re-creations of his poems (and perhaps the poems of other males who take on similar elements of the gender-charged ethos of our time). In this specific way, then mine is an effort at ethical criticism in Boothian terms.

3. A closely related poem, "In My Grandfather's Grocery, a Moment for Dr. King," appears in the *Oxford American* (January/February 2001: 28). Using the same setting, some of the same named characters, and certain repeated images, this much shorter poem suggests Bottoms' ongoing interest in the subject matter of race as it relates to his childhood world.

4. See especially in *Armored Hearts* "Naval Photograph: 25 October 1942: What the Hand May Be Saying," "The Anniversary," and "The Desk" and in *Vagrant Grace* "My Uncle Sowing Beatitudes" and "A Sunday Dinner."

5. The depiction of the mob mentality implied by the noise here, in addition to the parents' fierce impulse to protect the child and the poet's memory of the young girl who can tame the angry male population, suggests that the poet may be working with a very specific scrap of his culture here. The tone and imagery in this section of the poem evoke Harper Lee's *To Kill a Mockingbird*, another classic southern text about the effort to come to terms with our past regarding race.

6. Although Bottoms is a few years younger than Noel Polk, his assessment of his relationship to his southern partriarchal heritage is similar to the project Polk undertakes in his memoir *Outside the Southern Myth*. In that book Polk, like Bottoms, wants to be clear about the limitations of widely accepted notions of southernness, especially male southernness. Polk says, "The Southern Myth that I have lived outside of is that popular vision of the South that both controls and is controlled by media: those various images that depict the entire South on the one hand as an ongoing national farce, a sort of charming caricature of itself ... and on the other hand as a tragedy brought on by its own peculiar brand of pusillanimity, racism" (ix). Both Polk and Bottoms describe the South of their childhood as, to some extent, a place "too busy trying to make itself urban and middle class" to devote itself to the conscious project of being southern" (xi). However, ultimately, Bottoms' poems do honestly address the complexities of his position vis-à-vis regional history. Polk sees himself as "[bearing] a reality ... imposed on [him] by the group photo" (9) while Bottoms understands that he is willingly of the group even as he conducts an ongoing examination of his relationship to it. It is, however, the ways in which these two southern men figure the father that most separates them in their analysis of self and regional history. Polk sees his father as typical of a generation of southern men who attempted to live as Faulkner's Flem Snopes lived, who "mastered their culture not by subduing it but by yielding completely to it, by absorbing it, becoming it" (45). In his poems Bottoms is celebrating the ways in which his male forebears, particularly his father and grandfather, found the strength to resist the most insidious elements of the southern masculine identity. By specifically stating his desire "to lose" his father (71), Polk clearly distinguishes his relationship with his father from that represented by Bottoms in his poems about his father and other father-figures.

7. In an interview with Ernest Suarez, Bottoms essentially agrees with an observation made by Fred Chappell about the chief difference between Bottoms and James Dickey as poets. Chappell characterized Dickey as a poet of "expansion" and Bottoms as a poet of "compression." In this interview Bottoms agrees that his "best poems ... tend to focus and compress the experience"

(89) But "Country Store and Moment of Grace," "Homage to Buck Cline," and other more recent poems suggest that Bottoms is moving toward a more expansive sensibility as the cultural complexity of his subject matter becomes more central to his thematic and aesthetic concerns.

8. "Homage to Buck Cline" takes as its narrative skeleton an evening when the teenaged Bottoms is stopped for speeding by Cline, a Canton police officer and, like Bottoms' father, a veteran of World War II. When the officer sees Bottoms' name on his license, which is also his father's name, he lets the boy go after the speaker assures the man that he does not think that he can "whip [his daddy's] ass" or the officer's ass (32) By turning the speaker loose, Cline seems to acknowledge that the senior Bottoms is an effective patriarch, that he will instill the proper code of manhood in his only child. In so doing, Cline also — consciously or not — endorses the new masculinity that is the subject of this essay. According to Joe Dubbert, "Individual accomplishment and being a hero were secondary to the vast majority of soldiers [in World War II], who fought more for self-protection than for personal glory or adventure, the kind of quest for action that had characterized a Hemingway or Dos Passos in 1917" (234). By aligning himself with Bottoms Senior in this incident, Cline then becomes one of a number of surrogate patriarchs that appear in Bottoms' poems and also demonstrates the mindset that Dubbert claims as the predominant one for males of his generation. Michael Kimmel also provides insight that allows us to see Cline's treatment of the young Bottoms not as the great stroke of luck the youngster reads it as but as part of a pervasive cultural pattern. He writes that after World War II, "It was often as fathers that men sought to anchor their identities as successes as men." He goes to say that "In the increasingly suburban postwar world, fathers embodied masculinity" (226–27). Thus, Cline and Bottoms Senior may depart from the rigorous traditional concept of the southern male, but they also participate in a different pattern that is culturally pervasive for men of their era.

Works Cited

Booth, Wayne C. *The Company We Keep: An Ethics of Fiction.* Berkeley: University of California Press, 1988.
Bottoms, David. *Armored Hearts: Selected and New Poems.* Port Townsend, WA: Copper Canyon Press, 1995.
_____. "In My Grandfather's Grocery, A Moment for Dr. King." *Oxford American* Jan./Feb. 2001: 28.
_____. "Turn Your Radio On: The Spirits of Influence." *Southern Quarterly* 37.3-4 (Spring–Summer 1999): 85–92.
_____. *Vagrant Grace.* Port Townsend, WA: Copper Canyon Press, 1999.
_____. *Waltzing Through the Endtime.* Port Townsend, WA: Cooper Canyon Press, 2004.
Clemens, Samuel. *Adventures of Huckleberry Finn. Norton Anthology of American Literature.* 5th ed. Vol. 2. Ed. Nina Baym, et al. New York: Norton, 1998. 28–216.
Dubbert, Joe L. *A Man's Place: Masculinity in Transition.* Englewood Cliffs, NJ: Prentice-Hall, 1979.
Jewett, Sarah Orne. *The Country of the Pointed Firs and Other Stories.* New York: Norton, 1981.
Kimmel, Michael. *Manhood in America: A Cultural History.* New York: Free Press, 1996.
Lee, Harper. *To Kill a Mockingbird.* Philadelphia: Lippincott, 1960.
Polk, Noel. *Outside the Southern Myth.* Jackson: University of Mississippi Press, 1997.
Suarez, Ernest. *Southbound: Interviews with Southern Poets.* Columbia: University of Missouri Press, 1999. 85–103.
Stafford, William. *You Must Revise Your Life.* Ann Arbor: University of Michigan Press, 1986.

Warbling with TV in the Background
Robert W. Hill

Early in David Bottoms' career, it was easy but wrong to identify him as a shit-kicking would-be cowboy from Bibb County, Georgia, a mimic of James Dickey with a gift for narrative, an eye for detail, and a boyishly (though beardedly) appealing blues-bluegrass riskiness, a picaroon. Some people in Macon think he actually did vandalize Rose Hill Cemetery as described in "Wrestling Angels" (3) though he insists that he did not. The fact is, Bottoms is from Canton, Georgia, reared in a middle-class family on the dwindling, receding periphery of the rural, less than an hour's drive from downtown Atlanta, and his poetry is a remarkable record of the confluence of rural and urban-suburban currents in the contemporary South.

In the poem "Armored Hearts" (113) we see the narrator's reluctance to watch all the ramifications of domesticating the wild. He wants a pond in his subdivision with living creatures; he wants living creatures in and around it. But he prefers loggerhead turtles to ducks, and he retaliates against the pistol-packing neighbor who shoots from a tree at the turtles. The narrator's sense of suburban claustrophobia is made clear as he fears, or actually hears, bullets ricocheting in the direction of his house. No matter how neighborly the shooter might be otherwise (there is no gunfight, as Bottoms likes to evoke momentarily), the other guy's view of nature in the suburbs is to have ducks; the poet's view is to let the turtles kill. Both men are caught in homemade manipulations of the environment for very temporary results.

In a National Public Radio interview, Victor Nunez, director and screenwriter of *Ulee's Gold*, said it was the writer's job "to explore what's left of place when it's not all there anymore." He was referring to his own background as half first-generation American and half long-term resident of North Florida. His point was both pragmatic and imaginative (speaking as an artist), morally responsive, but reluctantly so (speaking as a citizen). He would give us people living in — caught in — places where flux is pervasive, where unanticipated cultures crop up and grow, shifting, breaking old soil, riving old pathways and settled hearts; those people are the source of the writer's strength, the source and treasure-house of humane adaptability. Nunez would not argue that the synthesis is easy nor that it is universally good. His comment clearly implies some regret at what may have been lost ("what's left of place when it's not all there anymore"), but his perspective as an artist has deepened as he has assimilated others' experiences into his own.

Nunez' comments triggered yet again for me a recognition that the sort of "quiet desperation" people experience nowadays is unlike Thoreau's in mid-nineteenth-century New England. That is, Thoreau's "desperate men" were struggling with tried-and-true spiritual conflicts, the kind that pits flesh against spirit, selfishness against social responsibility, Gradgrindian "Facts!" against the claims of the imaginative soul. But they were doing it within a relatively homogeneous society, certainly by our standards. Thoreau's protests were mounted against the sorts of dangers that romantics always mount against — institutional power, doctrinal tyrannies, materialism, the simple staving-off of mortality as we wind along, more and more distant from innocently insightful childhood, from our finer instincts that might be fostered by poetical attention to nature.

But Thoreau never saw Atlanta's I-285 at Spaghetti Junction at rush hour. He missed out on variously named exoduses to the suburbs — white flight, bright flight, "right flight" (referring to Gingrichian Republicans), and other millennialist flights yet to be named. The people in the world Thoreau describes may have had newspapers and the Post Office for him to warn against, but THIS? — these cell phones, faxes, internet, search engines that may find us hunched up with one shoulder to our ear and satellite-mapped voices telling us to go back go back, we missed our turn. This world is in such constant change, such radical uprooting, such endemic eclecticism, such pervasive mixing and matching, that old admonitions to simplify-simplify-simplify may not catch the tone, walk the walk, see the bottom line that our complex, dangerous, contemporary American — even Southern — living requires.

When *Armored Hearts* appeared in late 1995, a much wider readership could see David Bottoms' genuinely complex view of the rural and suburban, a traditional but dynamic philosophy that he repeatedly tests against the realities of the contemporary world, a world in which even the most rural can hardly escape television's almost unmediated channeling of "out there" to "in here," from them to us.

Situated in the suburbs, aspiring to some idea or memory of the peace and order of the pastoral rural, somewhat world-weary and regretful, Bottoms seeks a place not isolated — oppressed — by mass, urban society. His poems do not rage against the shallow materialism of suburban; they imply as much. They do not mount bitter tirades against the loss of the old ways; they meditate and memorialize. And they are not neo-Fugitive; they are firmly grounded in the contemporary. These poems mark the reality of the contemporary South even as they momentarily — consciously momentarily — remind us of rural values, such as loyalty, solidity, industriousness, and reverence, and they place us spiritually among the trees and waters. For Bottoms is irrepressibly human. He doesn't transform us into other creatures, as Dickey does and Ted Hughes tries to do, but Bottoms absolutely does bring us face to face with creatures of nature — bears, wolves, fish, ducks, and vultures.

Bottoms' work is centered in the country, not only in non-human nature, where peace may be visited among rural people. From the safety of, and another kind of isolation in, the suburbs, the poet may observe, pick and choose from among forces of extinction, high passions, religious ecstasies — all from which to pick and choose — to be a snake-handler or not, a runner-away in a U-Haul or not, a poet or not.

His narrative, poetical fulcrum has always been the human (and more so now as he considers the impact of urban, suburban, and rural values upon his young daughter); therefore, when he writes about nature, he marks the trail back to human condition. In "My Perfect Night" (139), for instance, he shuts the door of a "dark house" to which we know he'll return; and the wolf who wanders onto the scene "to lick dew off a stone" is faced with "extinction," not only the simple death of all things but also the extinction implied by human encroachment.

When Bottoms won the 1979 Walt Whitman Prize for his first book, *Shooting Rats at the Bibb County Dump*, Robert Penn Warren, the contest judge, observed that those poems set the protagonist in the position of observer, a human seeker after "illumination." Warren was rarely wrong in what he saw in poetry, calling Bottoms "temperamentally a realist," not a transformer, not a transmogrifier. He doesn't enter the natural world, letting it possess him in some atavistic urge to magical power.

Bottoms seeks peace more than roiling energies, order more than demiurgic chaos, confirmation more than cosmic questioning. Bluntly, while Dickey often proclaimed himself to have a "religion of sticks and stones," Bottoms is profoundly a Christian poet, with almost medieval scholastic impulses to understand without cashing in his heart, to make sense without presuming to be God. It is ludicrous to think of Bottoms even considering to write something as thunderously challenging to created heavens as Dickey's *The Zodiac*.

In "Occurrence in the Big Sky" (in *Poetry* magazine's eighty-fifth anniversary issue), Bottoms delineates in three sections some of his most persistent ideas about the clarity and solidity of rural values, including signs of mournfulness and isolation, particularly of women in those settings. The poem begins with details of a log house left unfinished or unrepaired by a man who has died. But the house is now—like it or not—finished, finally expressed as far as it shall be to the woman — probably his widow — who remains. "Logs uncaulked, walls all stud / and rough board, plumbing dangling like loose bones" recall Theodore Roethke's greenhouse poems, "Cuttings I," "Cuttings II," and others, whose animated roots loll obscenely in stinking dirt but foreshadow growth in their profusion. Bottoms' opening scene bares the guts of this lone house; "The faucet ticks" while "the wind rakes," and an "old woman with a weak heart ... / ponders/ the congested emptiness, at a loss / among hammer and power saw, chisel blade and level...." Church people appear fleetingly in one line, "late with her supper," so the mourner's isolation is nearly perfect (7).

The little monodrama is rural, all right, even bleak, but this opening section bears the burden of rural thingness, of the presence of physical things, physical acts — even those not completed, only potential, intended. As the widow memorializes her loss, she does so by cataloguing the things around her in the room where she sits: deadbolts, "an overturned thermos," a handkerchief, a sawhorse, "an unlaced boot," etc. One could say that she does not remember him, only his things, but they bear him still. Her section ends as she "dreads the cleaning out of closets, / the smell of old shirts" (7).

Section two ponders the condition of the dead man's spirit, where it is, how it must feel, what it must wonder about, but pondering takes the form of simple speculation, declaration, not mystical immersion. That sort of magical realism is not the rural world that Bottoms knows. Spirit is real but it isn't messily blending and dissolving into some Oversoul or other. His narrator speculates, "how hard for the soul / to put down the hammer, to understand the last nail / is never driven /...." He wonders at the wonder a soul must feel who must "brush off desire / and responsibility." "How dizzy the soul must be, / floating in that first violent gust of timelessness," he says. "How it must [want] ... something as solid as a bar of chocolate / or a hand across a table." And finally, to close the section, he declares, "Still the soul / must grow happy singing under the hill / in that network of roots..." (8).

In Section three, having parsed out the widow's grief and puzzlement and the possible or likely adjustment, or coping, of the dead man's soul, the poet turns to an emblem in the Big Sky of his title, where he sees "something ... like a page from Revelation" (8), two birds in flight tugging at a snake, balled up, dropped, unraveling, flailing, "a few seconds of horror, or ecstasy, / or beauty, / before an eagle plunged / and caught it, rose and broke the clouds" (9).

While Robert Penn Warren once spoke of Bottoms as "waiting for the world to speak to him," this poem suggests more that he waits for his thoughts and feelings, his imagination, to gather force and apply to the world — lay on the world — what makes sense. Bottoms is more akin to Elizabeth Bishop in "At the Fishhouses" or Wallace Stevens in "The Idea of Order at Key West" than to James Dickey in "Encounter in the Cage Country" or Gerard Manley Hopkins in "The Windhover." Bottoms' explosions of spirit are tempered, mediated through the poetry. As Joel Connaroe shrewdly observed, this poet is "clearly a meticulous craftsman whose highest pleasure is not in shooting rats or gigging frogs or killing squirrels ... but in finding a language, supple and evocative, to communicate the implications of these experiences" (4).

Now this is not to say that Bottoms raises no troubling metaphysical questions, but they are less directed at God and the universe than they are at himself, at people rather than principalities and powers of the air. In the mostly tired-sounding movie *Contact*, Tom Skerritt's ambitious sonofabitch character says to Jody Foster's character Dr. Ellie Arroway something like "It's too bad, but that's the way the world is," and Jody Foster responds, "I always thought the world was what we made it."

David Bottoms is realist enough to know that Tom Skerritt speaks the truth, but he's a seeker after truth enough and increasingly a father wanting the world to be better for his daughter enough that he tries to believe the peace, the order, the spiritual presence, the confirmation that may be perceived or created in close encounters with the world of society which is set down like an exotic plant in the midst of reformed, domesticated nature — a place we call the suburbs. There he can pause, observe, regroup his spirit, mind, and poetry, thereby setting at least some small part of the universe right, the world as he can make it, guided by scenes and senses carried from Canton, the rural in transition.

At a conference on "Writing the Rural" at Brewton-Parker College, Robert Morgan spoke of his youthful desire to get away from a literal one-horse farm in the Blue Ridge at least partly because of the "violence and meanness" he saw in the people who lived there, "Farming doesn't guarantee you'll be a good person." James Dickey has said, "In poems I can be a better man than I am." For David Bottoms, poems are a soul-tending way — one might say almost a religious way — to have a better world — rural, urban, and suburban — than we actually do.

In "A Home Buyer" (135) the poet begins, "I was so glad to be living in my own house again," where he walks, "exploring / my pond of ivy, shadows of maple and dogwood," and we recall Ralph Waldo Emerson's narrator in "Hamatreya," who proclaims his ownership of my land, my hills, my dog, but whose legitimate deeds are overturned by the Earth's Song of universal mortal cycles.

In "In Heritage Farms, Settled" (82), Bottoms' narrator views the suburban world as it settles, is settling, and therefore is threatening his spiritual relationship with "whole colonies of mushrooms, the stinkhorns, / the devil's urns," his earnest — if not desperate — search for the creek's "cargo / of debris," for things "small and changing, / the delicate white maggot," the tadpole, the hornworm, the phoenix moth. Such seeking for nature in the apparently heartless heart of the suburbs reiterates itself throughout Bottoms' poetry, at least since *Shooting Rats*, and stands as a testimony to the persistent clarity of image and the desire for truth this poet possesses.

But home ownership is ambiguous as a virtue, as well, for homes must be maintained, at great cost, including psychic cost:

> Then one night two policemen knock
> on your door and show you your hands, swollen, bloody,
> show you the battered plaster
> of your bedroom wall ["Home Maintenance" 120].

This chilling story of a frustrated, violent man — homo domestica — is one of many signs in Bottoms' poetry that issues of house, home, and family in today's world are unresolved — as they always are — and that those moments of temporary resolution, beauty, peace, and grace are very much moments. I hesitate to invoke T.S. Eliot's "The Waste Land"—"These fragments I have shored against my ruins"—but the glimpses of rural, of urban that intersect and mediate the world of the suburbs are a major contribution by this poet—one who seeks and memorializes the warbling of nature but who also hears at his back, through the loose screens, doors, and partitions of his suburban home, TV's cabled "chariot hurrying near."

Finally, to recall the poet's pursuit of the world, society, and the self, his effort to make or discover meaning, I close with the last lines of "Last Nickel Ranch: Plains, Montana" (124):

> I know what I've valued.
> Last night I heard a coyote howling off the ridge
> and went to the window.
> In the darkness behind the glass
> I saw myself, and behind my eyes the stars flew
> into the pines.

David Bottoms takes in the real world, as transcendent as it is, not as he desires it to be or forces it through art to be. He sees it, wherever he lives, and sings it to us for our lives.

Works Cited

Bottoms, David. *Armored Hearts: Selected and New Poems.* Port Townsend, WA: Copper Cannon Press, 1995.

———. "Occurrence in the Big Sky." *Poetry* 171.1 (Oct.-Nov. 1997): 7–9.

Connaroe, Joel. Rev. *In a U-Haul North of Damascus. Washington Post Book World.* 7 Aug. 1983: 4.

Morgan, Robert. Panel discussion on "Writing the Rural." Brewton-Parker College. 14 Oct. 1997.

Nunez, Victor. Interview. *All Things Considered.* Natl. Public Radio. 25 June 1997.

Roethke, Theodore. *Collected Poems of Theodore Roethke.* Garden City, NY: Doubleday, 1966.

Warren, Robert Penn. Dust jacket. *Shooting Rats at the Bibb County Dump*, by David Bottoms. New York: William Morrow, 1980.

A Real Mix: Rebirth and Gender in *Easter Weekend*

Marshall Bruce Gentry

At the end of David Bottoms' second novel, *Easter Weekend*, which has earned praise from Andre Dubus III as "profoundly successful" (1), things might not look so successful for the protagonist, Connell Holtzclaw. The last time Connie saw his girlfriend, Rita Estes, he repeated his excuse for the behavior of his older brother, Carlton, who recently touched Rita sexually (80), and Connie and Rita argued over his untruthful explanation of what Connie and Carl might be doing to raise money (77–78). Connie is now hiding in a crypt in Macon's Rose Hill Cemetery. He does not have the money in question anyway, money he had hoped to use to leave Macon for a new life in Montana. Connie's cooperation with brother Carl's kidnapping scheme has resulted in a spectacular failure: Carl is now dead and handcuffed to another dead body, that of kidnap victim Max Sheely. They were shot after being discovered by a group of local gangsters looking for Carl because of the money he owed them. As a result, the police are likely to consider Connie the number-one suspect in the killings, and the thugs want the $200,000 in ransom money they believe Connie has. Connie does not have the money because it was taken from a briefcase by Pop Ledford, an old man who showed Connie the well-hidden crypt where Connie now hides out. And one last problem: the gangsters know Rita Estes is Connie's girlfriend. So, as the novel ends, on Easter morning, while Rita is likely to start off the day wondering whether her unreliable boyfriend will be inspired to drop by, she is likely to be reached first by the thugs.

Since the novel's title refers to Easter and the novel ends on Easter morning, one must ask what sort of rebirth or resurrection of Connie Holtzclaw is suggested. However, one possible answer to this question is rather straightforward—perhaps Connie *cannot* be reborn, as reviewer John H. Hafner suggests: "...the main reason Connie cannot escape is that he lives in a world where escape may not be possible. There's a terrifying fate at work in *Easter Weekend*. Connie is trapped in a life that is as inevitable as the grave" (251).

A more common view regarding the possibility of resurrection is that the ending is completely ambiguous. Reviewer Eloise Kinney says that "...who will rise to live again after this *Easter Weekend* is anyone's guess" (1068). Another straightforward possibility is that perhaps Connie has been reborn because in the novel's final pages, he has learned to be a real fighter, taking on not only the gangsters, but also, and more importantly, his bullying big brother. In this reading, in other words, he has become a real man, and we may decide that he achieves a certain tragic stature, despite his ultimate losses. He *almost* managed to acquire $200,000, and he would still have the money if a fit of vomiting had not forced him to leave the briefcase full of money with Pop Ledford (thought to be a friend) for a few minutes.

I prefer a different answer to the question of how this novel addresses the sense in which Connie is reborn. He might realize, on a profound level, what a loser, what a bum, what an unmanly man, he is. In this view of *Easter Weekend*, rebirth is a matter of moving away from hypermasculinity and toward a mixture of masculine and feminine traits. It appears that this thesis amounts to positing that Connie is reborn as the unmanly Pop Ledford, and to a large extent this is true; however, like the old man, who also "lost a lotta money one time" (159), Connie can now hide in the cave awhile, knowing how to escape by hopping a train that travels by the cemetery. Indeed, this option may be the only practical course of action remaining open to Connie at the end if he chooses to leave the cemetery. But I would also claim that the novel calls on Connie not just to be led by Ledford (Pop's surname suggests that Connie should be led to ford a river?), but also to realize his similarity to the novel's other losers, to learn from hurt, and to improve on the old man's model.[1]

Arriving at a clear sense of Pop Ledford's personality and figuring out how Connie can fulfill that role more thoroughly — be a better bum — is important to our sense of Connie's potential rebirth. Pop Ledford's musings include a philosophical statement that the novel encourages the reader to reinterpret. Ledford claims that people are "a real mix" (50) in that they are sometimes good and sometimes bad and that they are unreliable. To make life worth living, one must have faith in people, even though one cannot completely depend on them. While there is truth to Ledford's philosophy, Ledford himself uses his statement for questionable self-justification, turning the mixed nature of humans into part of an excuse for his bad behavior. If he can cite the Bible as saying "Brother'll deliver up brother ..." (43), an idea he could have found in Matthew 10:21 or Mark 13:12, then maybe Pop is not too immoral when he takes advantage of his figurative brother, Connie. When Pop follows up a comment about how he dislikes money with the admission that he likes "what it buys, all right" (48), he may be justifying his own desire for cash. When Pop says "It ain't nothing to me if [Connie] stole [what is in the briefcase]" (158), we see the old man rationalizing the stealing he is about to do himself. If, as the old man says, "One man ain't gonna turn nothing around" (158), then no individual crime matters much.

At the same time, Pop Ledford has a number of good traits we might associate with his status as bum — being grateful for gifts, and being generous with what little he has. Connie summarizes several of these traits after his first major meeting with the old man:

> ...Connie liked the old man.... The old guy knew what he was and he was up front about it, honest. He was glad to get the shirt, glad to get the hamburgers [all of which Connie gave him at a Waffle House]. And he gave back some of what he had. Connie liked that.... There was something different about the old man. Connie remembered the way he'd acted at the Waffle House, how he didn't want to cause a stir, how he wanted to do everything just right [66–67].

This moment provides the most explicit communication of the idea that if Connie too is a bum, he needs to realize it, even though he regularly tells himself that he does not want to become like the old man and objects almost violently when explicitly called "a *bum*" (39).

Pop Ledford also respects "tenderness" in a way Connie respects, although Connie is shocked that the old man is willing to bring up the topic while living in a grave. Pop describes his fondness for his dead friend Kenny:

> He had a tenderness about him. He cared a lot about folks, how they felt, what they thought. He'd sit up all night with you, Kenny would. He cared about things. That's all comfort is, a tenderness. He said that, Kenny did. You can have a tenderness around and live real fine just about anywhere [160].

Pop's association of tenderness with a male friend here may be somewhat surprising, since this quality of profound tenderness is more traditionally associated with females. The point seems to be that life as a bum can make a man more like a woman. And the old man does have very strong connections to his concept of women, although he has poor recollection of the specific women in his life. When Connie asks Pop whether he has a wife, Pop says "I might have, maybe, long time ago. I can't remember much" (41). He is equally vague on the subject of sisters and a mother (41–42). The most important female in Pop's life is a woman with "red hair" who sang religious songs about rivers (55). Additionally, he recalls the "softness and warmth" of her church singing (22). She is surely the reason that he likes gospel music better when it is sung by a woman (21). The old man may confuse Easter with Christmas, but he believes confidently in the resurrection because it is taken for granted throughout the red-headed woman's songs (161–62).

The old man's faith in the red-headed singer benefits him most at the end of Chapter 9, the last of the three chapters narrated from the perspective of the old man. At a moment when Pop is tempted toward revenge against a man who may have been involved in the death of Pop's friend, Kenny, the act of violence is prevented by Pop's hearing the red-haired woman's voice and dreaming about her face (132). His attraction to this female becomes, arguably, the old man's best characteristic and a large part of his value as a model for Connie. Of course, stealing $200,000 from Connie is a sign not only of Pop's cleverness but also of a superficial sort of resurrection of Pop: at the end of the novel, Connie imagines him sleeping "in some boxcar on the way to Atlanta" (198). The old man, a rather folkloric figure, is a real mix, and most of his goodness derives from his female traits; the question is how much Connie can improve on the old man's model.

The signs that Connie needs to move away from masculine traits and toward feminine traits are more clear than the signs indicating that he has actually started to make such a move. Under the heading of tenderness and generosity, good traits that can be associated with Pop as a role model, one can find evidence of similar traits in Connie, though it is interesting that Connie's tenderness and generosity are most frequently expressed by Connie when he is interacting with his fellow bum, Pop (and not with any females). At the beginning of the third chapter, Connie, in spite of the pressures placed on him by his big brother, Carl, generously and tenderly gives the old man food and clothing and draws him into a detailed, personal conversation. Connie's gift-giving may be complicated by his desire to act against the interests of his brother and his girlfriend; however, the concern in the questions Connie asks the old man and the honesty in Connie's revelation of himself (41–44, 48–50) suggest genuineness. Pop thanks Connie by showing him his cemetery crypt and by giving him a lucky coin (59–63). Later in the book, when Connie uses the old man's crypt to hide from the thugs, he rather generously gives the old man between $1000 and $1200 of the stolen ransom money (166), and then even thinks that perhaps he should have given the old man more money (172). Of course, if Connie had taken an expandedly hypermasculine view of the situation and kept all the money for himself, he would have kept the old man from acquiring even a hint that the briefcase held money that the old man could steal.[2] But surely the novel praises Connie for this generosity, however limited.

The novel's opening scene, in which Connie's behavior is much less admirable, also points to how he could become a better person if he were less macho. *Easter Weekend* begins with Connie's terrorizing the kidnapped Mercer University student Max Sheely with a speech about cockroaches, a speech that concludes with Connie's eating a roach to prove he is as ruthless as his brother, the kidnapper Carl (4). Even as he prepares to use the cockroach to frighten Sheely, Connie shows the reader a capacity for genuine softness, gentleness. Looking at the cockroach, Connie is

> amazed at the delicate twitching of the tiny feelers — feelers and legs so thin they didn't even cast a shadow. And the way the roach seemed to want to touch everything before it walked out toward it, the way it wouldn't trust what it could only see, struck him as a real study in caution. It really wasn't such an ugly thing either. The faint yellow stripe near the head, the reddish-brown wings you could almost see through, the tiny hairy spikes along the legs, all these things gave it delicacy [2].

Connie's observation of beauty in a cockroach, while foreshadowing his ability to befriend the bum Pop Ledford, also alerts readers to the idea that we might see good in Connie if we look beyond his macho display. Is it because of or in spite of Connie's work as an exterminator (48) that he can appreciate cockroaches? In their childhood, Carl placed spiders in Connie's bed on more than one occasion, causing Connie to fear spiders (61) and perhaps to choose to work as an exterminator. Consequently, Connie's ability to appreciate a cockroach may be seen as a sign of his ability to overcome his brother's influence, a sign of Connie's ability to see the good in himself.

Where one *expects* to find Connie most able to display gentleness, tenderness, generosity — in his relationship with his girlfriend — one finds little evidence of genuine feeling. Connie recalls that he has a mother who "never raised her voice" (44) despite all the provocation she received from Connie's father, and even though Connie claims he wants a new life, it often appears he wants to force Rita into playing the mother role. One of

Connie's fondest childhood memories is of his mother's saying "Just over this river I'll bet we'll find Paradise" each time the family crossed the bridge into Paradise, Montana; Connie believes that there was love in her voice, even though he knows that her joke "was a laugh at the whole family" (71). Now Connie wants to take Rita to Montana, where he somehow unrealistically hopes she will accept the landscape — despite her insistence that she would like to stay in Macon — and lovingly accept him as his mother did. Connie fears Rita's becoming serious about her desire "to make something of herself" (138), because she would likely decide to find herself another man. It is easy to conclude how Rita Estes would be better off with a different boyfriend.[3]

Everywhere there are signs of problems in this relationship. Connie's most powerful emotional response in relation to Rita is pain over the prospect of "losing her" (75). They have a sex life, but she initiates the novel's only lovemaking between them (74), and when Connie describes the best aspect of their relationship, he oxymoronically calls it "good darkness" (162). The only way Connie can imagine being truthful with Rita is to fantasize about a conversation that he places firmly in the future; he spends much of the novel thinking up fresh lies he hopes Rita will accept.

At the end of the novel, Connie has a vision of the sort of relationship he thinks he could now establish with Rita:

> And suddenly it seemed as though all he'd ever wanted was light. Long days of it accumulating into years, a fortune of it, a fat wealth he could draw on like a bank account. He and Rita, rich on sunlight, rich on warmth. He thought of it breaking over the balcony and through the window of her apartment. She'd be waking now, rubbing her eyes, kicking the sheet to the foot of the bed. He wanted to watch it spark off the rings in her ear, wash red through her hair as she rolled on the pillow. He wanted to feel its wide shaft warming his legs and chest, to lie quietly beside her and bathe in that wealth [196].

This is a glimpse into the sort of rebirth the novel recommends for Connie. (Notice that the mythical paradise of Montana is missing here.) The question is whether this is a vision Connie can hold on to. The moment of apparent insight is idealized, and Connie probably still believes, as he said earlier, that Rita is unrealistic.

> Rita just thought that everything always had to be hugs and kisses. Always hugs and kisses, sugar and spice. Well, that's just not the way the real world works. He wished now that he'd thought to tell her that. Hugs and kisses, that's not the way it always works. It was like the old man said, folks are a real mix. And not just bad and good people, but bad and good mixed up in people, mixed up in everybody [95].

Connie must find a sense of mixed-up reality that he can live with, and Rita is probably not part of that reality for Connie.

As I suggested earlier in this essay, at the novel's end, Connie's failure to contact Rita is probably endangering her life. Rita's sad situation is part of a larger pattern of the victimization of women by men throughout the novel. Connie has stolen from a woman and gone to jail for it (48). The mother of the kidnap victim dutifully awaits commands from the kidnappers and obeys all commands, but at the end of the novel Connie does nothing to help the police locate the mother and her murdered son (190). Connie's mother is victimized by her drunken husband; Connie claims his father "killed my mama in a car wreck" (42). As I mentioned before, the old man values women's voices, but he steals tapes of women's singing. Connie's brother has had a girlfriend named Thelma, but when Connie praises her and says she may have become "tired of getting knocked around," Carl acts offended and makes critical comments about her (11). The only fault of these women seems to be their toleration of men's flaws.

Connie has much in common with these victimized women, and he needs to realize it. Of course, his relationship with his brother presents Connie with a related dilemma. Carl has constantly belittled Connie, and one suspects that a comment by Carl to Connie—"You ain't got any balls, you know that?" (103)—is common in their relationship. How did Connell Holtzclaw come to be called by a feminized name like Connie, anyway? The dilemma, in other words, is that Carl (and much of the rest of the culture in which Connie finds himself) has been telling Connie that he is womanly rather than manly, that he is a bum, all his life. For Connie to discover the good in being a bum and a woman, he must first unlearn a great many of the lessons he has been taught. Throughout the novel are accusations of homosexuality, accusations used by men to deny any value to any state other than hypermasculinity. Connie has held on with an animal's claw to his sense of his manhood, and he needs to let that go. It is as if he must die to be reborn.

Another dilemma Carl presents to Connie is one in which Connie must escape from his own dream of escaping Carl. Throughout the novel, Connie tells himself that he wants to get away from Carl by running to Montana. But psychologically, to return to the childhood home of Montana is to remain stuck in a childish, unhealthy relationship with Carl. Truly to escape Carl by running away, Connie should travel anywhere *but* Montana. It was in Montana that Carl saved him from abuse, at least from others (95), and there that Carl saved Connie from being sent to a "foster home" (43), and these memories inspire most of Connie's toleration of the abuse his brother dispenses. Another sign demonstrating why escaping to Montana would do Connie no good becomes apparent when Connie recalls a Christmas in Montana when he was six. Lying in bed, Connie, hearing his brother moving about, imagines that Carl might be "Santa? Or maybe a burglar?" (124). The dose of abuse Carl delivers—"You're so ugly.... If Santa Claus brings you anything tonight, it's because he feels sorry for you" (124)—is probably less significant than the fact that Connie continues to see his brother as both his benefactor—his Santa—and as the sort of criminal who could easily harm Connie. Montana, with its misleading connotations of manly living, would surely be the site of continued entrapment and neurosis for Connie.

What Connie needs, then, is a way to discover his bum/female nature that is not limited by the various distortions imposed by his relationships with Carl and Rita and even Pop Ledford. And he needs a new setting for his rebirth. The appropriate landscape for Connie—and I say this regardless of how one feels about Connie's ultimate success—is found in Macon's Rose Hill Cemetery.[4] According to this novel, the cemetery (as a viable character itself) eventually confronts Connie with all the qualities that he needs to recognize and learn to adopt.

One thing the cemetery represents is independence: although Connie is intrigued early on by how he could make the cemetery useful to Carl as a delivery spot for the ransom money, Connie eventually learns that the cemetery is the best place to escape both Carl and the group of thugs. Although Connie is introduced to the cemetery by Pop Ledford, the old man's disappearance with the ransom money proves he will not return. And Connie's flight to the cemetery at the end of the novel means his relationship with Rita is probably at an end.

Another valuable trait of the cemetery as Connie's destination in *Easter Weekend* is that it is a haven for a bum. As Connie takes over the crypt abandoned by Pop Ledford, Connie surely knows that he is now in the land of the bum (and of the dead, of course). There are references throughout the novel to how the local bums find in Rose Hill a place to escape from the mainstream of civilized life in Macon, Georgia. Maybe Connie can now admit that being a bum is not so bad. And of course, a landscape associated with death inevitably will teach Connie that his old life is over.

Probably the most important quality of Rose Hill Cemetery is that it is female. More persuasively than Rita's managing to transform Connie, the graveyard will show Connie his connection to the feminine. One is tempted to say that Rose Hill is the novel's major female character, perhaps the counterpart for Connie to Pop Ledford's hymn-singing woman. (Not that Connie sees the femaleness of Rose Hill immediately: his initial inclination is to masculinize it, by relating it to Gen. George Custer and a Montana town referred to as "Hard On" [54].[5]) Nevertheless, there are a various ways in which the connection between the cemetery and the feminine is strongly established. Connie notes at one point that when one sees a car in a cemetery at night, it is likely to be a boy and his girlfriend "looking for a place to park" (140), and he also notices scratches on cemetery walls, "dozens of names and initials" left by lovers (57). Another sign that Rose Hill is female is its wealth of female statues and images and statues of angels. The angels suggest ambiguous-to-female gender, as with the reference to "a marble angel *or* a woman" (53; emphasis added). Many of the statues are damaged: "an angel with one wing" (146), "a huge angel with broken arms" (147). That Connie feels a connection to the cemetery's females is suggested when he passes "a marble woman on a large pedestal" and experiences "an odd feeling ... as though she had gestured to him somehow with her eyes, a sign of understanding or recognition" (146). Connie even suggests at one point that it is possible to become a statue: watching one of the thugs walking through the cemetery, Connie "noticed something. Whenever he stopped, whenever he stood still, he became very hard to see among the stones. The darkness turned him into a statue" (137). This passage clearly suggests that Connie is figuring out that he too can turn into one of Rose Hill's females.

Another indication that Rose Hill is female is found in the descriptions of the cemetery's land. The final chapter (ironically numbered thirteen), in which Connie makes his final return to the crypt, repeatedly uses the feminine word "pink" to describe the cemetery on Easter morning. Moreover, throughout the novel's descriptions of the cemetery, emphasis is placed on the curvatures of the land, and the complicated path to the old man's crypt suggests a passage toward a symbolic vagina:

> At the bottom of the hill the land flattened into a wide triangular gorge — grassy banks on two sides and on the third the graveyard sloping down to the river. A narrow creek ran out of the far bank and down the middle of the gorge, and beyond the creek, huge brick and marble crypts were cut into the face of the bank.
> "Up this way," the old man said.
> Connie followed him up the gorge and into a thicket of brush and small

trees. They seemed to be moving toward the point where the two sides of the gorge converged, but in the thicket the moon was no help [58].

Entering the old man's grave, I am suggesting, is entering into the female.[6]

The ultimate effect of Connie's confrontation with Rose Hill is that he is presented with the lesson that he is one of its broken females, its broken bums, and the potential good in this lesson is suggested by passages about how Connie has benefited by experiencing severe hurt. To some extent, this is a matter of the hurt he inflicts, as when Connie repeatedly feels remorse for hitting the stripped and helpless, and therefore feminized, kidnap victim, Max Sheely. Connie is sorry he hit Max Sheely (whose name even has a female pronoun in it) because hitting Sheely is "like hitting a woman" (43), and Connie's memories of Max's sufferings are only intensified when Connie finds Sheely and Carl handcuffed together and executed with gunshots to their heads.

Another example of learning from hurt has to do with Rita. The most persuasive description of a genuine relationship between Connie and Rita relates his being able to talk sincerely following one of his losses in the boxing ring:

> ...he remembered the morning he'd first tried to tell her how much he cared for her, a morning after a bad loss, a TKO. He'd had his mouthpiece knocked out and had bitten clear through his tongue — three stitches. It was so swollen he could hardly talk, but he'd tried and he'd meant what he said, and what came out with those garbled words truly surprised him — something he never wanted to lose. Tenderness, he guessed, was as good a word for it as any [160–61].

Perhaps a more effective demonstration of Connie's learning from hurt is a less direct one. After being confronted by a promoter, Eddie Carano, over the fact that Connie had had sex with Carano's wife, Connie loses his next match badly to a strong boxer, Rick Hugo (perhaps a reference to Montana poet Richard Hugo?), whom Carano substituted at the last minute. Despite spending two days in the hospital after the fight, Connie decides

> ...it didn't have anything to do with getting even. It had to do with pain and fear. It had to do with helplessness, desperation, sickness, with loving a woman so much you couldn't imagine a life without her. And Connie knew now that the beating he'd taken from Rick Hugo was nothing like the beating Eddie Carano had taken from his wife, and it was nothing like the beating he might take from Rita [128].

We should be skeptical of this anecdote as proof of Connie's love for Rita, but it seems reasonable to conclude that Connie sees most deeply when he sees through pain.

Pain is what is foremost in Connie's psyche at the end of *Easter Weekend*, and while the novel's final line emphasizes the sinister — "The darkness closed around him like a room circling a drunk" (198) — there is plenty to indicate that the way for Connie to learn is not through his fight for his manhood but through his recognition of what he might interpret as a loss of manhood. Connie Holtzclaw is Max Sheely, he is Pop, he is any of the novel's victimized women. Connie needs to learn that his rebirth involves seeing himself as a real mix of the masculine and feminine.

Notes

1. Jane Hill discusses the development of David Bottoms' views of masculinity in his poetry, and she uses several poems set at Rose Hill Cemetery to develop her case.
2. Reviewer Daryl Frazell states that Connie "has compassion and crude strength, but they do not serve him as well as ruthlessness and cunning might."
3. Reviewer Dan O'Brien, who praises *Easter Weekend* as "honest and convincing," has an opinion quite different from mine about taking Rita to Montana: that the reader is surely "desperately hoping that ... Connie ... can manage to get Rita out of Macon and up to Montana, where he can wet a fly line, chill out" (34).
4. Some photos of Rose Hill Cemetery are available at http://rosehillcemetery.org/.
5. Christopher Lehmann-Haupt takes this section of the novel seriously, as Bottoms' use of "the novel's landscape to evoke the American past."
6. While I would like to agree with Lehmann-Haupt "that Mr. Bottoms is far too shrewd a writer to use that empty grave as the medium for Connie's rebirth that the story seems too obviously preparing it to be," I think the grave is indeed the medium for Connie's possible rebirth.

Works Cited

Bottoms, David. *Easter Weekend*. Boston: Houghton, 1990. [Note: This novel is also available, in paper, as part of the "Voices of the South" Series — Baton Rouge: Louisiana State University Press, 1998.]

Dubus, Andre, III. "Safe with Her in the Darkness." Rev. of *Easter Weekend*, by David Bottoms. *Los Angeles Times Book Review* 28 Jan. 1990: 1.

Frazell, Daryl. "Taut Thriller Explores a Crime that Dreams Are Made Of." Rev. of *Easter Weekend*, by David Bottoms. *St. Petersburg* [FL] *Times* 11 Feb. 1990, city ed.: 7D.

Hafner, John H. Rev. of *Easter Weekend*, by David Bottoms. *America* 13 Oct. 1990: 251.

Hill, Jane. "'To Own My Father's Name': Not Hiding the Masculine in the Poems of David Bottoms." *Studies in the Literary Imagination* 35.1 (2002): 25–59.

Kinney, Eloise. Rev. of *Easter Weekend*, by David Bottoms. *Booklist* 1 Feb. 1990: 1068.

Lehmann-Haupt, Christopher. "A Kidnapper with Schemes and Dreams." Rev. of *Easter Weekend*, by David Bottoms. *New York Times* 12 Feb. 1990, late ed.: C 16.

O'Brien, Dan. "Brother Hoods." Rev. of *Easter Weekend*, by David Bottoms. *New York Times Book Review* 25 Feb. 1990: 34.

Signs from My Fathers
David Baker

Poets use stories to tell stories. Inside, outside, or alongside the particular narrative of a poem, other frames of reference inevitably operate. This is a feature of serious poetry that especially attracts and compels me — not just the local situation of a poem, but those larger stories, too, obvious or suppressed, allusive or mythological, active or psychological. How complex, after all, are our local narratives? A lover woos, or is abandoned. Someone grieves. Another complains or accuses or, walking down the street, meditates on a cool autumn evening. The details may vary endlessly, but our stories themselves — or the rhetorical and referential structures of those stories — are relatively few.

A poet's style and voice derive from those local narratives, but perhaps even more from the surrounding, larger schemes he or she brings to bear — the worldly material by which the poet articulates and measures the local matter of a life. This dynamic gives a poem its distinct, and occasionally distinguished, features. Sometimes, as in the richness of baroque and metaphysical poetries, a surface complexity may itself be the dominant story, where the machinations of conceit supply the narrative drama. Sometimes, as in plain-style poems, there is almost no surface, no distinguishing features of a larger scheme, as the poet ushers us transparently toward the archetypical. Always what's fascinating to me is the manner by which a poet matches stories, influences, and styles, the local and any larger narratives.

David Bottoms is one of the most recognizably narrative poets working today, employing many of the traditional story-telling tactics of Southern poetry. We encounter real people as they undertake dramatic events, often in eccentric detail, through narrators with a penchant for the pleasures of folktale and an ear for colloquial diction. Since his 1980 volume, *Shooting Rats at the Bibb County Dump*, Bottoms has measured the dimensions, at once personal and collective, of the oral and performative traditions; in "The Drunk Hunter," from this first book, the speaker's own account of a stumbling and doomed huntsman is picked up and extended by the wider narrative of the group: "In two or three days, / they will tell what found him in the deeper woods."

For Bottoms the telling of tales is itself a delightful task. Just so, I have been delighted by his work from the beginning — from his catfish and gators, his diverse cast of farmers, bluegrass pickers, boatmen, and neighbors — and grateful for his regional devotion. But I have also been fascinated by the subtle yet central evolution from his early to his more recent work, as he has shifted some of the fundamental components of the stories he tells. I shall look at this development by examining Bottoms' second book, *In a U-Haul North of Damascus* (1983), alongside his fifth, *Vagrant Grace* (1999).

The region staked out in Bottoms' poems is located persistently in the deep South, from the swamps of his first work to the suburbs of his recent. With *In a U-Haul North of Damascus*, he presents a physical and emotional travelogue down the back roads, across the black waters of Florida and Georgia. Like nearly all the poems of his first collection, *Shooting Rats at the Bibb County Dump*, about half of these poems are short, sharp, dramatic excursions:

> Arms finned-out across the water,
> he floated face down in the crotch of a fallen oak...
> Then I drew the boat closer,
> watched the slack of his blue jeans roll in my wake,
> his head nod gently against the thick oak branch,
> long hair tangled in the branch-twigs.
> I eased the paddle out and touched his heel.
> He didn't turn or move, only gazed straight down
> into the deepest part of the Etowah
> as though fascinated by something I couldn't see.
>
>   [from "The Drowned"]

In his shorter poems Bottoms combines a hard, clear lyric voice, a typically long line, and an ability to turn a brief incident, characterization, or observation into a type of representative statement. Since even his shortest poems demonstrate this ambition, Bottoms' technique, while rewarding, is risky — the poems can seem too meaningful in their need to summarize, to draw idea from action and incident. Occasionally through this book Bottoms does seem to strain for the connections his poems desire. One such moment is found in "Hiking Toward Laughing Gull Point":

> Once I saw a gull catch a bait in midair.
> Climbing until the slack ran out,
> it snapped back like a white feather on the end of a whip
> and fell into the sea.
>
> We've all swallowed a line or two,
> a real estate deal, some bad investment of faith....

Here, as occasionally in his early work, Bottoms tries too hard and too directly to establish and extend his metaphor by a kind of rhetorical over-determination. Usually his control is less directive and more subtle. Indeed, at their best, his poems are characterized by sure, effective technical control: a rough though purposefully understated tone; an inclination to reveal rather than interpret; an eye for the crucial image yet an ear for what Whitman termed the "common language of the people"; irregular, even jagged-lined stanzas that yield precise, smooth sentences. In "A Home Buyer Watches the Moon" we find these strengths enacted in a poem that shows Bottoms stepping, for a moment, farther away from the primordial toward a more settled or civilized scene. The rich irony here is that this very settlement produces a tangible anxiety, unsettling the speaker's spirit:

> The whole neighborhood is quiet.
> The architect who lives across the street
> is now the architect of dreams, his cedar split-level
> still as a crypt on the landscaped hill.
> In the brick ranch house
> the city planner turns another spadeful of dirt,
> a groundbreaking for his own monument. And I,
> who can no longer afford to live
> in my two-story, have come out into the street
> to stare past the mailboxes at an abrupt dead end.
>
> Quietly now the bats jerk
> in and out of the streetlight, their shadows
> zipping across the grass like black snakes.

And the moon lies balanced on the roof of my house
like a new gold coin, or the simple face
of an angel in a colonial cemetery.

As the neighbors fall into sleep, their occupations continue to haunt their dream lives. The architect's creation is now his crypt, the city planner's proud construction becomes his "monument"—more tombstone than public testimonial—and the "dead end" street seems a darkening of prospects for the speaker himself, no longer able to afford his own home. At this moment of imagined dying, the old world emerges once more, coming into visible life in the form of animals under the abiding light of the moon. Above and below, in the air where bats fly and in the grass where snakes zip, Bottoms compares the transience and folly of the human world with its commerce and constructions to the enduring, primitive nature his early work so often reveres. It's a moment of quiet comparison: Even the moon is "balanced" for an instant on the fulcrum of the speaker's roof—no accident its monetary gold light, no accident its illuminative visage like an angelic reminder on an ancient tomb. Bottoms has yet to depict fully the existential doubt of his own scene, yet his unease is palpable as he searches for a place, a home, where the complexity of the human condition may find full expression.

Like many other young Southern male poets of the time, Bottoms draws on the powerful work of poets like Robert Penn Warren, James Seay, and James Dickey. In fact, Dickey stands as the primary forebear and influence of these poems, as he was the fundamental guiding force in the early work of such poets as Dave Smith, Rodney Jones, and T. R. Hummer. Bottoms learns particularly from Dickey's sense of raw naturalism, his dramatic (and eventually melodramatic) rhetoric, and his sense of the world that pits one man against the perilous, often ferocious, forces of nature. This impulse embodies something akin to a hunter's isolation and a warrior's power. In his best work—that is, before 1970—Dickey's sense of danger leads him to discoveries of sublime beauty, where nature threatens but also potentially provides a primitive, almost primordial transcendence, and thus a recasting of identity, as in "The Poisoned Man": "When the rattlesnake bit, I lay / In a dream of the country, and dreamed / Day after day of the river." Here, having cut his wound more widely open to rinse out the venom, Dickey also "open[s] his soul to the water." He literally becomes part of the landscape itself, in the mingling of his blood with the "freezing river," though the price of Dickey's soulful transcendence is of course the threat of the body's death: "I felt that my heart's blood could flow // Unendingly out of the mountain."

Dickey's rattlesnake becomes, for Bottoms, an equally venomous snake. "The Copperhead" (appearing in *U-Haul* in a slight revision from its appearance in *Shooting Rats*) is one of Bottoms' finest and most characteristic early poems. Here Bottoms' speaker is alone, fishing among "oak and poplar stumps rising out of the water / like the ruins of an old pier," when he sees like "a dwarfed limb / or a fist-thick vine" the snake sunning like "part of the tree." Such animals rise like totems in Bottoms' early work, representative icons of the hunter's world, reminding the speakers of their own fundamental natures as animals, as both predator and prey. The powerful vision in "The Copperhead" seems as primordial as Dickey's dream where he opens "[his] soul to the water." In each poem, the speaker pauses for a moment to observe the blood-pulse of an older life, a life, as Bottoms says, "all spine and nerve." Both poets often situate their heir speakers in such settings: drifting in a canoe on dark waters, taking target practice in a landfill, confronting alligators, poisonous snakes, and other treacherous creatures and situations. It's a decidedly male setting, and Bottoms' best early work is typified by these traits, passed in a ritual, as it seems, from father to son. If Bottoms had been content in *U-Haul* simply to continue the technique of the short, natural allegory he introduced in *Shooting Rats*, I would have enjoyed this second book. Not only does he maintain that powerful (if sometimes limited) capability, but to complement his shorter pieces Bottoms adds here a further powerful dimension to his work in the form of eleven longer (multi-paged) poems. Some are arranged in sections while others are single stanzas. Poems like "Under the Boathouse," "Sleeping in the Jon Boat," and "In a U-Haul North of Damascus" represent some of Bottoms' best work at the time; he retains the control and clarity of his short poems while extending and deepening the narrative and meditative events. Not just in size are these poems bigger, but *because of* their size Bottoms can more fully examine the landscape of his poetic region and the lives of his characters.

Short or long, Bottoms' poems may be typically right in their sense of control, but again, as in Dickey's best work, there is always something wrong in them. This is a world in which "nature doesn't specialize in mercy," where people with their troubled lives are always on the move, where the fisherman senses "the reptile that moves beneath [him]." Even in "Turning the Double Play" the softball player standing "out here at the edge / of middle age" knows that "nothing is won back for more than a moment." Bottoms' sense of balance accounts in these poems for his very theme. The people here feel bound to the natural world, like the fisherman above in "The Copperhead" who "wanted more than once to drift into the shaded water, / pull myself down a fallen branch." They look to the wilderness for answers, for a way to live. But they ultimately know, or at least sense, that something separates them from the raw and natural. Something always prevents the transcendence or unity that Dickey's own earlier work often captures. This uncomfortable humanness, this awareness of mortality, produces what Bottoms calls "the trembling in us all."

Such knowledge also leads to the restlessness and agitation at the center of Bottoms' early work. In this book's title poem, the narrator literally is "half-lost, / sick and sleepless / behind the wheel of this U-Haul truck parked in a field on Georgia 45." One of Bottoms' longer pieces, this poem is a powerful meditative "prayer" on moving, physically and emotionally:

> Lord, what are the sins
> I have tried to leave behind me? The bad checks,
> the workless days, the scotch bottles thrown across the fence
> and into the woods, the cruelty of silence,
> the cruelty of lies, the jealousy,
> the indifference?

As he mentally catalogues the qualities of life he has tried to leave behind, as well as all the belongings he has brought with him, the protagonist realizes that the pain of the past will not be surmounted, that "suffering [may form] a stronger bond than love." But the day here is beautiful with "the after-scent of rain ... as though the world really could be clean again." Doubt balances with hope. This poem concludes with a series of questions revealing both the narrator's fear and his sense of promise — as if in a fitting summary to the vision of Bottoms' earlier poetry:

> Somewhere behind me,
> miles behind me on a two-lane that streaks across
> west Georgia, a light is falling
> through the windows of my half-empty house.
> Lord, why am I thinking about all this? And why should I care
> so long after everything has fallen
> to pain that the woman sleeping there should be sleeping alone?
> Could I be just another sinner who needs to be blinded

> before he can see? Lord, is it possible to fall
> toward grace? Could I be moved
> to believe in new beginnings? Could I be moved?

These lines most directly identify the anxiety that marks a central change in David Bottoms' work. The earlier landscape fades in the darkening sky; the assertive, sometimes even dramatic voice has turned into a questioning one; and the primitive or animal power now sounds a more Biblical — if civilized — intonation.

Vagrant Grace is Bottoms' third volume after *Shooting Rats at the Bibb County Dump*. Though nearly twenty years pass between the books, Bottoms' newer poems seem at first consistent with his earlier subjects and narrative methods. With their crisp syntax, irregular lining, and closed strophes, most are just over a page long, focusing on a single personal event or impression, while several others are longer (usually three-part) works which combine narrative episodes into a kind of multiple-exposure. As in "A Family Parade," the dominant subject is connection, the various avenues between the present and the past:

> ...I know this is about eternity,
> this circling, this following,
> and, of course, that irredeemable taunt of memory,
> without which we'd have no ghosts to lead us....

From the beginning Bottoms has explored the binding, haunting properties of memory, yet in *Vagrant Grace* I note several subtle but central evolutions. His earlier work depicted a fierce natural world, dangerously beautiful with its swamps and its wild, sometimes predatory, growth. In turn, again as in James Dickey, the speaker in those poems learned to recall or intuit the most ancient and tribal of mysteries: "An old reptile at the top of my spine / knows about hunting / and leads me to this creek," as he says in "Hunting on Sweetwater Creek." Memory for him was bodily and rapacious, reptilian, and its codes of behavior were naturalistic and agnostic. Making poems, like the survival of the fittest, meant to attend with vigilance to the perilous and often merciless operations of nature. But the natural world found in *Vagrant Grace* has turned considerably more suburban, its wild past recessive, even repressed. In "A Family Parade," Bottoms rides his memory "down the streets of the suburb, / clowning for a block with my feet on the handlebars, / tipping my sombrero at kids / dodging sprinklers, barbeque jockeys saluting / with their spatulas." He clowns now where he once hunted, his vehicle a bicycle instead of a jon boat or pickup. His details are comprised of backyard implements, not gigs and guns; likewise Bottoms' protagonist here is shadowed not by feral land or water animals but by all manner of birds — eagles, owls, cockatoos, and in "Heron Blues" "a spread of giant wings drag[ging] a shadow over / the rooftops." Bottoms' protagonist has evolved into a family man and homeowner, an apparently civilized citizen-neighbor whose home is no longer rough country but the modern development. His remnant loneliness is not desperate but clearly mournful, as he still looks to the sky for signs:

> For a long time after
> I stared at the clouds
> and puzzled the talent the world shows for mystery,
> sending these glimpses on wings.

Such "glimpses on wings" portend natural developments and losses, as the human world encroaches, ruinous and busy, with its malls and subdivisions. But such glimpses also suggest a view of human destinies, and more specifically, human spiritual truths, for angels fly here among the birds, as do the visionary spirits of lost family members and friends. Everywhere this speaker sees both "wings and haloes," as he says in "Our Presbyterian Christmas." The shift from naturalistic to Biblical tropes is Bottoms' most significant and risky direction. Occasionally his drive to expand a natural figure into a larger spiritual one can result in sentimental inflation, just as that same drive to connect in his earlier work sometimes resulted in melodrama or over-determination. Here, as in "Occurrence in the Big Sky," Bottoms' birds seem pressed into symbol: "I saw something in the sky like a page from Revelation —/ high against a white ridge of clouds, two eagles / fighting over a kill." "In the Wilderness" shows how his elevated metaphors may lean toward the over-heightened: "And the wind is up, / the west wind, out of the wilderness, / and true to the season / the whole sky is overcast with God." But he is looking for size, for an expanded spiritual connection — "grace," as the title attests.

In his longest poem, "Country Store and Moment of Grace," Bottoms mixes his capability with story together with his newer, deeper meditative sense. This eighteen-section poem is a spiritual autobiography, recalling the speaker's childhood up to his present circumstance. The first crisis of the poem invokes the gods of narrative, as it reanimates the *ubi sunt* convention: "Where were the storytellers I'd grow up / to hear about?" That is to say, Bottoms is still seeking his fathers. Eliding story and meditation with great efficiency, Bottoms deepens his quest for connection as the crises deepen. He traces his memory's "little scraps of consequence" back to the questionable charms of a rural Southern boyhood, from the warm "pot-gut" stove of a grandfather's grocery store to Little League baseball and the "shoulder kick" of target practice. Each charm is mitigated by a deepening complicity and by a vivid hunger for confessional "self-acquittal." We find, side by side, the small humiliation of a stolen Montgomery Ward catalog and the tragedy of a mother mourning her son lost in the Pacific theater of World War II. We witness the public shame of corrupt judges, a little girl tormented by poverty's cruelty, and ultimately the South's deepest sin — the acute racism of friends who here enjoy "*Nigger knocking.*" To confess such transgressions is, of course, to propose forgiveness. Thus the poem moves toward its complicated acceptance of the past, as the speaker strains to say "Amen finally to what can't be changed."

Both in syntax and theme, Bottoms' recent tactics are powerful. "On Methodist Hill" once more finds Bottoms in a scene which seems similar to the moving nighttime scene in "A Home Buyer Watches the Moon" from *U-Haul*. Here he accompanies his daughter into a local graveyard with its "Shab of plundered tomb, crust and leaf-stain, / litter of wet newspaper, sandwich wrapper..." to find the weedy graveyard a dump for trash. But Bottoms loads his scene here not just with a counterpoint between the living world (its "chained up doors" and "traffic on Main") and a lost or primitive one, but also with a more mature inward vision as well as more directly religious inquiry. Stacks of hymnals, "olive trees / blue in ... the tumble of clouds," and even "Christ in his purple agony of glass"— these will be the materials with which Bottoms replaces the alligators and rats, those naturalist and primitivist totems, of his earlier work. Perhaps echoing Yeats' great "The Second Coming" with its severe Christian anxieties, Bottoms here notes that "surely some violence / is closing a fist" while even "in the breathing / of his friends he hears his loneliness." The poem's final lines replicate the "dusty road to Emmaus," where two traveling disciples met the resurrected Jesus but did not recognize him. Likewise Bottoms and his daughter seem like characters in Christ's own vision:

> For an hour he prays,
> but already he's foreseen — the rubble

of the temple, the three denials,
the trial and scourge, the veiled
and dusty road to Emmaus,
and maybe even as far as this church
hollowed and crumbling on a hill of weeds
where a four-year-old climbs a vandalized angel
as her father begins, unaccountably, to weep.

Bottoms' newer work is becoming more mature in its social and community connections and clearly more informed by Christian mythologies, as if in partial replacement of his solitary and primitive ones.

With his precise Southern tuning, his compressed or "sprung" narratives, as well as his need for spiritual clarity, Bottoms' *Vagrant Grace*—as is typical of his later work—reminds me much more of the work of Charles Wright than of the naturalistic (and eventually bombastic) work of James Dickey. He has become more inward, a typologist who hunts not for physical survival but for existential meaning. He is ultimately less metaphysical than Wright; Bottoms is not going to interrogate the *meaning* of meanings. A poem from Wright's collection *Appalachia*, published a year before *Vagrant Grace*, shows Wright's metapoetic urge to speak and his capability to negotiate the borders between language and erasure, as between image and abstraction. Wright articulates an anxious search for meaning even with the self-aware knowledge of meaning's elusive identity. In "All Landscape Is Abstract, and Tends to Repeat Itself," Wright's speaker is a "whisperer start[ing] to whisper in tongues" about "remembered landscapes … left in me / The way a bee leaves its sting." For the hyper-aware Wright, such these landscapes are "Untranslatable … Non-mystical." Where Dickey poured his blood into the freezing river in "The Poisoned Man," losing himself in a dizzy swirl of the near-transcendence, here Wright's memories are "insoluble in blood"; they act as opposite "To the absolute, whose words are solitude, and set to music."

I think it's accurate to suggest that a whole generation of younger, middle-career poets have moved, like Bottoms, farther away from the decidedly male Southern bravado of James Dickey toward the more complex and elusive poetics of Charles Wright. This transition may be traced in several parallel ways in Bottoms' work: from the savage natural scene in his earlier work to the familiar settled land of pasture and suburb; from the dramatic enactment of narrative to the more inward tones of meditation; from a kind of rhetorical certainty to a more fundamental doubt. In

"Night Strategies," a poem that fuses the familial (seen in the tenderness of a father bathing his young daughter) and the political (seen in the horrible attack of "a girl in Sarajevo, sixteen," surrounded by battle and raped by an enemy soldier), Bottoms confesses now that "the only answer I have / is this nervous / exaggeration of tenderness, / and that every ministry of my hand, clumsy / and apologetic, asks her / to practice such a radical faith." Wright's influence is large in Bottoms' recent work. It is to Wright's own impressive credit that he is able to envision both spheres — the worldly and the metaphysical — and to articulate them so clearly, as in the closing lines of "Indian Summer II," "We live in two landscapes, as Augustine might have said, / One that's eternal and divine, / and one that's just the back yard, / Dead leaves and dead grass in November, purple in spring."

Bottoms' best new work also mediates between the two "landscapes" that Wright identifies. It is a type of religious vision — to perceive the shape or light of the holy world through the landscape and detail of the physical one. Here in *Vagrant Grace* and even more deeply in his most recent book, *Waltzing through the Endtime*, this perception of the holy within the physical provides Bottoms with a rich new complexity and metaphysical disease. (In *Waltzing*, Bottoms extends a further point of influence by Wright, as his sense and application of form — line-length, indentation, and stanza structure — become clearly more akin to Wright's than Dickey's.) "A Walk to Carter's Lake" finds Bottoms once more revisiting the kind of natural scene we find in his early work. But his earlier drama (and occasional melodrama — of predatory animals and a fear for personal safety) now is replaced by a spiritual doubt akin to Wright's:

> Look, above the creek, hummingbirds in the trumpet vine.
> Not too close, wait. See the green blurs
> stitching the leaves?
>
> Here at the edge of the millennium
> I don't imagine
> you'd call them anything as archaic as angels.
>
> But aren't they agents of a sort...?

Bottoms even enjoys the witty self-reflection that Wright relishes, too, the metapoetic wink. Here he may be directly addressing the expectations of the readers of his earlier work: "I know, / you thought you knew me, /

and now to hear me talk this way...." The ethereal hummingbirds provide a literal image of the angels he imagines in this scene, so fleeting. They also provide an agency for the holy. "What else," he asks, "can promenade in the air?"

In "Steve Belew Plays the National Steel," Bottoms more deeply explores this manner of vision where the material and physical world, even as it grows "smutty" and trashed, may virtually shimmer with the metaphysics of grace:

> For beauty we sometimes have to close our eyes —
> as I do now, rocked
> against the railing of this deck,
> hearing in these sparks of glass and steel
> a woman dragging the Dumpsters
> of the Claremont Hotel.
> Down alleys off Ponce, in a peacoat
> and cap, she parades under smutty windows,
> not drunk, I think, but slightly dazed
> by her own vagrant grace....

Paradoxically, when the speaker closes his eyes, he sees. This is both a Christian and a Classical trope: Blinded, the prophet can envision the otherworldly, just as he can detect through the language of nature the music of the divine:

> All over the yard, the bottleneck loosens
> the tongues of trees...
>
> Who knows what promise floats over these shadows
> or whether it rings as true
> in that refuge of boxes,
> though I hear her fingers fumbling the neck,
> fretting for a key,
> until somewhere above the long alley
> a window opens.

The open window suggests that point where language ceases and a passageway appears that may lead to the "promise [that] floats over these shadows." Bottoms' embrace of the physical world — wildly natural at times, settled by the human at others—has led him ultimately to a visionary brink. Or as he says in the concluding lines of "Country Store and Moment of Grace":

>   these shadows
>   of house and pine
>
> and fence and maple becoming one shadow
> *where the shadows of this life...*
>   yes,
> lengthen into the shadow of memory,
>
> and finally
> to that shadow, Amen.

This may be the clearest expression of faith in David Bottoms' recent work. For all the threats embodied by the feral physical world, for all the anxious doubt accompanying his metaphysical and religious investigations, this poet's ultimate gesture is an act and articulation of acceptance, where the apparently dual worlds "[become] one shadow," where the shadow itself is the figure of quiet unity.

David Bottoms has deepened his portrayal of the American South beyond alligators and county fairs to a place of genuine spiritual searching. Such are the tactics and successes of the poems of *Vagrant Grace*: "Listen, here in the foothills / above the suburban skirmishes of apparent Armageddon, / I can't turn around without having / to untangle parable" ("My Uncle Sowing Beatitudes"). Bottoms' best poems contain the two worlds of wilderness and settlement, animal power and human doubt (with its emerging shadow of acceptance). He may be more civilized now in the suburbs of the new South, and his rhetorical means may have shifted subtly to include both active narration and interior meditation, but the poet is as agitated, probing, and readable as ever.

Works Cited

Bottoms, David. *In a U-Haul North of Damascus*. New York: William Morrow, 1983.

———. *Shooting Rats at the Bibb County Dump*. New York: William Morrow, 1980.

———. *Vagrant Grace*. Port Townsend, WA: Copper Canyon Press, 1999.

———. *Waltzing through the Endtime*. Port Townsend, WA: Copper Canyon Press, 2004.
Dickey, James. *Poems 1957–1967*. Middletown, CT: Wesleyan University Press, 1967.
Whitman, Walt. "Preface 1855 —*Leaves of Grass,* First Edition," *Leaves of Grass.* Eds. Sculley Bradley and Harold W. Blodgett. New York: W. W. Norton, 1973.
Wright, Charles. *Appalachia*. New York: Farrar, Straus and Giroux, 1998.

The Logic
of the Original Dream
WILLIAM WALSH

This interview was conducted at Georgia State University in Bottoms' office on two occasions, August 3rd and November 18th, 2004.

Walsh: I'd like to start this interview with a discussion of metaphor in your poetry. Is the metaphor consciously there or does it derive from the poem as you work through it?

Bottoms: It's both, I think. Often the poem is born out of a metaphor, out of a figurative device. As a matter of fact, that's usually the way poems come to me. And it's the most fortunate way. For instance, my poem about the vulture tree — that notion of the vultures as "dwarfed transfiguring angels" was actually the seed of the poem, and the last line —"with mercy enough to consume us all and give us wings"— was the first line that came to me. Sometimes, though, the figurative will find an unexpected way to rise out of the poem. I'm thinking here of the word play that occurs in that old poem about bunting ["Sign for My Father Who Stressed the Bunt"] and the way one pun sort of gave rise to the next.

You have several favorite metaphors—things you keep coming back to. One is water as spiritual transcendence. I think you said somewhere that your first encounter with figurative language came from church.

Yes, I believe I said Sunday school at the First Baptist Church in Canton, Georgia. When I was a boy my mother was superintendent of the Primary Department, and so I spent a good deal of time there. Those old hymns, I suppose, were the first place I ran across language being used in a figurative way. "Shall we gather at the river," that's still one of my favorites. Or "I'm gonna take a trip on that old gospel ship." There are dozens and dozens of those old songs. And, of course, in scripture. Mostly, the psalms, I suppose. But there's so much water imagery in those hymns. It's the whole beautiful notion of crossing over, of getting to the other side. This imagery, of course, is ancient, and not uniquely Christian, but I suppose Sunday school largely accounts for my love of it, and the gospel music I listened to as a boy. My grandfather owned an old country store on Highway 5 just south of town. We had one radio station and he kept it on all the time. It was mostly always gospel music. So the spiritual metaphors came early. Also, as you know, lakes and rivers make such a wonderful metaphor for the psyche — the conscious mind and the unconscious, the surface and that hidden realm below the surface. I tried to say something about that in a recent poem called "Melville in the Bass Boat," a poem that wants to say something about the creative process, about the unconscious and the way the idea hits, the way it springs out of the unconscious mind and surprises you. It's about a guy out on a deep lake, fishing, at night. He's trying to "conjure one small mystery caged in the bones of a fish." But nothing is happening. Oddly enough, as if he'd anticipated his luck, he's brought along a copy of *Moby Dick*. He begins to read by lantern light and his mind drifts into Melville's story. Suddenly the "dream-fish" strikes "far out, like a thought." The poem plays on a line from Melville —"…Meditation and water are wedded for ever."

Metaphorically, fishing has always been important to you. As well as animals….

I had a grandfather who was a fisherman and so I grew up with it. He lived next door to us and Lake Allatoona was only a few miles away. We fished there pretty often. Also our neighbor had a little pond, actually it was more like a large mud hole, but it had some catfish and bream in it. I used to fish quite a lot, especially when I lived in Florida back in 1980–81 when I was in grad school at Florida State University. I loved those little rivers around there. But I haven't been fishing in years. I stopped when my daughter was young. I tried to get her interested in it, but she thought it was boring. The world got busy and I sort of let it go. But I've always been very attracted to it, and as you say, to the turtles, snakes, rats, and other creatures that you find around lakes and rivers. Someone told me once that Warren and Dickey took all the noble animals — the eagles, the owls, the horses — and I got stuck with all the creatures of a somewhat lower order. It's true, I suppose. But they tell their own special story, don't they? The reptiles, I mean. And the amphibians. They're wallowers in the muck and slime. They talk about beginnings and transformations, and

I'm very interested in that, and the ways in which we're still connected to them.

How's that?

Oh, there's still a lot of the primitive inside us, I think. Maybe the first time I ran across this in poetry was in Roethke. You know that little poem called "The Slug"? "Loose toe from the old life," he calls it. Isn't that great? Then he says, "I'm sure I've been a toad, one time or another … I rejoice in the kinship." And there's that little poem "River Incident," where he's standing in the water and he says, "And I knew I had been there before,/In that cold, granitic slime." He's deeply interested in origins, and all through his work you see an affinity for the primitive. He calls it his attraction to the "minimal."

You have some poems in your first book that deal with this. I remember what Robert Bly said in Leaping Poetry *where he discusses the reptilian and the mammalian brains and if you can transcend away from the reptilian brain which is the fierce warrior (which Dickey sort of embodied as the hunter) to the mammalian brain that elevates, actually transcends, a person to a level of thinking where you have this pure clarity of thought, almost as though it were a tunnel to the answers.*

That's right, a section called "All the Animals Inside Us." But I haven't thought about those poems in a very long time. They came out of a book I'd read by Carl Sagan, *Dragons of Eden*. In one part he sort of distills the notion of the triune brain—the notion that our brain developed as three separate brains, sort of one on top of another. The first is what he called the old reptile brain, a little mass of tissue at the top of the spine. This supposedly accounted for the sex drive and ritual, and maybe something about eating. I can't remember. On top of that formed the limbic brain, or the old mammal brain, and on top of that came the neocortex, which accounts for abstract thought. Anyway, I don't have much of a background in science, but I was struck by the fact that we still have that old reptile brain. And I got the notion that occasionally it rears its head and make us aware of our relationship to the lower creatures—snakes, turtles, frogs, and as Roethke would say, slugs.

The centerpiece of the new book is a poem called "Homage to Buck Cline." It's about you getting stopped for speeding, but it's also about your father.

Buck Cline was the chief of police in Canton, Georgia, when I grew up there in the sixties. Buck was literally 6'5" and weighted around 280. He had a reputation for being about as sour and generally mean as a human being gets, and he'd made that reputation by keeping the young toughs in line. Everybody in our high school feared Buck Cline like the devil himself, even the guys who considered themselves "tough," which of course, I didn't. The poem focuses on a night in my life just after I turned 16 and got my driver's license. I had a steady girlfriend, who was fifteen or sixteen. Her mother was teaching her to cook — food was still thought to be the way to a man's heart. Anyway, my girlfriend especially liked to make spaghetti suppers, and her mother encouraged her by supplying candles and a bottle of Mateus Rose. That was very adult, you know. So one evening around 12:30 or 1:00 in the morning, after a couple of glasses of Mateus, I was driving home and stopped at the traffic light on the edge of town. Across the street, about fifty yards to my right, I saw Buck Cline parked in his patrol car in the shadows of the North Canton Store. Buck was keeping an eye on the would-be hoods circling our one hamburger joint in their jacked up Chevys and Fords. Well, I was feeling a little too full of myself, on the Mateus, I guess, and I got the strange notion that if I pulled through the light and put about fifty yards between Buck Cline and my car, I could floor it, spin some rubber for the guys at the burger joint, and out-run Buck to my house, which was only about three miles away. The poem centers on what happened when Buck pulled me over about a mile and half down the highway, took my license, and found out my name. My father was a veteran, a sailor who was severely wounded at the naval Battle of Guadalcanal, and like most men of that generation, Buck Cline was a veteran also. Canton was a small town, but I had no idea they knew each other. What I discovered was the secret bond that existed between those veterans, and that there are relationships in the world that were formed way before our time that affect us in profound ways.

You call him "Saint Buck" at the end of the poem. Quite a shift in opinion.
   That's right. "Saint Buck/of the handy blackjack." He was, I suppose, at that particular moment, a very unlikely vehicle of grace.

It's interesting if you look at the vultures transcending and your earlier poems all the way up through Vagrant Grace *where I think you have a major transition in your work up to and including this new book,* Waltzing Through the Endtime. *There's a shift, a spiritual transcendence, away from the animals in the earlier poems. The animals are still there to some degree in the new book, yet the metaphor is more spiritual, and the animals are employed more as backdrop. I mean, if a person didn't know the new book was written by you, he'd most likely not guess. That is, outside of a few titles such as "Shooting Rats in the Afterlife."*

The new book is much more of what I've always wanted my poems to be. I'm interested in what you said about this spiritual shift. I don't really think the poems have shifted so much toward the spiritual — I think I've always worked toward that, at trying to be what Warren calls a "seeker." But there is a significant shift toward a Christian outlook. *Waltzing Through the Endtime* is a quirky sort of book. It's apocalyptic in many ways, and it deals with wacky speculations about the afterlife and the problems of living a spiritual life in a secular and scientific age. The poems have also evolved stylistically. They've stretched their muscles a little. They've grown longer. The stories are still there and they remain central, but the poems pause to think about them more, and to think not only about their consequences for our everyday lives but to think about their ultimate consequences. For instance, what does it mean that in 1977 a woman in Phoenix, Arizona, pulled from her oven a tortilla scorched with the face of Christ?

That's from your poem "Vigilance." Where did that poem come from?

A number of things. My fascination for other wacky appearances of the Deity, a dream my mother-in-law had, but mostly, I think, the seed was a talk I had with my friend Barry Hannah, the Mississippi novelist. A few years ago I saw Barry at the Sewanee Writer's Conference. He'd just finished a bout of chemotherapy and was getting strong again, and he told me that when he was in intensive care in Oxford, Mississippi, Jesus had appeared to him. He looked up, he said, and Jesus was standing at the foot of his bed, a big man with a barrel chest. Barry was very sincere, and I was moved by that. He looked at Jesus and said, "I've neglected you." And Jesus said nothing, or smiled. I can't really remember. Anyway, it was a moving story, and it brought up a memory of my father-in-law, who was a pretty strict fundamentalist, and how one night way out in the boonies of Montana he'd seen Christ standing on the shoulder of the road. I wove these stories together with several others, including a dream my mother-in-law had about floating down a river on an outhouse — true — which I paralleled with a little line of scripture about the second coming: "If the goodman of the house had known in what watch the thief would come." You'd have to know my mother-in-law, but she said it wasn't the Jordan

River. But she took it somehow as a sign of the end. "If the owner of the outhouse had known when the river would flood," says the poem.

It seems like you're doing something different with the animals in your new book. There's the snake in the poem "Little Drop of Wickedness." It's used much more mythically there.

Yes, that poem wants to be about evil, I suppose, and about the origins of evil. And the snake has always taken the rap for that. In Christian myth, I mean. So in the poem, it sort of works metaphorically in that way. When the persona runs across the snake in his backyard, it sparks a number of memories — questions about evil and the horrible things folks do to each other. And, of course, it asks the question about origins. The snake takes the rap. Someone has to, right?

Satan actually turns up in this poem.

He turns up selling dope in a Saigon bar. Witnessed, I believe, by my old friend Steve Belew, who served in that war. Again, evil incarnate.

You give him a snazzy red blazer and a salt and pepper beard. He's sort of hip, right?

I've just always been fascinated with the various ways we imagine him. Two of my favorites are literary. I love that section in *Brothers Karamazov* where he appears to Ivan. I forget how he's dressed there, but I think I modeled him after Dostoevski's devil. Actually, the devil in Thomas Mann's *Dr. Faustus* was also a model. He's fairly gaudy, I think. I remember Mann has him wearing a pair of yellow pants, too tight, and worn-out shoes. He says he looks something like a pimp. I like that. What might at first look snazzy, as you say, or sophisticated, becomes gaudy and shabby on a closer look, which says something, I think, about sin, about evil. And then there's the question of reality. In both of those novels we're always kept a little off balance, aren't we? What's really happening here? Ivan is feverish, very much out of his head, Leverkuhn is syphilitic and moving toward insanity. Is this confrontation merely a disturbing hallucination? Something rising out of the diseased mind? Even so, is it any less real? And what does that say about the origins of evil? The kingdom of God is inside you, says Christ. And also, no doubt, the kingdom of the devil. Didn't Jung say that the primary thing that kept folks from looking inward was the fear of Hades? Or something like that.

Let's go back to this notion of the poet as "seeker." You talked about that recently in an essay. That phrase is from Warren?

Actually, he may have used the word "yearner." But I take the words to be synonymous. He said that in an interview he did with Peter Stitt, back in the seventies, I think. He said he was a yearner after meaning. He didn't have any particular theology to assign to the world, but he was a yearner for meaning. I like that very much, and I think that all serious writers are yearners. They're seekers after the big answers, what Warren called the logic of "the original dream." We'll never know those big answers, of course, because we're only a part of the dream, not the dreamer, but the serious writer yearns nevertheless. And what the writer yearns for, what he or she seeks, is a sense of consequence in the world. The world is constantly teasing us about this, constantly dropping little clues to the mystery. But the world is very coy, I think. It doesn't want to give us the whole story, not in one piece anyway. You've heard me say this. I remember Dickey telling me that he occasionally experienced these little epiphanies, these moments of clarity in his life, when he felt that if he could just connect them all together, like you might connect the dots, he'd have a perfect blueprint of reality. The key here, I think, is the word "felt." We feel sometimes that we might actually break through the fog of the world into some ultimate clarity, yet we're severely limited. Nevertheless, we yearn for that breakthrough.

Going back to what you just said regarding writers who are searching for the mysteries when you look at it in those terms, what mysteries are you, personally, trying to unravel?

What I am trying to unravel is sort of the ultimate reason for everything, and as Warren said, "the logic behind the original dream." But, you know you are not going to be able to do that because you didn't dream the original dream. You are only a part of it, which is an interesting irony, and yet, there is something that compels you to keep searching.

What was your relationship with James Dickey like?

We were friends. We always got along well. He liked to assume the role of father figure with young writers he liked. He'd say, "You're one of mine" and such stuff. We were friends for about sixteen years, I guess. I've always heard stories about Dickey's outrageous behavior. You know the stories — Dickey got drunk and insulted so-an-so, or made a pass at a professor's wife. Or pulled off some equally obnoxious stunt. But, truthfully, he never behaved badly in front of me. He stayed at our house several times back in the eighties. The first time he came, his wife, Debba, phoned me to ask that I not take him to a liquor store. On the way home from the airport Jim asked me if she'd called. What could I say? And how could I tell him I wasn't going to take him to a liquor store. He suggested a compromise, a sort of pack then, and we stuck to it. I'd not tell Debba he was drinking, and he'd only drink beer at my house. Actually, I think it was Country Club Malt Liquor. Anyway, that's the way we played it. Only malt liquor. We had a good relationship, though I didn't see him much during the last few years. I'd talk to him on the phone occasionally, and I talked with him a few days before he died.

I remember one time at his house, Dickey told me that the stories about himself—and this is what he felt killed Hemingway, this macho pose, the bravado—he said these stories about him were highly exaggerated.

Well, they were. He exaggerated them. I've always found this interesting. If you go back and look at the back jacket flap of *Deliverance*, you'll see that it says he flew a hundred missions over Japan in World War II. Well, he really only flew something like thirty-eight. I can't remember. The real number is in that Henry Hart biography. But think about that — thirty-eight combat missions is nothing to sneeze at. That's thirty-eight bombing runs over Japan with a whole lot of people trying to shoot you out of the sky. Now if you'd done that thirty-eight times, why would you feel the need to exaggerate that number?

Did you ever read one another's work in the early stages? Would he hand you an early version of a poem?

No, he'd never do that. He wouldn't have been able to give up that sort of authority. And even if he did, I wouldn't have known what to say to him. I didn't care much for his later poetry, but I certainly couldn't have told him that. We talked about poetry, of course, but not much about our own. Actually, we probably talked more about music. I've played guitar in several little bluegrass and country bands, and he was interested in that. He loved folk music. Southern folk music, I mean, bluegrass and mountain music. He loved guitars and owned a bunch of them, but wasn't really much of a guitar player. Ironically, he didn't have a very good sense of rhythm. He was also very interested in sports. Football and boxing, I remember. I believe he and my dad actually played football against each other in high school. I remember Dickey asking me a few days before he died on the telephone what I thought of his poems. He was questioning his own success and what he had left.

Did he know he was close to dying?

Yeah. He told me several times over the last couple years that he thought he was going to die. He had just gotten out of the hospital and I didn't know really how serious it was, but yeah, he knew. He wanted to know what I thought about his poems. I told him what I always did. I told him the story about when he and I had lunch with Peter Taylor. Taylor was a good friend of Robert Lowell's, and Taylor was telling us what a jealous man Lowell was and that Lowell was jealous of no one more than Dickey. And of course, Dickey just loved that — that Lowell would have been jealous of him. But, I think even at the end of Dickey's life he doubted himself, he questioned the quality of his own work. I think it is only natural because you never know what people are thinking.

What was your relationship like with Robert Penn Warren?

Well, I really didn't know him. After he chose *Shooting Rats* for the Whitman Award, we swapped a letter or two, but I never got a chance to meet him. I have to say though, that his work moves me more consistently than any other American poet. Years ago Dave Smith and I would argue about who was the better poet — Warren or Dickey. I always defended Dickey. Over the past few years, though, I've come to see a depth in Warren that Dickey didn't possess. Dickey had a marvelous energy, and a wonderful gift for drama and language, but Warren's work has a deeper spiritual depth, a great sense of awe for the natural world.

Warren's "yearning" for answers?

Yes, and it really didn't flower in Warren until late in his career. I'd say until "Audubon." Those later poems have a powerful and beautiful sense of consequence about them. That's not to say there aren't touches of it all through his work, but it really comes into full bloom in that last great spurt of energy. In his constant questioning of the world you see a philosophy develop that unites the whole body of his work.

Would you say that Warren's longer poems were an influence on Waltzing Through the Endtime? *Structurally, I mean.*

Of course, "Audubon" is one of my favorite poems in the world. I love the way he caught the man's life and character in snapshots, and the way the poem lets Warren think about the various implications Audubon's life has for all of us. Another influence, of course, is Charles Wright, those beautiful meditations he's written for years. In many ways, though, I think my poems are much different than Charles.' I just don't have his gift for language, and nobody does really. My poems are much more narrative, though they've become sort of fractured, I guess. Still, they're born out of the world, out of events that happened in the real world. What distinguishes them from my older poems is that they don't focus around a single event, but pull together several events that tend to form a kinship.

When I read your poems I do not see a person who is particularly humorous as I would say Fred Chappell, although I know you are quick to laugh and can be funny. Have you ever attempted to work in that area?

No, although I think you will find that some of the poems in the new book have funny parts in terms of irony. I've always had sort of a serious notion of what poetry was all about. I don't mind laughing. I like to laugh, but the poem is more than laughing. Yeats talks about the poem as being almost a religious experience. Warren talked about the poem being a search for the logic of the original dream. Poetry is a way of doing that. I hold poetry to a pretty high standard and it's a serious business as we look for our own sense of humanity, our own sense of reality in the world, and language is one of those ways we search that out. Warren always referred to himself as a searcher, and I was trying to make the case that the greatest poetry and fiction is that which searches after ultimate meanings. I think that is true. It's doesn't trivialize it, which is not to say that you cannot be humorous and still do that. I'm sure you can. But, I've always liked best those writers, both poets and fiction writers, who are examining the mysteries. As Ed Hirsch says, "In praise of the mysteries."

You've taught poetry writing for a number of years.

Twenty-two or three, although sometimes it seems much longer than that.

What's the single greatest mistake you see young poets make?

That's very tough. The mistakes keep changing. But there is one thing that continuously distresses me. I don't know if I'd call this a mistake, maybe a flaw. But so many poems I see by young writers, actually so many I see period, just don't have sense of necessity about them. They don't communicate a compelling need to have been written. Either they memorialize some very uneventful event or they try to express some vague feeling the poet has had. They just never develop into art that suggests a significance, a need to be. And here's a thing too, especially about young poets — a large number of them, at least the ones I see, tend to confuse poetry and philosophy.

You mean they want to write philosophy?

That's right. They want to write ideas and not poetry. Someone asked me once in a class, "Hey, but can't the poem be an idea?" I said no, absolutely not, and I stick by that. On the other hand, it can express an idea, and it usually will if it's any good. Karl Shapiro puts this well in an essay called "What is Not Poetry." He says, "If poetry has an opposite, it is philosophy. Poetry is a materialization of experience; philosophy is the abstraction of it." I love that, and it's a point I try to get across to all my students. Okay, this is simplistic example and won't stand up in court, but think about this. Here's a story I like to tell. Karl Shapiro and … give me the name of a philosopher. Anybody will do.

Heraclitus.

Okay, I've forgotten everything I ever knew about Heraclitus, but Karl Shapiro and Heraclitus are walking across Woodruff Park in Atlanta, going over to Fairlie-Poplar for some Thai food. When they reach Peachtree Street they see a yellow flash go by then hear a gigantic crash under the traffic light at Five Points. A yellow MG has tried to beat the light and smashed into the side of a Macy's furniture truck. It's a mess. Shapiro and Heraclitus rush over and try to help. A crowd gathers. Somebody on a cell phone calls an ambulance. The driver of the MG has been thrown into the street. The sports car's a tangle of crushed metal. Gasoline, blood, and glass are everywhere. Heraclitus, the philosopher, takes it all in and immediately abstracts. He thinks Chaos, Accident, Fate. Shapiro, however, whips out his notebook and writes down everything that happened. The yellow flash on Peachtree Street, the smell of the burning brakes and gasoline, the sound of the impact, the blood in the street. He goes back to his apartment and puts it all down on a legal pad as vividly as he can, then he types it up into a poem, and sends it to *Five Points*. Megan Sexton likes it and publishes it in the next issue. We get our copy a few months later and turn to a poem called "Auto Wreck." We read the poem. We ponder it for a few seconds. We think Chaos, Accident, Fate. Okay, as I said, this is simplistic and won't stand up in court, but it touches on the fundamental difference between philosophy and poetry, and illustrates pretty well the function of poetry. The point is simply this — the poet and the philosopher are traveling to the same city, but the poet is simply taking the scenic route. The poet is trying to make the world materialize on the page, so that the reader can participate, can abstract for himself and take for himself what meaning the world offers.

I read not long ago, that if we had never invented poetry or if we never wrote another poem, it would make very little difference in the lives of most people. Do you agree or disagree?

That sounds a little like something Auden said, that poetry never makes anything happen, or something like that. I think that probably isn't true. Poetry makes things happen in the human heart, and that changes what happens in the world. Without poetry, without art, I think we'd generally be much poorer spiritually. Even if a person doesn't read poetry, he or she benefits from a culture where other people do. Even if I don't go to museums and look at great paintings, I benefit in many ways because other people do. This is true because the human imagination is being exercised. It's turning itself into art, and art, because it brings consequence into the world, exerts an influence that is powerfully contagious. It does, indeed, change people's lives.

Recalling the poem you mentioned, "Sign for My Father Who Stressed the Bunt." That poem has gotten around a lot, and I think it's one of the finest poems ever written about sports. But when you go back to it now, a poem you wrote more than twenty years ago, how does it read to you?

That poem has been anthologized more than any of my other poems, not because it's my best poem but because it's so teachable. It's built on a series of puns that tie the game of baseball to family sacrifice. The bunt, you know, the sacrifice. And so it provides a way to teach students how language works on various levels. It's still a pretty decent little poem, I think, and has held up well enough over the years. I read it not long ago, and thought if I had it back I'd certainly change the line breaks and maybe work on the first stanza some. Basically it does what it set out to do. It has gotten around, though, and it turns very odd places. A couple of years ago it even showed up on some standardized test for high school students in Missouri. But I'm a little tired of it now, as you might imagine.

Back to Dickey for a second. I'm very interested in poetic influences and how they sort of create a lineage of poetic history, like a strand of DNA. You're often associated with Warren and Dickey, with the narrative line in Southern poetry. Who do you see as your most crucial influences?

That's hard to say. Their influence came relatively late, I think. When I started writing poetry as an undergrad at Mercer, that would be in the late sixties and early seventies, I was very taken with Dylan Thomas. Everybody was then, it seemed. Anyway, all of my poems had very heavy sound devices. Unfortunately, they didn't make much sense, and I was really aware that making sense was a necessary element of poetry. Then I met the poet James Seay, who came to Mercer to do a reading. He'd just published his first book, *Let Not Your Hart*. I really didn't know anything about contemporary poetry at all, but I was very impressed with Jim. I started reading his poems, and he put me onto Dickey. This may sound odd, but for years I didn't think Dickey was all that good. I see now that my judgment, or taste, or whatever, was a sort of safety mechanism, a defensive mechanism that allowed me to go on and write without the shadow of Dickey hovering over me. So, I never felt intimidated by him. Also Dickey was much older than I was, a full generation.

In a recent biographical sketch it stated that you are one of the South's leading writers. At this point in your career, do you find the term southern writer limiting or inviting?

That's a good question, but I don't know what it means to be one of the South's leading writers. There are so many writers in the south, and so many really good ones, I don't find it limiting at all. As a matter of fact, I was talking to my wife, Kelly, in terms of the 2004 Presidential election. I mean, this country is so big — we were thinking how could anybody possibly have a handle on everything going on in this country? It's not really one country, but about four countries. It's the northeast, the southeast, southwest and the northwest. Those areas seem more like something you can get a grip on. How do you get a grip on the whole thing? It terms of literature, over the last few decades we've characterized ourselves in that way. We now teach classes on southern literature and western literature. It's almost a literary country in and of itself. It's much easier to get a grip on the characteristics of southern literature than, say, Irish literature. It's much easier than American literature. I mean, what is American literature right now? It's just a big patchwork quilt. There's so very little consistency of theme or whatever, but with southern literature you can say things and it's not limiting because what you are after is the universal through the regional, through the specific. Your landscape may be southern, but your intent is universal. You move from that specific landscape and into the global landscape or spiritual landscape, a universal landscape. I don't find it limiting at all. It's probably beneficial in terms of feeling a sense of tradition and having a tradition from which to work, a culture out of which you work.

One of my favorite quotes from Robert Penn Warren is "Since my idiot childhood the world has been/ Trying to tell me something./ There is something/ Hidden in the dark." That something hidden in the dark is that mysticism. When did you first discover the power of his work?

About the time I published my first book, I think. Roethke was a big influence then, especially the poems in *The Far Field*, and so was James Wright. I'm thinking of *The Branch Will Not Break* and *Shall We Gather at the River*. There were strong stories there, and wonderful language, and the poems were trying to work figuratively. And some of William Stafford was important. And Elizabeth Bishop. But Dickey was later. And Warren was later still. I found Dickey's collection of four books, *Poems: 1957–1967*, to be just dynamite stuff. All the way from the early war poems like "The Performance" and "Fire Bombing" to the animal poems.

In the past year or so, for work, I have been to where you grew up in Canton, GA about a dozen times. One day I drove by the K-Mart and pulled into the parking lot to look out over the terrain, just imagining what the area must have looked like with your grandfather's store and your house.

That's it, the K-Mart. The whole area, that whole parking lot was land that belonged to my grandfather. He had an old country store that sat there for about fifty-two years. That Kentucky Fried Chicken is exactly where my house was. Of course, it was a two-lane road back then. There was a ball field right across the street from our house. Behind the store there was a barn. He always had a walking horse he used to show. There were some chicken houses and dog lots. He raised beagles up above that.

I went into the Kentucky Fried Chicken and I mentioned to the kid who waited on me the fact that this area used to be a farm and your house was directly where he was standing. I got just this dumb blank stare back at me then he asked what I wanted to drink. (laughing) I like to think about the things that occurred, the life that was lived, and everything that has been buried under and built upon. How do you reconcile that?

I don't know that you do. It doesn't really matter whether you do or you don't. It's just that way. It's like all things pass away. Like in that D.H. Lawrence poem (it's not a great poem, but a poem that is very important to me) that goes something like "we're dying, we're dying, all we can do is be willing to die." There's nothing you can do about it. It's just gone. I regret that they sold it. I regret that it's paved over and I regret that there's a stupid K-Mart on it, but what do you do? Time moves on. The town that I grew up in when I was a kid was a beautiful little town but then as so many towns in the South have done when a little money came into the town, they developed too quickly and only in cheap ways. Nice landmarks fell to car washes and fast food restaurants. So that is pretty much what happened to my home town. I think they are trying now to save a little of what they once had. I would go to the old library up at the head of the main street from when I was about seven years old. It was a beautiful old Victorian house turned into a library, just gorgeous architecture. Of course they plowed that under and put up a little pill box that looks like it ought to have gun turrets on top. R.T. Jones, who started the Canton Cotton Mills and owed just about everything in Canton, built a beautiful two-story brick house with a red tile roof near the center of town. I spent a lot of my childhood there because my best friend was his grandson. It was a gorgeous house, a landmark. Well, they tore it down to put up a cheap post office. One hardly knows what to say about it. You have a notion that you want to preserve the past in some way, but it takes money to do that.

But, the place is still in my head, and I think that is a point that *Waltzing Through the Endtime* tries to make about memory and the roll of memory. One of the poems speculates that maybe if there is an afterlife, the only thing we carry into it is memory. This is not a new notion, of course, but to sleep, a chance to dream, that sort of thing. We keep these things alive in our memory. One of the poems calls memory "pocket charms against oblivion." In my head, I have the store, the house, the chicken houses, the barn. It's still there. I remember it just about everyday. I think about that landscape a lot. At night, when I'm trying to go to sleep I'll play that landscape over so as not to forget it.

Since I brought up Canton, Georgia, I want to ask you a question that I have had since about 1983 when you published North of Damascus *in a U-Haul and it has to do with the poem, "The Desk" and how you broke into the Canton Elementary School to steal the desk top your father had carved his name into when he was a boy. Did you really break into the school and steal the desk top?*

I'll tell you and I will tell nobody else. I went back and the desk wasn't there. (laughing) They had renovated the building and had taken all the desks. The story about the desk is true, but when I went back the desk wasn't there. I went back and actually tried to talk to the people in the building to see if the desk was any place else, but they had disposed of all of them. I think they saved one room sort of as a museum piece but the desk wasn't in there.

Did you actually break into the school?

Yeah, I think I may have, but it wasn't the way it was in the poem. It might have been an open door or an open window around the back of the building. But I didn't break any windows as in the poem. (laughing)

The Rolling Circle: Memory and Maturity

Edward Byrne

Finally, yes, I know this is about eternity,
this circling, this following,
and, of course, that irredeemable taunt of memory,
without which we'd have no ghosts to lead us....
—"A Family Parade"

Ever since David Bottoms' first book, *Shooting Rats at the Bibb County Dump*, was selected by Robert Penn Warren for the Academy of American Poets' Walt Whitman Award in 1979, readers have come to expect certain traits or patterns of action in his poetry: a clear and credible voice offering accurate and evocative descriptions of nature, as well as the natural activities of everyday existence, often mixed with wit and irony, as he searches for understanding of the higher spiritual significance among the commonplace or ordinary events of life. In retrospect, with nearly three decades of Bottoms' career behind him, these signature features are even more readily apparent in an accumulation of outstanding lyric narratives.

As the title of his initial collection might indicate, some of Bottoms' most characteristic works during the earlier years of his poetry offered narrators in risky situations, outsiders and individuals barely on the ragged edge of society somehow engaged in activities that were rebellious or defiant. From those earliest poems and through some others that followed in subsequent volumes, readers have been introduced to characters stealing ornamental ironwork and vandalizing gravestones in a cemetery at night ("Wrestling Angels"), getting high on pot in a crypt ("Smoking in an Open Grave"), hot wiring a friend's car in the middle of the night so it later could be rolled into a river to claim insurance ("In the Black Camaro"), breaking into an old elementary school to cart off a scarred desktop carved with names ("The Desk"), or raping a young woman in a hayloft ("The Farmers").

The Rolling Circle (Edward Byrne)

Many poems have presented portraits of the lost or lonely: "The Drunk Hunter" secretly hopes "someone has heard his shot, / takes time to warn he's hunting posted land"; "A Trucker Drives Through His Lost Youth" searches "again for the spirit / behind the eyes in his rear-view mirror"; "The Lame" boy dreams "he feels fish gnaw the swollen ankle, / carry off in their bellies chunks of his deformity." Even those poems in which the description and circumstances of the narrator most clearly suggest identification with Bottoms — and in which the speaker appears to have undergone some sort of self-discovery, a moment of illumination or imagination he may have been seeking — an absence and a separation from others always seem to have emphasis. Bottoms writes "In a Jon Boat During a Florida Dawn": "you feel an old surprise surfacing / in and around you. If you could, / you would cut the outboard / and stop it all right here...." The speaker concludes "In a Pasture Under a Cradled Moon," by "studying the way the light drops into the trees, / the way so much love can be learned / from loss." "In a U-Haul North of Damascus" the narrator finds himself "on the road from one state / to another, what is left behind nags back through the distance." In "Paper Route, Northwest Montana" Bottoms recalls an early glimpse of "a stunned white wolf" drifting down the river on an ice floe, and he concludes, "sometimes in loneliness, I claim it / a blessing...." And alone on another river in "Under the Vulture-Tree," he imagines the black birds filling a dead oak as "transfiguring angels," figures "who pray over the leaf-graves of the anonymous lost...."

The scenes depicted in Bottoms' poems have always carried a strong sense of authenticity and credibility as they carefully catalog even the most ordinary items in everyday life, yet present them in a lyrical language that lends an elegance to everything that matters, especially those objects too often overlooked because of their commonplace appearances, but that are nevertheless essential.

Appropriately, in "Appearances" Bottoms recounts once listening to a radio reporter's narration of sheriff's deputies searching a hay field in a curve of headlights: "I curl under my blanket, / watch the yellow dial on the radio, the stars hanging / in the black panes of the window. This is real...." Indeed, the more "real" the images and events chronicled in Bottoms' poems, the more he seems obligated to choose musical phrases with convincing metaphors or similes that persuade the reader of their significance, and the reader is richer for it. Bottoms' ability to transform the ordinary into the extraordinary can be seen in one wonderful work after another among the pages of his various collections.

"Under the Boathouse" is a remarkable example. In this lyric narrative effectively written in one extended stanza of nearly fifty lines, Bottoms' narrator describes how he and his wife had arrived at a lake for a picnic, his "wife / rattling keys, calling for help with the grill, / the groceries wedged into the trunk." Instead of assisting her, he ran to dive into the lake, but as he "cut through water" into the "junked depth," his "right hand dug into silt and mud," and his "left clawed around a pain." "Caught by the unknown," his "lungs collapsed in a confusion of bubbles, / all air rising back to its element." He describes it: "Halfway between the bottom of the lake / and the bottom of the sky, I hung like a buoy / on a short rope, an effigy...."

Suspended in water between the mud beneath him and the sky brightening the surface above him, the speaker finds himself out of his element, "a curiosity among fishes, a bait hanging up / instead of down." His world has literally been turned upside down:

> In the lung-ache,
> in the loud pulsing of temples, what gave first
> was something in my head, a burst
> of colors like the blind see, and I saw
> against the surface a shadow like an angel
> quivering in a dead-man's float,
> then a shower of plastic knives and forks
> spilling past me in the lightened water, a can
> of barbequed beans, a bottle of A.1, napkins
> drifting down like white leaves,
> heavenly litter from the world I struggled toward.

Like Frost's swinger of birches who climbs black branches toward heaven and then comes back "to begin over," Bottoms' narrator also comes back with a renewed vision to begin again. In the final act of this metaphoric baptism and rebirth, death and resurrection, there is a welcoming by "a shadow like an angel" and a shower of "heavenly litter." The narrator describes the moment when he discovered himself returning to the elements of his world:

> Into the splintered light under the boathouse,
> the loved, suffocating air hovering over the lake,
> the cry of my wife leaning dangerously

over the dock, empty grocery bags at her feet,
I bobbed with a hook through the palm of my hand.

Rising into the light and once more able to see the world, now "like the blind see," with its "suffocating air" he had hurried to escape, the narrator is greeted back by the wife whose plea for assistance he'd ignored — even risking falling herself as she leans over the lake toward him to offer help, her silhouette against the bright sky above, taking the shape of an angel on the water's surface. Those groceries, the everyday items that suddenly matter so much more, have become "heavenly litter from the world" to which he is struggling to return, although he will carry a scar in his palm as a souvenir of the experience, as well as a constant reminder of what he ought to value.

The use of religious symbolism — images of angels, heaven, and even the wound in the palm of the narrator's hand — and references to spiritual redemption or renewal are not isolated to "Under the Boathouse" and "Wrestling Angels." In another example, "Cemetery Wings," a worker allergic to bee stings is attacked by a swarm while mowing grass among monuments in a cemetery. As the worker is digging "into his pocket for the bottle" of "blue pills for allergy," the poem's narrator arrives as a witness wanting to assist:

> If he knew me, I couldn't tell. He only stared
> over the terrace at the thin cloud lifting
> around the faces of angels, his eyes
> wrinkled toward a question,
> as though puzzled
> at being carried away by such small wings.

Like those other Southern poets — James Dickey, Robert Penn Warren, Dave Smith, and Charles Wright — most obviously influential in his poetry, Bottoms often uses such religious allusions. In fact, Bottoms' emphasis on the spiritual and his reliance on religious allusions have not only accumulated but perhaps grown over the years. Indeed, the allusion to Christ's stigmata in "Under the Boathouse" appears more completely in "Last Supper in Montana," an important poem among the new works included at the end of *Armored Heart: Selected and New Poems* (1995), in which the speaker's "father-in-law begins the feast / by reading a few verses from the Gospel of Matthew." He then "breaks the body into thumbnails

/ and passes the plate among us, pours the blood / into plastic pill cups." Using similar images, but in contrast with the tone of "Under the Boathouse," Bottoms writes:

> I swallow, and glance at my palm, the tangle of veins
> in my wrist. A minute drips into an empty pan,
> then a guinea screeches from the barn.
> Prayer breaks out on the sofa,
> and finally I see how a wound could bleed
> for centuries, could trickle enough
> to fill this cup.
>   Years ago, after my divorce,
> I looked for my own way of renouncing
> the world. I sat down in my kitchen and scratched
> a list on a grocery bag,
> every desire linked
> in red, then carried a shovel into a grove,
> wadded the bag and buried it.
>
> But that was Florida, smothering heat,
> bouts of booze and fever,
> so what can I say for sure about surrender
> or that lightness of heart?

  The narrator recounts another metaphoric death at the conclusion of the poem as he reports "something / left me, and the wind knocked me down," and the speaker lies sprawled on his back "across that grave." Indeed, it is as if Bottoms' poetry near the end of this collection reflected a transformation and signaled a renewal of spirit, a death followed by a rebirth of the self.

  This can easily be seen in a contrast of two poems with similar titles: "A Home Buyer Watches the Moon," which was printed early among the poems of *In a U-Haul North of Damascus* in 1983, and "A Home Buyer," which appears near the end of *Armored Hearts* in 1995. In the early poem the narrator reflects upon the feeling of total loss (perhaps even of life itself as suggested by the line break after "live" and the image of a "dead end") symbolized by an inability to keep his house: "I / who can no longer afford to live / in my two-story, have come out into the street / to stare past the mailboxes at an abrupt dead end." "A Home Buyer Watches the Moon" concludes with another series of superb images, typical of Bottoms' lyrical and evocative poetry, that again speak about an angel and bring to mind the scene depicted in "Cemetery Wings":

> Quietly now the bats jerk
> in and out of the streetlight, their shadows
> zipping across the grass like black snakes.
> And the moon lies balanced on the roof of my house
> like a new gold coin, or the simple face
> of an angel in a Colonial cemetery.

The lone figure wandering at night dejectedly observing ominous images and the speaker's use of similes suggesting loss or death in this early '80s poem are already familiar to readers of Bottoms' poetry. However, a dozen years and three collections of poetry later, Bottoms offered a different view. Bottoms begins "A Home Buyer" with a couple of lines reflecting happiness and renewal: "I was so glad to be living in my own house again, / glad for a few rooms to wander through, a place to sprawl." Although this poem also begins with the figure of the speaker wandering at night ("I walked all night from room to room, / onto the deck, into the yard, exploring / my pond of ivy, shadows of maple and dogwood"), the mood has been reversed. The narrator now feels content: "settled, finally, in the striped chair of the study / as a blue daybreak leaked like bar light / through the curtains." The onset of a new day's brightness causes him to recall another time of "happiness, confidence, like a saint" — or perhaps, similar to the kind of persona who often was seen in Bottoms' previous poems:

> ...some cowboy off the ranch in Rygate
> who's driven into town for a Legion Hall dance,
> some slicked-up kid with scuffs on his boots,
> smart enough and handsome, a hard worker
> who believes in virtue,
> and knows the value of a dependable truck.

The pairing of "virtue" and "value" seems significant in these closing lines, as does the speaker's feeling of being content with becoming "settled," which could be applied in its many definitions: settling into the new house; settling down to an end of restlessness; settling up a debt; as legally defined, settling his property; perhaps even as a consequence of learning compromise, settling for what he needs.

Certainly, the following poem in the collection, "Sleepless Nights," at first suggests a return to the dejected wanderings as the narrator tells of visiting his old house at night while the woman he left "was out of town, or drunk herself / in a fast sleep." However, he reveals: "In middle age you strike your bargain with shame, / and I leaned back against that tree, happy / and hurt to be trespassing." Further, the poem's conclusion presents proof of the narrator's transformation toward greater wisdom and new concerns, voiced not only in this poem, but seemingly emerging in the development of Bottoms' poetry at the very end of *Armored Hearts* and soon to be realized further in future work. He confesses:

> ...I'd look back at myself
> out of another night, pacing another darkness
> ringed with geese and black sheep
> and swans, singing again,
> laughing, shouldering the complaints
> of a newborn daughter.

Bottoms' relationship with his daughter Rachel, who is named in the poetry, and his focus on comforting and protecting her become central themes in his work. In "A Daughter's Fever" Bottoms addresses Rachel, but his comments reflect a new vision and a new attitude toward the world and his position in it. After reading books aloud and trying other distractions to ease his daughter's discomfort during an illness, Bottoms states:

> Rachel, about the little girl
> who started home late
> across the darkening woods...
> Someday I'll give you the words I used all night
> to guide her home. So many ways
> to enter the forest and never return.
> But happily that's another ending.

Perhaps a darker ending might have been the kind of conclusion readers would have seen in Bottoms' earlier poems. Instead, in this poem, Bottoms states, "I lean to your blanket / and hold my breath." After all the previous images of death and loss in Bottoms' poetry, of the self seeking independence, his life — indeed, his every breath — has now become dependent upon the safety and well-being of another, his daughter.

Although the closing stanza of the poem switches to third person, creating an ambiguity of memory and distance, almost as if the narrator has now become a character in one of those tales told to the daughter, he concludes with an image that contrasts with the darkness of the poem's opening stanza, which begins with the following lines: "Dark ivy draws a wave across the yard, / even the shadows / are streaked with rain."

In this wonderful ending, once more his breath is dependent upon his daughter's, and even with a small curled finger, her hold on him continues:

> Her father watches
> new light clothe the trees.
> In his orchard
> the crows out-cackle the squirrels.
> He holds his breath to hear
> her breathe, around his finger
> small fingers curl.

Published in 1999, two decades after his first collection was selected for recognition by Robert Penn Warren, *Vagrant Grace* was David Bottoms' fifth book of poems and the first to follow publication of *Armored Hearts: Selected and New Poems*. Although many of the characteristics identified with Bottoms' fine poetry over the past twenty years remained, this collection possessed an identity of its own. In fact, coming after the 1995 retrospective volume of selected poetry, *Vagrant Grace* appropriately displayed many poems that represent a new movement forward in content and in tone toward a direction first suggested by those closing poems of *Armored Hearts*.

Vagrant Grace is organized symmetrically in five sections. The first and last sections contain a trio of three-part poems each. Sections two and four have ten poems, each a short lyrical work and none separated into parts. The third section, literally the centerpiece, is one poem, "Country Store and Moment of Grace," nearly twenty pages long and broken into unnumbered parts separated by horizontal lines. This center section also uses the "drop line" popularized by Charles Wright, and clearly resembles in style and content some of the longer poems found in Wright's recent collections. Therefore, it is not surprising to note that one of the epigraphs at the beginning of *Vagrant Grace* is from a poem by Charles Wright: "All things aspire to weightlessness, / some place beyond the lip of language, / Some silence, some zone of grace...."

All three poems in the opening section continue the emphasis on a father-daughter relationship that emerged in the closing poems of *Armored Hearts*. In fact, the first poem of the collection, "Bronchitis," carries similarities to "A Daughter's Fever." Once again, the narrator's concern is for the safety and well-being of the young girl who "breathes the little noise of wheels / on dry axles." As he sits nearby and reads a book about the Civil War, the speaker acknowledges his worries: "All the loose uncertainties of fatherhood grate / in the joints of my chair." He is absorbed by the story of another young child, a three-year-old girl killed with her dog by shell fire during one of the Civil War battles, though mentioned "only as a footnote in the abstract / strategies of war." He imagines the situation, "shell crater and spaniel, / powder stench, geyser of dust settling / as her mother staggers." He reveals the one vulnerability he cannot avoid, and which now appears again and again in Bottoms' poetry, a fear of any danger that might affect his daughter.

Almost as if Bottoms has intentionally taken his poetry full circle since his first poems twenty years before, the second poem in *Vagrant Grace*, "On Methodist Hill," displays a viewpoint in direct opposition to "Wrestling Angels" (from *Shooting Rats at the Bibb County Dump* and the opening poem presented in *Armored Hearts: Selected and New Poems*). On this occasion, father and daughter visit a boarded-up church and a cemetery that have been vandalized, allowed to fall into ruin:

> Shab of a plundered tomb, crust and leaf-stain,
> litter of wet newspaper, sandwich wrapper, pizza box, stench
> of sardine and wine—
> in the wind it hisses slightly,
> or sighs like a choir before the first note sung,
> then nothing much as I walk my daughter up the marble steps.

The tone of regret in this new poem should be heard in contrast with the defiant voice at the end of "Wrestling Angels," where the speaker and his friends have vandalized a cemetery, and the persona comments on further damaging monuments during their departure: "We break their arms and leave them wingless, / leaning over graves like old men lamenting their age." By the closing of "On Methodist Hill," the scene has become one evoking sorrow from the narrator rather than defiance, "this church / hollowed and crumbling on a hill of weeds / where a four-year-old climbs a vandalized angel / as her father begins, unaccountably, to weep."

The final poem in the opening section, "A Family Parade," completes a trio of triptychs involving the father and daughter. Filled with detailed description of townfolks and objects one might find in any small community's parade "somewhere up Main Street," and rendered in the clear and lyrical language now expected from his poems, Bottoms' lines invite the reader to ride along with him, his wife, and daughter Rachel as they weave on their bicycles through people along the parade route:

> Rachel banks on a training wheel, veers
> toward her mother, then cuts away,
>   flag of the fifty states
> ruffling from her basket, a bouquet of balloons
> off her fender...
>
> A rolling quack
> and rattle, bulb horn, mouth harp, tambourine,
> Sousa-blasting boom box bungeed
> to my carrier,
>   I circle them down the streets of the suburb....

Bottoms repeats the action of "circling" a number of times in the poem, obviously suggesting the circular patterns of nature's seasons in his description of the weather or flowering trees, the repeated rituals like this holiday parade, the renewal as evidenced by "the antebellum library waiting / to be reborn in brick and glass," and the circular pattern of life itself. As he watches the motorcycle corps, the narrator thinks back to a memory of his father:

> Finally, yes, I know this is about eternity,
> this circling, this following,
> and, of course, that irredeemable taunt of memory,
> without which we'd have no ghosts to lead us...
> the way my father leads his pack into the Snake Slither,
> the Rolling Circle, the Figure 8.

Remembering his father reminds Bottoms of another circular pattern — of family, of his own role now as father, as he turns "to catch Rachel's eyes."

Throughout *Vagrant Grace*, other poems return to the father-daughter relationship, the carefully crafted lines of poetry as much lines full of caring poetically crafted. The fear of harm coming to the daughter arises again in "My Daughter at the Gymnastics Party," where Bottoms watches Rachel perform in "a lower-school gym" by climbing a rope "until she'd cleared the lower rafters." This time, she is the one "glancing / toward the bleachers to see" if he is watching. However, Bottoms is unable to observe without fear, without thinking of other scenes:

> ...that boy
> with the waffled skull, stiff and turning blue
> under the belly of a horse,
> or the Christmas Eve skater on Cagle's Lake,
> her face a black plum
> against the bottom of the ice.

Another moving poem, "Night Strategies," demonstrates the father's fear for his daughter's safety. While bathing his young child, the narrator is unable to escape a radio report, even more disturbing than that in "Appearances," he'd recently heard about warfare in Europe. Much like the girl killed by the shell fire of a Civil War skirmish who haunts the father in "Bronchitis," the father in "Night Strategies" is haunted by the image of another girl caught in the midst of battle:

> I kept brushing the cloth over the pouch of her stomach,
> the cherubic and slightly chafed
> folds of her hips,
> remembering the voice rising off my radio,
> a girl in Sarajevo, sixteen,
> quivering between a translator and the thuds
> of local shelling.

The girl had been attacked by soldiers. She describes a rape that resembles a scene in Bottoms' early poem, "The Farmers." However, if one compares the two poems, the second-person narration and the distance created by the tone of the poem in "The Farmers" has now been replaced — even though the rape in this new poem is reported secondhand through memory of an account from a radio — by the intimacy of a first-person narrator, the father ("clumsy / and apologetic") shaken by such a tale of violence to someone else's daughter:

> They left her naked on a bloody cot.
> She wept, she said, but not inconsolably
> like her mother, who clawed all night at the tiles
> of their mosque.

The father realizes he is powerless in any desire to protect his child her entire life from such a vicious world as this. (As the speaker offers in "A Walk to Carter's Lake": "Small wonder the angels are said to despise us.") He is at a loss to explain such actions to her — perhaps, to himself as well. For the moment, he can only continue to bathe his young daughter:

> I lathered the cloth with our wafer of soap
> and dabbed at my daughter's stomach ad thighs,
> knowing the only answer I have
> is this nervous
> exaggeration of tenderness...

The centerpiece poem of *Vagrant Grace*, "Country Store and Moment of Grace," offers a welcome opportunity for Bottoms to be expansive, even more than in the terrific triptych poems from *In a U-Haul North of Damascus* and again present in this collection. Like Charles Wright, whose longer poems in the collections since *The Southern Cross* this work resembles, Bottoms' ability over the years to compress so much descriptive detail and dramatic tension into shorter lyrical poems has been admirable. However, as in those lengthier poems by Wright, the longer form used for "Country Store and Moment of Grace" appears to allow greater complexity and more gradual development. Indeed, the South of Bottoms' childhood is precisely drawn in the numerous scenes that follow one another in this nineteen-page poem that turns on the actions in his grandfather's store:

> Pot gut stove and wood sizzle,
> and the raw smell of bologna and cheese, rack
> of Slim Jim and jerky, Tom's snacks,
> peppermint, drift of kerosene from a paint can,
> and from where he sits,

> glassed sweetness
> of stacked tobacco, Chesterfield and King Edward,
> Beechnut, Red Man, Bull of the Woods.

The men who congregate in the store, those men "brooding or tongue-tied, / worn-out in their walked-down boots and overalls shabby / with clay" are depicted with equal precision. With the luxury of expansion, the narration drifts across years, even generations, and back again, as Bottoms watches his daughter gather leaves for burning: "Rachel rakes a few into a pile the wind disperses, / and again I'm drawing parallels / to the memory...." Bottoms seems once more brought back by the "taunt of memory" that gives "ghosts to lead us." However, a larger issue exists behind all the pleasant memories he recalls and the lessons of love or the meaning of grief they offer, and a darkness lies just outside the door of his family's house despite the appearances of security or comfort at home:

> ours is the scrawny house of green shingles, rusted screens
> on the side porch,
> rock arch around the door.
>
> Television in the living room, Arthur Godfrey
> or Ed Sullivan, and a juggler spins plates on tall sticks
> as my father and I watch from the couch...
> Sweet smell of corn
> and barbequed chicken,
>   which means it's Sunday...
>
> Horns blare from the highway, south from the Trading Post,
> loud and louder,
> then right outside our door
>   a legion of noise.

The larger issue is displayed throughout the poem in images of racism and possible violence, some as subtle as the "black noose of fuchsia / dangling" from a bedroom planter or the more threatening symbol of the noose "looped around the rearview" and "hanging like a pair of dice." Other indications are as overt as the racist statements by the country store regulars or "the two cars / burned / on the curb in front of the Canton Theater." A parallel is developed between the grief his grandmother felt when Bottoms' father was reported missing ("Whenever I think I know about grief, / I imagine an only son lost / in the Pacific"), presumed dead for fifteen months, and the loss felt by a black mother who prepares holiday decorations as she waits for her son late from school because he is off cutting a tree for Christmas. Instead, the woman sees:

>	the road behind her house
>	the dull yellow star on the door of a Chevy
>	and feels down her nerves
>	 the ice
>	of her whole head frosting white, a shiver
>	against terrible weather.

The whole theme of racism, threats of violence, and resistance to integration lead to a single incident of great significance witnessed by Bottoms — though not part of "the noise of headline and newscast," but "the real thing" as it "plays out quietly somewhere else." It is December of 1960. A black woman enters the country store amid the threatening expressions of all the regulars, and the grandfather gets up out of his chair:

>	 not gauging their faces,
>	not glancing at me watching, stunned, from the feed room
>	as the woman fingered coins
>	and lifted from the drink box of Coca-Cola,
>	so that suddenly at the scripted moment
>	the script fell away,
>	 his hand simply opening,
>	his head nodding slowly
>	as she dropped the two nickels and faded
>	in the drizzle, in the shiver and groan of muffler,
>	the crunch of tires on gravel.

That simple act by his grandfather signals an end as well as a beginning. Bottoms doesn't decide whether the act was "failure of nerve / or heart, or among those hardening glares, that victory / of nerve or heart," and it does not seem to matter. What matters is the "passing into memory / and Amen to its passing again out of memory." That old South he once knew has been replaced, even the grocery store torn down to make room for a K-Mart. Bottoms says "Amen to leaving behind of places / that might have been less lovely and often are." Consequently, they may merely exist in a "fractured afterlife of memory."

Bottoms considers the nature of memory and its vagaries throughout *Vagrant Grace*, suggesting "there's always uncertain light in a memory like this" ("A Room on Washington Avenue"), and "in middle age the memory circles" ("My Uncle Sowing Beatitudes"). In fact, Bottoms acknowledges this collection contains poems of middle-age in "A Morning from the Gospel of John":

> This morning in my bathroom mirror, I glimpsed the slope
> of my shoulders, my chest thinning to a hint of ribs,
> the hair of my pouching belly
> black and beaded with water,
> and pondering myself limp and priestly,
> laced with blue veins, I judged nothing threatening.

The poems of *Vagrant Grace* are written with the achieved wisdom and maturity of middle-age. Readers who enjoyed Bottoms' shorter lyrical works in his four previous collections were not disappointed by the twenty poems in the two sections of this collection still filling that description. Moreover, the two sections containing a half dozen triptychs and the centerpiece section of "Country Store and Moment of Grace" presented a diversity of options for Bottoms to explore more complex issues or situations, as well as his emotional responses to them, with greater depth. In many ways, over the first two decades of Bottoms' career, the poetry turned full circle; however, like the Rolling Circle pattern his father maneuvered on a motorcycle in Bottoms' memory, with the circular motion there had been a correlative movement forward.

In a poem titled "At the Grave of Martha Ellis," where a statue of the twelve-year-old (made famous in the song "Little Martha" by Duane Allman) looks down over her grave, Bottoms decides "in middle age rebirth isn't such easy work." However, rebirth and renewal gradually appear as primary themes in Bottoms' poetry, and although it may not be such easy work, the more mature works of poetry created by Bottoms exhibited a renewal of spirit.

The centerpiece and longest poem, comprising an entire middle section of the three in David Bottoms' *Waltzing through the Endtime*, focuses on an incident the poet remembers happening "one night in '65." In "Homage to Buck Cline," a seven-page eleven-part piece of personal recollection from four decades ago, Bottoms elaborates upon a fairly ordinary occurrence in order to provide source material that allows him to muse upon elements "lit in an uncluttered niche" of memory. The work winds its lines of reminiscence and speculation around a teenage experience in which the speaker, "stoned on a glass of Mateus rosé," is pulled over for running his father's Impala through "the traffic light at the corner of the North Canton Store, / where sour Buck Cline / sat in the dark patrol car with the gold badge / of the Canton Police stenciled on his door." Out of respect for the boy's father, whom the officer recalls with reverence as a tough high school football star wounded in World War II, the teenager is let off without arrest or the need to answer to his father for his recklessness.

However, this narrative of actual events does not represent the most significant aspect of the poem. Instead, the various mental associations for the poet evoked by those actions present a pattern of thoughtful rumination that may fascinate readers, especially when imagination and memory are blended: "And imagination, of course, depends on so much ... // Take the polished memory of my grandfather's horse barn / and its hayloft full of jewels." In fact, Bottoms finds everyone holds "something divine in the memory," perhaps even when we are reminded of painful moments in our history, as when the father's war wound can be felt with each step he takes "across the concrete garage / on that splinter of a bone / the Japanese navy left in his leg." By the end of this poem, the poet declares: "memory toughens us up for that tumble / and drift of eternity, for the unpatrolled landscape / of the psyche unfurling."

Indeed, throughout this mature collection, David Bottoms patrols those crossroads where memory and imagination intersect, as in "Kenny Roebuck's Knuckle-Curve," a boyhood recollection as extended metaphor where "once again the world isn't what you think, / and the memory, already wobbling, knuckles off / into voices, laughter, jeers." In "Black Hawk Rag" the speaker plays notes on an old mandolin as he tries to revive the images and sounds of his grandfather hunched with a "fiddle / under chin" in a garage beside his store; although, the speaker believes it may be "silly to lean on the rhythms of memory, / which will hardly give back / even the threads of that rag."

Nevertheless, the rhythms of memory continually fill this book to revive characters and contexts from the poet's past, even to the point of reliving some circumstances similar to those in Bottoms' first book, *Shooting Rats at the Bibb County Dump*, but this time with his more mature perspective. In "Shooting Rats in the Afterlife" Bottoms insists "the memory is so persistent, and territorial. Take Macon, Georgia, 1971, / which I carry around in my head, like a classic video." The word "memory" appears repeatedly in this poem, as it does so often throughout the rest of the collection. Bottoms concludes: "through memory we create our own afterlives," those narratives of the former times that define for us who we are or where we have been. As the speaker recalls the situation of driving to shoot rats in a dump with his drunken buddies, he reveals: "We rode slow, / though everything moves slowly in memory. / Which is part of the act of savoring,…"

One set of memories arises when the poet visits a former home of his favorite musicians ("In the Big House of the Allman Brothers My Heart Gets Tuned"), where twenty-eight years ago he stood outside and listened to the band rehearse. He also recounts an episode during which — "stupefied / and afraid, skulking on all fours through those briary terraces / of Rose Hill Cemetery" — he sat at the "slab of Elizabeth Reed," the inspiration for one of the group's finest songs. (As readers recall, in *Vagrant Grace* a similar poem, "At the Grave of Martha Ellis," references Duane Allman's song, "Little Martha.") Ironically, two of the band members mentioned in the new poem, Duane Allman and Berry Oakley, were buried in the Rose Hill Cemetery upon their untimely deaths. But Bottoms also remembers those days when he could "hear through bricked Tudor wall / and blanketed windows an electric concussion of bass / and guitar," when he even met Duane Allman "eye to bloodshot eye / in a Kmart." Bottoms wonders whether remembering such activities constitutes "strung-out memory / or middle-aged panic." As the poet indicates, such memories overcome the transitions time has dragged with it, and when brought to mind, for him it is "as though the house, / my heartbeat, the larger night, were all tuning up for the lifting / of some curtain."

In *Waltzing through the Endtime* Bottoms again displays greater complexity when his meditative lyrics develop slowly in lengthier poems. As readers have gradually observed over the years, Bottoms appears mesmerized by the intricate nature of one's memories, especially when they are introduced or interpreted through the imaginatively manipulated renderings of the poetic process. Therefore, the longer form for most of the works in this book (which contains only 14 poems in its 59 pages) complements the contemplative temperament of the pieces' speakers.

Bottoms establishes early a relaxed, pensive, and reflective atmosphere in an excellent opening poem, "Easter Shoes Epistles," which contains a sequence of observations or narratives threaded together by images of shoes and statements that explore variations on the issue of faith: "we have to travel on faith, struggling not to notice the absence, / the stray shoe in the street." The speaker's mother even refers to faith as "just like an old shoe." However, memory remains central to the poet:

> It's odd what the memory smuggles into the afterlife —
> the squeak of my mother's shoes,
> or a baseball game from the fifties, my father's wing tips
> kicking up a coaching box — pocket charms against oblivion.

The last section of the poem brings together its different items — shoes, faith, Easter, memory — in a traumatic second-grader's situation, experienced by the speaker's wife when she was young and poor, "with one dress / salvaged from a house fire," and "ashamed of her shoes." Taken by a Sunday-school teacher to the mall, the cathedral for consumers, she is suddenly confronted by "fountains of brass cherubs, / chandeliers, skylights, and that one fragile storefront of glass / where every wall sparkles with shoes."

Additionally, Bottoms expertly combines the narratives' gritty realistic details with some subtle philosophical introspection. The poet's language comfortably accommodates natural colloquial conversation as well as lovely and lyrical description of nature. Apparently disparate sides of the poet adjoin smoothly with "Melville in the Bass Boat," where the speaker, unable to catch a fish despite hours "throwing deep runners, live shiners, / rattle-bugs and jigs," opens his "slightly soggy" paperback edition of *Moby Dick*. As the epigraph hints, "meditation and water are wedded for ever." Indeed, throughout these poems a number of literary figures are invoked and quoted by their speakers, including Homer, Blake, Whitman, Melville, Poe, Emerson, Coleridge, Jung, Rilke, Lawrence, O'Connor, and Warren.

Nevertheless, the most prominent quote is drawn from the poet's mother-in-law, whose phrase, "Waltzing through the Endtime," provides the book's title. In the closing poem of the collection, "Three-quarter Moon and Moment of Grace," Bottoms tells readers that the book's title phrase is what she calls his worrying and wondering about life, his habit of "wringing out my spirit / like a dirty dishrag." Near the end of this final work Bottoms once more turns toward the sense of recollection as a primary influence in our lives: "doesn't it all come down to memory...?" However, just like the book's first poem and others in between, this last poem also raises unanswered questions about faith and its mysteries: "and what are we dragging in that heavy sack / if not the cornerstones of Heaven, / or the charcoals of Hell?"

As witnessed in his previous volumes, David Bottoms frequently seeks spiritual significance from among everyday experiences or observed ordinary events, and he offers life lessons learned from scattered fragments of remembered adventures. With his matured voice, Bottoms also demonstrates a greater penchant for self-reflection in meditative language: "Days now I've pondered / what my mother-in law calls the Endtime" ("Vigilance"). Nevertheless, his poetry continues to be based in precise and persuasive descriptions, and the language remains narrative yet melodic. The poet's balance of vivid imagery and expressive lyricism nicely combines nature with art in *Waltzing through the Endtime*, regularly giving readers a sense of pensive composition, much like that "mandolin trilling out the indecipherable harmony" in "O Mandolin, O Magnum Mysterium" with its music of "melancholy little sparrow-cries / fluttering over the riffled water."

Works Cited

Bottoms, David. *Armored Hearts: Selected and New Poems*. Port Townsend, WA: Copper Canyon Press, 1995.
_____. *Vagrant Grace*. Port Townsend, WA: Copper Canyon Press, 1999.
_____. *Waltzing Through the Endtime*. Port Townsend, WA: Copper Canyon Press, 2004.

Searching for the Kingdom of Heaven: A Spiritual Journey

MICHAEL SOWDER

In a 2004 interview, David Bottoms spoke at length about Robert Penn Warren, the poet and author, who chose Bottoms' first book for the Walt Whitman award in 1979. Robert Penn Warren, Bottoms tells us, called himself:

> a yearner after meaning. He didn't have any particular theology to assign to the word, but he was a yearner for meaning. I like that very much, and I think that all serious writers are yearners. They're seekers after the big answers, what Warren called the logic of "the original dream."

David Bottoms' books of poetry recount a spiritual journey of yearning, a path towards an understanding of the original dream, one that Bottoms says can never be fully comprehended by any of us who are actors in the dream. Climbing in desultory fashion in the general direction of the celestial city, the poet-pilgrim of Bottoms' books is looking for clues, watching and waiting, negotiating the wreckage of a broken yet glittering world, one into which greater light begins to shine as he makes his progress through six books of poetry.

Along the way, we visit ruined houses, broken homes and broken men and women. We stop at abandoned churches, graveyards, impoverished farms and ranches, blossom-littered suburbs. The tracks of lowly animals lead us on. We float in fishing boats waiting for something to rise, for visions, symbols, "bony metaphors" ("Melville in the Bass Boat"). The music and voices of fiddlers, preachers, and healers, wives and daughters of the old and New South accompany us. But all tend inward toward that original yearning and outward again to the changing world, until in Bottoms' last book (to date) we find ourselves entering if not a new heaven and earth, then a heaven and earth newly seen, peopled with signs, suffused with the presence of "the Great Mind," and find our pilgrim "waltzing through the Endtime."

To explore the theme of spiritual journey and transformation in Bottoms' work, I take a particular tack. I begin with the assumption that the speaker throughout the books is a single speaker, and I do so for two reasons. First, while I do not assume that this speaker is literally the poet, David Bottoms, at the same time it is clear that the poet Bottoms does not write dramatic monologues, adopting the voices of various speakers. For example, there are no poems in the voices of women. Even when he is writing about women's experience, as in "The Voice of Wives Dreaming," the experience is imagined, filtered through the experience of a speaker whom we have gotten to know quite well.

Second, much of the echoing that occurs between and among the books loses its power if we do not take the speaker as one. For example, in the seminal poem, "Wrestling Angels," the speaker and his friends vandalize a cemetery, breaking among other things the wings and arms of stone angels. In later poems in different books the speaker returns to the same cemetery and reflects upon his past. For example, in the powerful poem, "On Methodist Hill," from *Vagrant Grace,"* he returns to the cemetery with his daughter, and the

> ...four year-old climbs a vandalized angel
> as her father begins, unaccountably, to weep.

The powerful effect of the father weeping for having been himself the one who vandalized the angel years before would be lost without the echoing among the books traversed by a single seeker.

The spiritual dimension of Bottoms' work has been only occasionally explored in the criticism, though I find it the dominant core of the poetry — at first a dried-up, buried seed in *Shooting Rats*, but one that struggles out of the dirt to rise through southern air and sun to break into blossom in *Waltzing Through the Endtime*. An essay of Don Russ's remains one of the few to take up the issue. In "'Up Toward Light': Resurrection, Transfiguration, Metamorphosis, and Evolution in David Bottoms' *Armored Hearts*," Russ identifies themes and images of transcendence and redemption in the poetry as being rooted in traditional, southern Christian culture and identifies images of metamorphosis that are rooted in classical sources. Russ maintains that these traditional sources of consolation fail to heal the disillusionment and doubt that pervade the work and instead suggests that by the end of the new poems in *Armored Hearts,* "David Bottoms' speakers seem to have come to a full appreciation of nature's own transfiguring power ... and to full appreciation of the wondrously transforming power of human regard for other creatures" (71).

Importantly, Bottoms' religious orientation does not reach towards a single religious tradition, though, as Russ has shown, the Protestant Christianity of the South provides much of the imagery and metaphors that enlighten the work. Bottoms has said that his earliest introductions to metaphor and other features of poetry came from the hymns and gospel singing that he heard both at the Canton First Baptist Church and on the gospel radio station that played in his grandfather's Canton General Store (Walsh). As the books progress, however, the spiritual register becomes more complex with the appearance of Catholic saints (unlikely in Southern Baptists traditions) and, eventually, Hinduism and the Buddha make appearances. Images and language from different religions eventually decorate the landscape like shrines, chapels, and stupas along the pilgrim's way. For this reason, I use the words "spiritual" and "religious" in a comprehensive way. Bottoms' quest is not toward an alignment, or realignment, with the orthodoxy of his childhood religion or any other. The faith toward which the poetry aspires is not that of intellectual assent to a set of doctrines, Christian or otherwise, but rather toward direct experience of the mystery manifesting itself in what Warren calls the original dream of the world.

As a search for direct experience of that mystery — what we may call the divine or transcendence — the spiritual dimension of Bottoms' quest can properly be called "mystical." We find support for using this term in the poetry itself, as in the first poem of *Waltzing Through the Endtime,* "Easter Shoes Epistle." There the speaker laments that even though "Every leaf [is] an oracle, sure, / [...] in the local phone book / not one listing under *mystagogue*" (italics, Bottoms') — a mystagogue being a teacher who initiates a seeker onto a mystical path.

Mysticism is an often misused and misunderstood term. Evelyn Underhill, the great scholar of Western mysticism, defines it as follows:

> Broadly speaking, I understand it to be the expression of the innate tendency of the human spirit towards complete harmony with the transcendental order; whatever be the theological formula under which that order is understood [Underhill, xiv-xv].

One can see here that the particular "theological formula" under which the "transcendental order" is understood is less important than the desire for direct, personal experience of that order. The "faith" our pilgrim is after is something more than doctrinal orthodoxy unto which he might give assent. Underhill continues:

> This tendency, in great mystics, gradually captures the whole field of consciousness; it dominates their life and in the experience called 'mystic union,' attains its end. Whether that end be called the God of Christianity, the world soul of Pantheism, the Absolute of Philosophy, the desire to attain it and the movement towards it — so long as this is a genuine life process and not an intellectual speculation — is the proper subject of mysticism. I believe this movement to represent the true line of development of the highest form of human consciousness [xiv-xv].

While Bottoms' seeker never achieves the heights of "mystic union," a persistent yearning for transcendence toward, experience of, and contact with the divine, propels the quest forward. He is doing more than looking for fragments of one of more religious traditions to shore against his ruins.

Shooting Rats at the Bibb County Dump: Wrestling with Angels

As noted, the seed of spirituality in Bottoms' first book, *Shooting Rats at the Bibb County Dump,* is buried, hardly visible. The book appears like a charred scrap of apostasy uncovered in a burned-over landscape. The poems feel almost post-apocalyptic, the speaker Nietzschean, Faustian, with a voice flaunting nihilism and at the same time betraying (partly-) repressed rage and despair. Titles point openly into the darkness: "The Lost Hunter," "Shooting Rats at the Bibb County Dump," "All Systems Break Down," "How Death Isolates." The spiritual remains a dark absence. This is not the "dark night of the soul" St. John of the Cross wrote of, for that night comes after an earlier awakening and many miles traveled on the mystical path. This is a darkness before awakening, before (in Protestant Christian terms) conversion, the darkness of the depraved soul of Calvinism. Augustine before his conversion, Dante in the dark wood. We begin at the bottom.

Shooting Rats nevertheless remains haunted by that very absence. The speaker cannot get religious ideas and imagery out of his head. He is a lost soul, but one preoccupied, almost obsessed, with things divine. The language of salvation and damnation fills the book. For all the cynicism painted thickly over the surface of the poems, our rebel, almost unbe-

Searching for the Kingdom of Heaven (Michael Sowder)

knownst to himself, is hunting, searching for something. One remembers the words of the great monk and mystic, Thomas Merton, that "[p]rayer and love are learned in the hour when prayer has become impossible and your heart has turned to stone" (133).

So we begin in graveyards, county dumps, bars and cheap hotels. The first section of the book, "Into the Darkness We're Headed For," begins with the poem, "The Drunk Hunter," whom we meet killing time, poaching, hunting on posted land. He has only a "whisky bottle [to point] out magnetic north," (not of course, "true north"). He can find neither his prey nor his way home. "[C]ome morning" his friends "will praise his patience." The religious diction, *praise, patience*, resonates clearly. "In two or three days / they will tell what found him in the deeper woods." So we begin our quest with the death of the hunter. A false start? A foreshadowing? A trespasser in his own journey? An entry into the underworld?

After this opening scene, we make our way fittingly to a cemetery. "Wrestling Angels" is one of the most important poems of Bottom's oeuvre, one to which he returns in later books, especially in *Vagrant Grace* and *Waltzing Through the Endtime*. In this poem, he plumbs the depth of the speaker's despairing rebellion. Cynically reenacting Jacob's biblical account of wrestling with an angel, our speaker and his companions come "[w]ith crowbars and drag chains" through the "valley of tombs." They come for ironwork that brings money, but while there, "if there is time" (bitterly echoing Marvell, Eliot), they will enact mindless violence upon the innocents. They "shatter the hourglasses," slaughter the "lambs asleep on children's graves," break the marble strings of lyres and the arms of angels, leaving them wingless "leaning over graves like old men lamenting their age."

In these acts of violence against petrified lambs and angels, we witness an acting out of some barely-repressed rage and despair our speaker feels at the absence of the light. His heart is petrified, too, has turned to stone, but instead of learning to pray, the stone heart will wreak its vengeance on speechless surrogates, traditional ciphers for the divine, for Christ, for religion and for poetry. This is not the famous *via negativa* of the mystics, this is nihilistic anti–theology. And yet, doesn't it also offer a dare? Don't these secret acts of nighttime effigy-murder and desecration throw down a gauntlet, daring the divine, the universe to do something, to make itself known, to come down from the cross?

Unlike someone such as Colonel Sutpen, for whom the divine and its memory have long ago been erased from every cosmic equation, our pilgrim is caught in Biblical allusion. Why take out vengeance on religious symbols? Even raging, our lost hunter can't erase from his head the memory of divine things, even when striking at the absence he feels must reside at the heart of creation. He strikes like moody, stricken Ahab daring whatever's there to strike back. No simple atheist, our vandal is wounded, almost heart-broken, and comes to rage against the death of the light and the author of emptiness, secretly hoping to rouse some kind of response.

From these futile acts of symbolic deicide we move on to some real violence in the bitterly sadistic title poem, "Shooting Rats at the Bibb County Dump." Having tired of the graveyard, we take midnight pickups to the county dump and "turn our headlights across the wasted field." Once again choosing the helpless for our victims, we fire vengeance on innocent rats. "Shot in the head, they jump only once, lie still / like dead beer cans." But our hero — a little more self-aware than he might wish to be — says of the rats (but, of course, of himself, as well): "It's the light they believe kills." The rats tolerate light no better than he can. This self-awareness almost undoes the fictional contract with the reader, except that it's the self-awareness of an alcoholic, of a drunk hunter. He knows he's lost, drunk, poaching. We never discover what wounded our pilgrim, what turned him away from the light. We only witness him later turning back toward it. For now, like the rats, he can only limp deeper into the darkness.

In this first section of the book, thus we gather in graveyards, dumps, and junked cars. We meet at county fairs and cockfights, wander the forgotten, dissolute byways of the South. Sheltered from rain in a rusted-out cab of a junked pulpwood truck, our seeker watches his dogs follow game into the darker woods, and speaks in religious diction: "white breath rising form their yelps like spirits / in that song land *where the soul never dies*" ("Below Freezing on Pinelog Mountain," Bottoms' emphasis). He yearns for such a place, but his companion's whiskey breath only "rises like gray smoke through rust holes in the roof." Similarly, in "Smoking in an Open Grave," he and friends get high, get drunk in a grave, but "choir out the old spirituals," and back at the landfill, even the scavengers hope "for the redemption" of things cast aside ("Scavengers at the Palm Beach County Landfill"). Then in "Coasting Toward Midnight at the Southeastern Fair," the speaker, lifted high above a banal and broken world, confesses how we all want to "break our orbits," "to take our lives in our own hands / and hurl them out among the stars." A buried yearning for transcendence and epiphany runs through this dark book.

The book's second section, "Country and Western," offers glimpses of down and out, lost and lonely southern souls: a trucker breaking down, a girl raped in a barn, busted up sots in run down bars. We find ourselves alone in a cheap hotel with nothing to read but the Gideons Bible. Our reluctant hero picks it up and then delivers a nihilistic sermon, perhaps protesting a little too much in "All Systems Tower and Collapse":

> Here's the natural gospel of it all:
> all systems tower and collapse, and we
> babble in darkness, seeking foundations
> for other reconstructions, knowing all
> along that what works always is nothing.

There is truth in this natural gospel. But it does not satisfy. We finish out this section by turning to religious healers, fit symbols for the persistent yet suspect features of religion and a submerged hope for the speaker's own healing. It's no surprise that the healings fail, but it's also no surprise that we can't shake these religious subjects.

The third part of the book, "All the Animal Inside Us," then takes a curious turn, deeply into the animal kingdom. I read this, in spiritual terms, as follows: Nihilism and apostasy ultimately do not satisfy our seeker; so, he turns to the natural, primitive world. If he cannot find fulfillment through the traditional religious paths, he will go elsewhere, down into an animal, reptilian, instinctual nature, resulting in poems about predation, hunting, cruelty, savagery, seduction, and barbarity. Bottoms has said that in these poems he was exploring the instinctual nature of what scientist Carl Sagan described as our "reptilian brain," located at the base of the brain, root of the primitive, instinctual foundation of our consciousness. Even in later books, as our pilgrim begins his ascent, a crawling out of the muck and into the light and air, he will often return to this primitive natural, animal consciousness.

The poem that ends this section is "The Copperhead," which Bottoms reprints in his next book, suggesting its importance. In it we feel a desire for downward metamorphosis. The speaker spots a copperhead. Not having had luck with the fishing, he lays his rod across the floor of the boat, and as shadows make the snake a part of the tree, a part of the water, the speaker "wanted more than once to drift into the shaded water, / pull [himself] down a fallen branch toward the trunk / where he lay quiet and dangerous."

Fishing is an archetypal activity in Bottoms' poetry, one that suggests a primitive relationship to the earth, but also a psychological sounding of the depths, a jigging of the unconscious, a baiting of fate, and we should remember the life of the first apostles before they became fishers of men. Interestingly, we have to read several of Bottoms' books before a fish is ever caught. Not until the speaker catches one for his daughter in *Armored Hearts* do we land the spiritual fish. But even here in this most reptilian section of the first book, our seeker is casting again and again, like Whitman's spider spinning filaments, hoping they might catch hold somewhere.

In the last two sections of the book, the speaker encounters actual death witnessed in the passing of his grandfather and grandmother. The first poem of section four—"How Death Isolates"—provides another sermon on nihilism as did "All Systems Break Down," ending with the line, "how deeply faithless we will always be." But the following poem, titled religiously, "Learning to Let Water Heal," closes with, "we must let the water turn an image back on us, / learn to look inside it and find what magic remains." Hope remains.

The final poem of the book, "Speaking Into Darkness," retells the resurrection of Lazarus, but halts the story with Jesus calling, "*Lazarus, come forth.*" Whether Lazarus, or the speaker, will come forth is never revealed, and the speaker tells his dead grandfather, "I am holding no true book. / I have no orthodox dream. / My head is a kaleidoscope of crossed images / ... / And saying all this is pain." The final line of the book confesses, "Speaking into darkness is the closest I can come to prayer." A book that began in nihilistic rage at speechless angels, rats, and lambs, ends on the word "prayer."

In a U-Haul North of Damascus: Watching and Waiting

After the first book closes on the word, "prayer," how fitting that the title poem of the second book, "In a U-Haul North of Damascus," is in fact itself a prayer. In this book we move away from the soap boxes of nihilistic rage and vandalized scenes of apostasy and rebellion into a different atmosphere. The poems of his second book are almost contemplative, as if written in shocked or puzzled patterns of waiting. The poems vacillate between scenes of hopeful, sometimes even reverential waiting and those of darkness and the reptilian instincts of the first book. But the predominant tone is a stunned and silenced watching.

Robert Penn Warren provides the first epigraph: "It is hard sometimes to remember that beauty is another word for reality." Some glimmering thing, a fugitive beauty, has been glimpsed at the edge of Bottoms' dark world. The epigraph may seem off-hand, one-sided, merely wishful thinking. But if we take a step back through American religious history we can find a possible origin for the sentiment. Jonathan Edwards, America's greatest theologian and eighteenth-century Puritan minister, in *Religious Affections* elevates beauty to the highest possible level in his theology. He calls beauty "first among the perfections of God; it constitutes in itself the perfection of all the other divine attributes" (298). Moreover, for Edwards, only God can be considered real; all created things are "shadows" or "images." God is the only true substance and only true cause. Scholars debate whether Edwards can be called a pantheist, but to find beauty as the first perfection of God and God the only true substance in the universe, we are but a small step from Warren's belief that "beauty is another name for reality."

A second epigraph, one from Malcolm Lowry, identifies the trajectory of the book, indeed of all of Bottoms' poetry: "Sickness is not only in body, but in that part we used to call: soul." The sickness, having now been named, may be subject to treatment. For that, in this book, we wait.

We begin with "Rest at the Mercy House." The speaker visits a house of refuge built long ago for the shipwrecked — because "nature doesn't specialize / in mercy[,]" (as it also did not in the natural gospel of "All Systems Tower and Collapse"). In its time, the Mercy House was "adequate to its vision." Now tourists stop for a rest where ocean meets shore, the archetypal site of liminality and vision in American poetry, according to Harold Bloom. At the end of the poem, we learn that here "nothing is molested, all blest. / For travelers like us, a tour of the house, a vision, / a momentary rest." The keys to the house are those to the book: rest, holding, watching, waiting, for vision. We have traveled a good ways from "The Drunk Hunter," with his whiskey-bottle compass. We may be wrecked, but have been found, rescued by mercy.

In "Hiking Toward Laughing Gull Point," a gull catches a bait in midair, and forever after the seeker searches "for my dream / vacation, only to find" himself like the gull, climbing "toward … / a hook, the end of the line." Earthbound and unfulfilled, still we are dreaming now, contemplating ascent.

And more mercy appears. At the end of "A Home Buyer Watches the Moon," "the moon lies balanced on the roof of [his] house / like ... the simple face / of an angel...." The angel once mindlessly hacked in cemeteries now returns to watch over his house and wife. Grace has come into the world, stalking him like the hound of heaven, fit reversal of the primitive hunting and fishing myths these books keep trying to believe in. In this book the speaker returns to graveyards but now no longer simply to get high or drunk or laid or to perpetrate iconoclastic violence, but "crouched under the arm of this angel / to wait for voices" ("Recording the Spirit Voices"). In another poem, "The Tent Astronomer," he's in a tent, makeshift augury, a sheet over a telescope tripod, and he's looking for stars. He cuts a hole in the sheet for the barrel of the telescope and lets "lens and mirror lift me up toward light." He has glimpsed light, and it no longer seems lethal.

In "The Boy Shepherds' Simile," the speaker and other children taking parts in a Christmas manger scene, "shiver in adoration," again watching, waiting. In "Light of the Sacred Harp," with comrades he warms himself with a fire in an abandoned church, and the church itself catches fire. But the arsonist can hear the old voices, the house of the Lord popping and burning with revival, "becoming pure spirit / of voices returning in the joyful noise / of the Sacred Harp, singing over and over / the good gospel news that men do rise from dust / and ashes." Something like hope is stirring in the heart of the pilgrim.

As mentioned above, the journey is not a simple ascent; our pilgrim climbs but also descends several times to the primitive again. In fact, the end of this book brings on a total collapse, a "dying" evidently necessary before the third book can open with resurrection and transfiguration. In the third part of *In a U-Haul,* he thus returns to powerful dark poems sprung fully formed out of the reptilian brain, including the nihilistic "Sermon of the Fallen," another bleak lesson in the vein of "All Systems Tower and Collapse." But on this descent we encounter fishing poems in which the speaker waits not only for edible finned things to rise from the dark, tanic-stained cypress water of the swamps and slow moving rivers of the coastal South, he also waits for "the dawn," "the one dream," "the mystery." "In a Jon Boat During a Florida Dawn" is set in a pre-dawn morning where "there are no real colors, only tones / promising change, a sense / of something developing," where "you feel an old surprise surfacing / in and around you," where "you would give yourself completely / to the holding." In "Sounding Harvey Creek," we learn what he loves "about water is mystery," "a beautiful danger," "the hours of awesome ignorance — / enough possibility to make me reel." Here, he listens "for absolute silence / in the unsoundable depth of all water." And while no fish is ever caught in this book, the speaker himself is hooked in "Under the Boathouse" when his hand is impaled by a buried hook after a deep dive into the muck. He rises as though some fisher of men had got him at last.

The last section of the book enacts a final descent into sorrow, loss, and total collapse. As *Shooting Rats* ended with poems about the death of the speaker's grandparents, this book ends with the death of the speaker's marriage. We learn in "In a Pasture Under a Cradled Moon" that his wife has had a miscarriage and he grieves not only the lost child but also the future that seems to be aborting as well. But he also experiences "the way so much love can be learned / from loss." From this poignant poem we turn to prayer. In "In a U-Haul North of Damascus," (my personal favorite of Bottoms' poems), we find the speaker having abandoned home and wife. Was he kicked out? Did he want out? We don't learn. But we locate him in a moment of stillness, waiting in his U-Haul truck where's he's spent the night at a rest stop in the rain. The dark metaphysical yearning and Nietzschean speculation of previous work gives rise to a simple prayer for grace to fall upon him as he falls out of his life. In a book of poems of stillness, of watching and waiting, now in this poem — a confession and a prayer for forgiveness — he asks to be moved: "Could I be moved / to believe in new beginnings? Could I be moved?" Having held fast throughout the entire book, he has realized he cannot move himself out of the darkness.

The book's final poem answers this prayer not with mild reassurances but with a hurricane. "Hurricane" comes as a personal apocalypse, like a voice out of the whirlwind:

> At the church site across the field, animation
> and rapture,
> lumber scraps rising out of the dirt like Baptists
> at the Second Coming.

It seems that everything must be lost before our seeker can find himself. And in this poem, after the hurricane has passed, we find signs of rebirth: "the half-moon scabbing above my eye / is a good sign." And like Thoreau's beetle of hope and rebirth burrowing out of a table top, here "the ox beetle gores up though blown sand." "Joys impregnate. Sorrows bring forth," said Blake, and it seems that after a long watch, only the final collapse of miscarriage, divorce, and a hurricane are able to wrest the seeker away from his old life and into the hope and resurrection about to be enacted in *Under the Vulture-Tree*.

Under the Vulture-Tree: New Beginnings

Under The Vulture-Tree opens dramatically in a new key, in a moment of metamorphosis, transfiguration, resurrection. A new energy and aliveness courses through the entire book. "In the Ice Pasture" opens as the speaker has gone out to rescue a horse that's fallen through. "What was he trying to become out there?" he wonders, "as though he wanted me to witness the beauty / of his change." But the good Samaritan, too, falls into these freezing waters of baptism and transformation, where the two of them hung "bodiless," until "the body of the horse rose under [him] / and what [they] were … broke / to the air…." They rise until "the night / crack[s] like an egg shattered in the storm / of two beasts becoming one, / or one beast being born." We begin with the speaker resurrected from death by water, reborn and rising into air, Pegasus-like.

After the darkness of the first two books, *The Vulture-Tree* surprises with its bright energy and power, poems with vigorous narratives and strong characters, lively voices, diction, and image. Poems of doubt, despair, and uncertainty appear, but more often the poems are celebratory. And the speaker is no longer alone. The speaker's new wife appears frequently, in addition to friends, father, family, and the usual cast of musicians, artisans, and other country folk heroes. An arc of empathy appears first at the end of the second poem, "White Shrouds," where the breathing of the speaker's wife in a cold room becomes the breathing of homeless persons in doorways and behind dumpsters everywhere. In "Ice," the speaker celebrates a neighborhood girl's skating on the ice of a pond. In "Voices of the Wives Dreaming," we re-imagine the death of a child drowned in the same pond. And when our seeker returns to cemeteries, he goes with his wife rather than drinking buddies intent on vandalism ("The Resurrection"). In Part II, we extend this circumference of honoring others, with songs and hymns, homages for fiddlers, banjo players, and numerous southern artisans. Part IV, through memory and dream, pays its respects to family members and childhood friends, and Part V honors the life of the speaker's father.

The most overtly spiritual poems of the book appear in Part III, the central section devoted to fish, rats, vultures, and an unidentified red-eyed bird looming on a midnight bough, the reviled, ignored, and often forgotten members of the animal kingdom. But now, rather than mindlessly murdering such creatures, he honors them. Perhaps most interesting is his return to rats. In "Rats at Allatoona," he comes back to them with cleared eyes and heart. On a lake where "stars scatter their crumbs of light," the speaker, drunk, hears the noise of rats rummaging in trash cans, who "pray a squeaky grace of fine nails climbing / the rusty sides of cans." The rats have become holy, now, or at least co-ritualists with him in this dream of redemption. He walks toward them, blind, "homing / on their rapture," dreams of lying down beside them, letting them crawl upon his body, and in the morning, waking

>   among cans
> and ashes, shreds of their sacrament, of fingering
> my hair and my face, waking
> to what I am in my dream and my body, whole
> and broken, having taken from the feast
> and given to it, the tip of a thumb, the lobe of an ear.

This is my body. This is our body.

The title poem of this book, "Under the Vulture Tree," emblematically enacts the speaker's, and all our deaths, our resurrection through the beaks of these ugly "transfiguring angels." Their heads "ugly as a human heart," their faces "wrinkled and generous, like the faces of the very old / who have grown to empathize with everything." Empathy, compassion — new tones in Bottoms' work. Like the rats, the vultures, too, "pray," but these pray "over the leaf-graves of the anonymous lost,/ with mercy enough to consume us all and give us wings." In contrast to the opening poem of *In a U-Haul* ("Rest at the Mercy House"), now nature does *specialize / in mercy*. The incarnating, sacramental eating and being eaten of poems in this third collection enact rituals of healing and redemption.

Armored Hearts and *Vagrant Grace*: Rest on Jordan's Shore

In the next two books — the new poems of *Armored Hearts: Selected and New Poems* and *Vagrant Grace*— we meet the speaker in a new condition. The journey of these book feels less urgent in its yearning, more like a place of refreshing, where our hero stops to enjoy the fruits of his labors. The tone is more at ease, more tempered, less anxious, often quietly celebratory of a life of marriage and fatherhood. Bottoms' persona seems to have reached a plateau of serenity and ease. Outward things are now seen not only as symbols for his personal quest but as they are in and for themselves. He is more involved in the social and historical worlds, the here and now, feeling compassion for others working and suffering. He's looking at family history but also at the history of Canton, his hometown, as well as the history of the South, with its legacies of religion, racism, war, and lynching, and the Invisible Empire of the Ku Klux Klan. The central poem of *Vagrant Grace,* the twenty-two page "Country Store and Moment of Grace," brings many these themes together as he recalls his grandfather's country store during southern desegregation.

And if less urgently spiritual and mystical, religious themes paradoxically find more explicit statement. The word, "God," appears for the first time; Jesus, too, appears frequently, and for the first time our fisherman actually catches a fish.

Notably, Bottoms opens *Armored Hearts,* his selected poems with the same Warren epigraph that opened *In A U-Haul North of Damascus.* A second epigraph comes from Augustine's *Confessions.* "My soul is like a house, small for you to enter, but I pray you to enlarge it ... remake it. It contains much that you will not be pleased to see: this I know and do not hide." As epigraph, it asks the reader to enter into the book, participate in its meaning making, but acknowledges that the reader will not like everything found there. Then we remember that Augustine's *Confessions* is a prayer, that the "you" addressed here that we have mistaken for ourselves is God.

The new poems of *Armored Hearts* return again to the lowly creatures of our world: turtle, snake, roach, opossum. Once gunfire sport for a callow rifleman, they now receive compassion from his hand and are ennobled with the same generosity that first appeared in *In a U-Haul North of Damascus.* In the first poem ("Armored Hearts") we find our pilgrim out at night stripping bait from the hooks a neighbor has set to snare loggerhead turtles that he thinks have been taking his pet ducks. It is an act of eco-activism in defense of a threatened species and a reaffirmation of the speaker's connection to the muck-loving creatures of the world; however, stripping bait from another man's hooks would hardly be the action of the hero of *Shooting Rats.* From this poem the book takes its title: "snappers

/ with their ugly armored hearts, who wallow / like turnips in the muck of the bottom, clinging / to their stony solitude." The turtle is of course a symbol for the poet, himself.

After this opening bow towards and ennobling of the lowly creatures of the earth, we suddenly encounter a sort of miracle — the resurrection of confederate soldiers on a battlefield as they rise at dawn out of mounds of snow under which they had slept the previous night. In another poem, one of love and desire, the speaker and his lover get tattoos and recognize in them "the desire for permanence / and the permanence of desire." Then follows a series of poems set in Montana, where Bottoms met his second wife. These poems celebrate other animals, the eagle, the coyote, the wolf, the burrow, a dead man's dogs.

In "Last Supper," a more traditional kind of religious poem, the father-in-law in a Montana ranch house administers communion, the wine of blood poured into paper cups. The father "breaks the body" and "passes the plate among us." "Prayer breaks out on the sofa, / and finally I see how a wound could bleed / for centuries, could trickle enough / to fill this cup." What follows this realization is an imaginative return to a scene of the speaker reckoning with his divorce. He recalls a night when he wrote down "every desire" burned up in divorce and goes out and buries the list. Then the winds knock him down and "sprawled on my back / across that grave, clutching the wet grass, / … the oranges / kept flying through the leaves." This literal and surreal image of oranges flying through the leaves enacts, if not a resurrection, then at least a vision of hopeful spirits on the wing.

"The Pentecostal" tells the father-in-law's story of having seen a vision of Christ walking along the side of the road, and comes home weeping about *"those eyes, those sad eyes."* His wife understands that the eyes of Christ he saw were also the eyes of their only son, "sixteen and curled behind the sofa, guarding / his ribs, cursing the boots and verses," and the eyes "of their child evangelical, / their twelve-year-old witness, their runaway daughter" (most likely this is the poet's wife). Here we witness a staggering movement toward forgiveness, a belief in redemption, a vision, a descent of tongues of fire. In "Free Grace at Rose Hill," the speaker says of grace: "It swirls where it wants to swirl. / If it touches us, / it touches us." In "Zion Hill," he acknowledges openly his desire for redemption, even if it has risen out of "despair."

"Shelves on the Clark Fork" performs a movement towards healing: "you need to let go / of the people who have harmed you, / you need to slip out of those bruises / and across these stones." And the final poem of the book calls to the speaker to "lay down [his] anger" on the green stones / beside this water." And with his anger, his ambition, "which is itself anger." In a Buddhist-like moment of surrender to the very moment, he says, "Nothing is more beautiful than your emptiness, / and over the lake / these three stars soaking up twilight."

It's no surprise that Bottoms' next book is titled *Vagrant Grace*, for grace seems to have been stalking him on through all of his wayward ways. We begin the fifth book with a poem of two daughters, "Bronchitis," in which our seeker is reading a history of Sherman's march into Georgia while his daughter sleeps fitfully in the next room, coughing. The first shell that whistled into the city of Atlanta, we discover, killed a three-year-old girl. He asks, "whose story this is?" And he concludes that it is ours, all of ours; the history, the memory, is ours.

But his daughter teaches more than lessons of history. She also teaches contrition and grace. In "On Methodist Hill," the speaker returns to Rose Hill Cemetery and muses upon the services once held at the dilapidated church, the faithful words and songs that once rang through the ruined structure. He stands with his daughter, and imagines again the scene of Gethsemane, Jesus praying with his disciples, Jesus betrayed and foreseeing the end. And here at last the speaker's heart breaks: his "four-year-old climbs a vandalized angel / as her father begins, unaccountably, to weep."

In *Vagrant Grace*, we encounter poems of family history, memory, legacy. We find poems of empathy and compassion, a memory he can't shake of a newborn in intensive care, "a little brown sack of twigs / curled under the glass, eyes bulging, trembling in the monitors." We come upon a poem I find among his very best, "Night Strategies," in which a scene of bathing his young daughter frames one of remembering a young Muslim woman's radio voice reporting being raped by Christian soldiers in Sarajevo. The poem ends with these haunting lines written in religious diction:

> I lathered the cloth with our wafer of soap
> and dabbed at my daughter's stomach and thighs,
> knowing the only answer I have
> is this nervous
> exaggeration of tenderness,
> and that every ministry of my hand, clumsy
> and apologetic, asks her
> to practice such a radical faith.

How do we teach faith in a world of rape and brutal violence, faith in the world, that not all men are brutes, that there is tenderness, that she may be safe in the world. In another poem the speakers' daughter receives the first fish caught in of any of Bottoms' books.

We then come to the middle poem of the book, "Country Store and Moment of Grace," which coalesces many of the themes of the book: compassion, forgiveness, history, religion, racism, memory, and redemption. The fragmented form, the dropped and broken lines, the scenic, imagistic, braided narratives, the mining of family lore, history, religion, and final questions all signal a new turn and look forward to the poetic and spiritual breakthrough of *Waltzing Through the Endtime*.

"Country Store" swirls like a solar system of memories and events around the wood stove burning in his grandfather's country store, while a gospel quartet weaves harmonies through the radio, at the time of the desegregation of the South. Here we meet Klansmen commenting with platitudes about the specter of serving African Americans: "Close it down … fore I let Lyndon Johnson run it." The speaker is a kid, but hears all, and witnesses the tokens of violence of these men, the noose hanging from the rear view mirror of a pickup he's pumping gas into, phrases like "nigger knocking" mouthed while pistol butts hang from pockets, the Invisible Empire parading in front of his house, some unrevealed violence committed by a judge's brother, and the brother brought to trial before the judge. But his grandfather serves the black woman who dares to come in the store, and the boy sees that, too. Around these central scenes orbit those of present days of the speaker with his daughter raking leaves around his suburban home, memories of his father at turkey shoots, an imagined scene of his father floating on burning water after his ship, the *Atlanta*, had gone down at Guadalcanal, until finally in the poem's last section, the speaker comes to some peace about the past. "We go on now / building on what they were obliged to build on, / pasting into memory / these little scraps of consequence / and self-acquittal, // so that it's Amen to what can't be changed." "Amen to the passing into memory / … Amen to the leaving behind of places / that might have been less lovely and often are.…"

> What's left in these last moments but memory?
> And what is memory
> but the mirror image of hope?
>
> So Amen also to hope

And finally, "when the shadows of this life ... / yes, / lengthen into the shadow of memory, // and finally to that shadow, Amen."

Waltzing Through the Endtime: A New Earth

The fragments of memory in *Vagrant Grace* receive new life in Bottoms' next book, *Waltzing Through the Endtime*. They become what we carry into the next life, "pocket charms against oblivion," for waltzing through the end of times.

At the beginning of this essay, I spoke of Bottoms' spiritual, mystical, quest as being one not shackled by any particular religious tradition or doctrine. The third poem in *Waltzing* "Allatoona Storm" makes this clear. Our pilgrim rests beside the lake where there's been a thunderstorm every afternoon for a week. This afternoon, he's reading a history of Egypt and learns that there is no evidence of the Jews ever having been there. He concludes: "No plagues then, no exodus, no forty years kicking around / in the wilderness." And after reading these historical, archaeological facts, he says, he might have gone on to quibble "with plenty of lovely pictures / in my illustrated Old Testament // but"—and this "but" signals the turn of the poem. We now shift into a telling meditation on what's left of faith when faith has been emptied of the old contents of faith — beliefs, dogmas, and doctrines. He concludes: "but the sun over the lake was slicing through the clouds / in such a miraculously thin veil, / and the rose trellis lifted to the thunderbolts / the waxy faces of penitents, and all evening / the stooped magnolia, leaves gray as sackcloth, trembled..." He has broken free of a faith limited by dogma and has moved into a more mystical awareness of the divine, present in nature, in every moment, in the lake, the sun, the clouds, the rose, the magnolia. All tremble before that presence. It cannot be named in any book.

On the journey of this book, he stops at the "Big House of the Allman Brothers" where his "Heart Gets Tuned." Now, at last, the once wounded angel, of whom he later sought a voice, who watched over his house, whose broken body he returned to with his daughter, now, for the first time speaks, says: "*Looking for the dead? ... / Don't look here, / nobody home.*"

Making amends with angels may be one of the more straightforward necessary acts of redemption on the way to the celestial city. But what of rats? In the extravagantly named poem, "Shooting Rats in the Afterlife," our contrite pilgrim muses long upon what may be the character of that city. He remembers the Southern Baptist belief that in Paradise, "every crown is jeweled, every jewel a good deed remembered, / a kindness rewarded." He thinks it must be jewels of memory we carry into the afterlife. Then, in a kind of rewriting of James Dickey's "The Heaven of Animals," the poem meditates upon the place of animals in Christian theology. He remembers preaching on a soap box as a boy to guineas and hens, like Saint Francis, bringing reverence for animals into Christian faith.

Then, in memory, we revisit the Bibb County Dump and learn that prominent among the memories our speaker will carry into the afterlife is one of his soldier friend, Leroy Lawson ("Leroy"—"the king," "Lawson," the "son of the Law") leaning into the pickup strategically parked at the dump and flicking on the headlights. There among the garbage shine "hundreds of startled rubies...." These jewels—that were rats eyes—have our shooter-poet riffing on the line from *The Tempest*, once heard in another famous wasteland. The poem ends in the hushed silence and ellipsis of those lights coming on. We do not hear the rifle slash. No rats limp away into the darkness, as though our pilgrim, now a kingly son of the Law, has been himself startled by the light, light he once thought killed, startled into reverence, silence, and awe. No guns in heaven, no death but transfiguration and ruby jewels that were rats' eyes, to decorate his heavenly crown.

If in this book angels can be healed and rats redeemed—or we ought to say angel-slayers healed, rat-killers redeemed—what else can be sanctified? "Homage to Buck Cline" redeems the Canton town cop, who taught the speaker in his teenage years something of mercy, something about his father, and by the end, is apotheosized as "Saint Buck," "a street cop, surely, in the City to come." Miracles appear everywhere in this book. In "Melville in the Bass Boat," our fisherman out at night in a boat lit by a lantern reads *Moby Dick* while seeking "one small mystery caged in the bones of a fish." And sure enough, by the end there appears the "spark and slap of the dream-fish, leaping far out, like a thought, / and the felt vibration in the nerve, / that trembling to know, to take / another crack at whatever might surface—that mind-flash, / that 'ungraspable phantom of life,' / that bony metaphor."

Along the spiritual arc of the book, we also keep in clear sight the suffering of human beings. *Waltzing* has a number of powerful, moving poems of compassion. The opening "Easter Shoes Epistle" begins in suburban contemplation of the ten thousand things of this world, seeing in "every leaf an oracle" and checking the phone book listings for *mystagogue*.

Among meditations on natural and suburban images, on the nature of faith and miracle, the central metaphor of the poem is "shoes," appropriate figure for a pilgrimage. The poem reaches its epiphany with a story about the speaker's wife. As a child, he tells us, she was ashamed of her clothes, of her shoes, and one Easter morning the Sunday-school teacher drove up the gravel drive in her Cadillac to take the girl to Palm Springs and the mall, "revolving / into a city of light ... / and that one fragile storefront of glass / where every wall sparkles with shoes."

"Vigilance" the second to last poem, returns to the theme of Bottoms' second book, to watching and waiting, but now overtly for epiphanies, for a second coming, though perhaps not in any traditional, doctrinal sense. Sitting outside by the bird feeders of his suburban home, he says, "Days now I've pondered / what my mother-in-law calls the Endtime... days now trying to make the Jesus of Mark / jibe with the Gospel of John.... All this searching for the Kingdom of God." Then, out watching meteors, he hopes one of them might turn out to be more than a "pointless sizzle," might be "a blue Parousia unfolding." We learn of his hospitalized, cancer-sick friend, the writer Barry Hannah, seeing Jesus appear beside his bed, and we remember the speaker's father-in-law seeing Jesus appear on the side of the road in Montana. But the vigilance here considers as well the folk appearances of God's face "on pastry and French toast, / on biscuits lightly burned around the edge." He quotes Blake's notion that *"every thing that lives is Holy!"* and expands the register of spiritual references with, "Which any backsliding Hindu could tell you." But whatever the caliber of these varied epiphanies, it's spring and the world has "re-upped on its lease." In the end, in this world of suffering, what counts is "Vigilance and virtue, or what we can muster."

In the final poem of the collection, "Three-quarter Moon and Moment of Grace," he contemplates the gospels of Bartholomew and John, and in valediction says, "Verily, verily, / doesn't it all come down to memory ... Bartholomew's / or John's, yours or mine? And what are we dragging in that heavy sack / if not the cornerstones of Heaven."

Bottoms says, "Listen, out of the crank and rut / of history, this opulent millennial stillness––/ as though the Great Mind / ... lingered on the edge of a thought" and "your hand rising with mine / on the same gust of wind...."

Having begun shooting helpless rats and vandalizing petrified angels, having descended into reptilian worlds and been moved by the brain that governs there, our seeker saw in the crisis of divorce the destruction of his old life and was resurrected through the guts of vultures to reborn Pegasus-like from death by water. He found his family and made peace with a troubled past, blessing both humans and the lowly creatures of the world, finding redemption for both rats and rat killers. All this searching for the Kingdom of God now has him waltzing through the Endtime, and so we wait expectantly for more news from the journey of our honest, brave pilgrim.

Works Cited

Bottoms, David. *Armored Hearts: Selected and New Poems*. Port Townsend, WA: Copper Canyon Press, 1995.
———. *In a U-Haul North of Damascus*. New York: William Morrow, 1983.
———. *Shooting Rats at the Bibb County Dump*. New York: William Morrow, 1980.
———. *Under the Vulture-Tree*. New York: William Morrow, 1987.
———. *Vagrant Grace*. Port Townsend, WA: Copper Canyon Press, 1999.
———. *Waltzing through the Endtime*. Port Townsend, WA: Copper Canyon Press, 2004.
Edwards, Jonathan. *Works*. Ed. John E. Smith, 16 vols., *Religious Affections*, vol. 2. New Haven, CT: Yale University Press, 1959.
Merton, Thomas. *In Seeds of Contemplation*. New York: Dell, 1946.
Russ, Don. "Up Toward Light: Resurrection, Transfiguration, Metamorphosis, and Evolution in David Bottoms' *Armored Hearts*." *The Southern Quarterly* 37, 3/4 (Spring/Summer, 1999), 66–72.
Underhill, Evelyn. *Mysticism: A Study in the Nature and Development of Man's Spiritual Consciousness*. 1910. New York: Penguin, 1974.
Walsh, William. "David Bottoms: The Logic of the Original Dream." Interview, 2004.

"Up Toward Light": Resurrection, Transfiguration, Metamorphosis, and Evolution in *Armored Hearts*

DON RUSS

Most of David Bottoms' earlier poems seem to have been set in a still transitional modern South and peopled with the local likes of young thieves and vandals, drunken hunters, aging truckers, cock-fighters, drug smugglers, and solitary fishermen. In a very real sense, though, he was writing about an altogether familiar larger world of twentieth-century disillusionment and doubt, a world in which thinking human beings — including eventually his uneasy suburbanite husbands — struggle to find meaning and even the seemingly unthinking are left suffering its absence. Gathered in a single volume, *Armored Hearts* (2005), his first three collections could begin to come across as a coherent and richly suggestive, unified body of work. With the addition of a generous portion of new work, his themes highlighted themselves, patterns of imagery coalesced, and the affecting progress of a remarkable late twentieth-century consciousness manifested itself. There was largeness there. For all its Southernness *Armored Hearts* was — and is — a spiritual autobiography for ours or any time.

Even in the most local of the poems' stories and scenes, Bottoms draws upon the Western world's time-honored Judeo-Christian and Classical sources for his imagery, at first ironically playing up the failure of the older systems of belief, but then increasingly suggesting new hopes and possibilities. And employed alongside Biblical and Christian imagery of transformation (baptism, resurrection, transfiguration) and Classical imagery of metamorphosis (or other transmutations), the imagery of Darwinian evolution — for many, one would assume, the very antithesis of traditional Western sacred meaning—comes to suggest something positive, allowing finally a consoling recognition of kinship with all evolved life and thus some sort of salvation from modern isolation, despair, and darkness. The book ends with a poem in which a man envisions himself as no longer separated by a sense of self from the natural order but at one with the world, at peace with the past.

Bible and Echoes of the "Good Gospel News"

In "Shooting Rats at the Bibb County Dump," the title poem of Bottoms' first collection, the wounded rats turn away from light and "crawl/ for all they're worth into the darkness" which the speaker seems to feel he and his drunken companions and perhaps all human beings in the garbage dump of the world are headed for. And in the two poems which actually open this corresponding first section of *Armored Hearts*, the speaker for still other such groups seems to be directly (if somewhat meditatively) mocking the trappings of conventional religion. The cemetery thieves and vandals in "Wrestling Angels" set upon the very emblems of Judeo-Christian belief, leaving, for example, the stone-angel reminders of Jacob's Old Testament destiny "wingless,/ leaning over graves like old men lamenting their age." And in "Smoking in an Open Grave" a group of friends "bury [themselves]" to drink, smoke, and sing such now meaningless spirituals of resurrection as "I'll [F]ly [A]way," their only ascent an alcohol- and pot-induced high.

Examples of such denial and disillusionment may be found throughout the section. As he drinks, the hunter in "Below Freezing on Pinelog Mountain" is conscious both of the logged and spoiled winter landscape around him and of the fact that the breath of his companion is not different from the "white breath rising from [the dogs'] yelps," breath which seems pointedly only "like" the "spirits/ in that song land *where the soul never dies*" (another reference, of course, to old hymns). And for the trucker in "A Trucker Breaks Down," whose road signs once "glowed in his headlights like true/ evidence of things unseen," faith is gone, and he now dreams only of his truck leaving the highway and carrying him into "absolute darkness," dissolving with him into mist.

While the husband in "A Home Buyer Watches the Moon" sees his neighborhood as little more than a dead-end street or dark graveyard, and the boy in "Sermon of the Fallen" hears at a funeral only the dismaying lesson of death and the decay of the body, Section Two contains a number of poems with less bitterly ironic religious references and some even suggesting a changing attitude. These are the poems of Bottoms' second collection, *In a U-Haul North of Damascus*.

The boy in "Sermon" learns that the deceased had come into the world only to die, and he begins to feel the fearful "trembling in us all." But only a few poems earlier, in "Recording the Spirit Voices," the speaker has placed a recorder on the grave of a young woman killed in a fire, and he waits, actually afraid he might discover evidence of life beyond the grave, afraid "her tombstone lied," afraid he might lose "the truth" which both he and the stone angel have apparently stood on: "*born* and *died*" — one life and no more.

But that, one might say, is just for starters. The hunter in "Light of the Sacred Harp" seems for the moment actually able to participate in something like a drunken religious ecstasy or at least in the drunken idea of a religious ecstasy. He and a group of friends have broken into an abandoned country church and, for warmth, begun to burn hymnals, then funeral-home fans (with their scenes from the New Testament), dead flowers, and perhaps the church itself, and while they kneel and drink around the fire at the altar they seem — at least in the speaker's imagination — to join the ghosts of past congregations in a fiery communion of song. The circumstances are highly ironic, but the burning of shape notes and of hymn words fuses with their bottled "plasma of visionaries," and these then fuse as if into a "light/ to see all things by." He says that they hear, "old voices"

> burning back from the graveyard
> in newfound harmony as the pulpit catches
> and becomes light, and we kneel
> for drunkenness and joy as fire climbs the wall
> and enters the Last Supper, the air filling up
> with psalm-smoke, the whole house of the Lord
> popping with revival, becoming pure spirit
> of voices returning in the joyful noise
> of the Sacred Harp, singing over and over
> the good gospel news that men do rise from dust
> and ashes.

However ironic, "Light of the Sacred Harp" contains Section Two's most explicit and extended treatment of ideas having to do with resurrection and spiritual transformation. The section then ends with a poem called "Hurricane." It somewhat comically describes the effects of a storm as a "rapture," with debris "rising out of the dirt like Baptists/ at the Second Coming," but then closes with "[l]ight gather[ing]" after the destruction and life literally rising again from the earth in "the ox beetle gor[ing] up through blown sand."

In the final two sections of *Armored Hearts* (poems from *Under the Vulture-Tree* followed by the selection of new poems), such ideas come into their own and are put to a variety of less and less negatively suggestive uses. Some of the poems are actually about religion, while others use religious allusions, images, and metaphors to make their points. There is, for example, a poem about children's belief called "A Tent Beside a River." It describes a boy and his young siblings or cousins performing their own private version of a church service meant to see their grandfather's soul away from his body and into the afterlife, across the metaphorical river which so preoccupies a number of these later poems. "An Old Hymn for Ian Jenkins," "Gospel Banjo: Homage to Little Roy Lewis," and "Homage to Lester Flatt" all directly or indirectly allude to the Jordan River, and in sometimes complexly suggestive, ambiguous, and yet somehow hopeful-sounding acts of language, they suggest an equation of the making of music (and perhaps of poetry itself) with the ever-compelling human dream of perfection, of life imagined beyond the grave, the old hymn's "mansion over the hilltop, [the] land/ of beautiful flowers where we'll never/ grow old" — a "dream flaunting the possibility of the dream,/ which is the joy of waking on either side of the Jordan." Then, in a poem actually entitled "The Resurrection," the specifically Christian concept of resurrection of the body comes up again — along with the concept of reincarnation — in a conversation about cremation which a disappointed and now rather reluctant lover has with the woman he is with. He at least tells her he believes in "the new life" and that he knows "the Lord could mend us ash by ash," but when he follows her into the "black mouth," the "jaws," of an open grave they have visited on his dare, the moment of the resurfacing of his old emotions is frightening, almost indistinguishable from dying. But the "pit" they are in is also called "that belly of earth," and what he begins to experience is indeed presented as the beginning of a rebirth, a healing, or at least the metaphoarical "resurrection" of the poem's title.

Section Three's climactic expression of the idea of resurrection and — now specifically — the idea and actual terminology of transfiguration occurs in its powerful title poem, "Under the Vulture-Tree." In it a boatman drifts under a tree of roosting vultures and experiences what might be described as a full-blown epiphany, a startling but nevertheless comforting revelation of the transitory place of death in the scheme of the natural world, in the realm of both animals and of humankind. If it is not specifically termed a religious revelation, it certainly seems a nearly mystical one and is expressed in a medium of metaphors drawn from traditional religion. Passing beneath the vultures, beneath "their dream," he sees its "wrinkled and generous" face and is reminded of "the faces of the very old/ who have grown to empathize with everything." He then says:

> And I drifted away from them slow, on the pull of the river,
> reluctant, looking back at their roost,
> calling them what I'd never called them, what they are,
> those dwarfed transfiguring angels,
> who flock to the side of the poisoned fox, the mud turtle
> crushed on the shoulder of the road,
> who pray over the leaf-graves of the anonymous lost,
> with mercy enough to consume us all and give us wings.

In a world of natural death no less than in the seemingly less natural world of human destructiveness, the vultures become figures of redemption, and the boatman's acknowledgement of that fact seems itself redemptive.

"Cemetery Wings" is another poem directly referring to death and to the soul's transfer onto some kind of higher plane. It appears among the new poems in Section Four and takes place among tombstones, where the speaker comes to the rescue of a grounds-keeper swarmed by yellow jackets. At first glance, it might seem merely ironic, but the wording is interesting: at the end of the poem, the victim stares "at the thin cloud lifting/ around the faces of angels," and looks "puzzled/ at being carried away by such small wings"—that is, not puzzled at being carried away, but only at the smallness of the wings.

Three pages later, "A Night, Near Berkeley Springs" recounts a Civil War scene in which the "'light of the future eternal' ... breaks on a life" in a different way. In a Virginia field a surprise snow falls upon Henry Kyd Douglas and his sleeping troops, covering them in a "suffocating / absence of dreams." But after waking, after a moment of fear at finding themselves buried in the dark, they experience—or the poet imagines they experience (even as he experiences with them)—a sense of renewal and, after night

and in the midst of war and death, a sense of life. The poet imagines "...
the awe, the simple joy"

> of rising up and shaking off that half-foot of snow,
> of seeing outstretched from your feet the whole white field
> mounded with graves,
> and one by one in the early light
> the glazed mounds quivering awake, each hopeless soldier
> sitting up, brushing off
> a fine dust, astonished to be rising from a cloud.

A final poem alluding at least indirectly to resurrection is again set in a literal cemetery—in fact, in Rose Hill, the setting of "Wrestling Angels," which opens the book. It is a meditation on grace and the history of the speaker's own knowledge of and experience with religion. It is called "Free Grace at Rose Hill" and describes his having never quite made it to full belief in his own redemption, even after finding himself—as an adult—capable of "listening suddenly/ with [his] heart" to the "promise of an old hymn." But even as he describes the movement of grace as being like the wind, swirling only "where it wants to swirl" ("If it touches us,/ it touches us"), he describes the "roses/ quaking in their terraces," life itself seen blooming from the grave.

Although "Wrestling Angels," with its physical attack on tradition, is in a different world from this final acknowledgment of grace, it is worth noting that nowhere in the entire volume following "Wrestling Angels" has the speaker ever actually ridiculed believers when they were the subjects of poems—whether faith healers, snake handlers, revivalists, radio evangelists, boy shepherds in Nativity scenes (who "since believing was easy" believed), the lame in search of healing, the millenarians heading for the hills, or even the abusively tyrannical head of a Pentecostal family. The title poem of the book's Section Two—"In a U-Haul North of Damascus"—even takes the form of a prayer. And in addition to the overtly theological subject of grace, the idea of Holy Communion is alluded to time and again, and its actual practice seriously examined for at least one entire poem. It is not surprising then that in "Zion Hill," the poem facing "Free Grace at Rose Hill," the speaker suggests that, if it is impossible for him finally and fully to believe, it is not because he is someone who "considers himself a physician/ equal to his own heart." He would like to be able to believe. "[W]ho could ever stop desiring/ that serenity?" he asks.

Classical Allusion: Old Stories
"Quick and Radiant as Revelation"

Although Classical allusions appear much less frequently, the general idea of metamorphosis pervades *Armored Hearts*, sometimes describing biological processes, sometimes occurring as metaphorical elaborations, and almost always suggestive of movement from death to life, darkness to light, a lower level to a higher. Even the rotting tree/corpse the boy in "Sermon of the Fallen" pictures contains larvae waiting to be transformed. And the too-settled suburbanite in "In Heritage Farms, Settled" actually goes looking for such metamorphoses — any good and natural change: "the delicate white maggot wagging in its cradle/ of turds, the tiny feet of the tadpole, every leg/ of the hornworm inching toward the wings of the phoenix moth." And in "In a Pasture Under a Cradled Moon," there are more fantastic imaginings of metamorphosis. In a passage filled with details suggestive of death-in-life and life-in-death, the darkly meditative husband of a wife who has miscarried sees "What might have been" as "an image/ almost solidifying, a cloud of fireflies swarming," "one creature/ almost becoming whole, molecular,/ but dissolving with the quickness of light." And in the final section's and the entire volume's title poem, "Armored Hearts," the apparently same Heritage Farms suburbanite praises (or at least empathizes with) the reclusive loggerhead turtles coming up from the muddy depths of a pond to feed on the neighbor's ducks, "rising when they're least expected/ into a panic of wings," angelically transfigured (in a manner of speaking, in a little miracle of inspired wording) in spite of their ugly selves.

However, there is an occasional direct Classical allusion. Even the "inadvertent" allusion to the phoenix in the name "phoenix moth" at the end of "Heritage Farms, Settled" should be taken as being made in full consciousness of its significance, and the boys praying for their grandfather in "A Tent Beside a River" may model their efforts after tent revivals and use a Bible and a Baptist hymnal, but in getting the old man's soul across the specifically named Jordan they are participating in something more, something less narrowly sectarian. It is his "shadow," the poem suggests — his shade — which their words "ferry" across, and it is therefore also across that other, unnamed river as well: the Styx, of course.

At least two poems draw heavily upon what might be termed Greco-Roman images of metamorphosis. One of them, "Red Swan," turns wonderfully mythological — however ironic, comic, and sad it is that settled suburban life (which includes a pond and tamed and tame-able bird-life) can experience again its lost sense of magic, of mystery in the natural world, only through an electric lamp in the shape of a bird, a lamp which a husband and wife wired up and planted one night at the water's edge. There that apparition "burned like a returning god"—perhaps like Christianity's Second Coming, but even more like Zeus incarnate, God, come once again and amorously to earth. And the earth is renewed. The poem ends almost reverently; the neighborhood's real goose

> ...still honks on the lake, all night,
> haunted. And in the stories
> of the neighborhood kids,
> the ibis is commonplace, the snowy egret nothing
> to speak of. There is only that sighting
> too beautiful to believe, quick
> and radiant as revelation,
> and all their stories tell of a night
> when lightning waddled down to the edge of the lake
> to burn for a moment in the shape of a swan.

Even the traces of irony have practically disappeared, however, in "In the Ice Pasture." There the suburban speaker goes to the rescue of a fellow creature, a horse fallen through the same neighborhood's pond, now frozen, and is transformed with the horse into a splendidly new, even magical being, something such as Ovid might have imagined. Seeing its struggle to get out, the speaker first asks himself what the horse is trying to become, looking like "an odd beast cracking its shell": something bird-like, of course—a winged Pegasus, perhaps. Then it looks to him like "half a white statue in a fountain of ice"—perhaps a baroque Italian re-creation of some Neptune's fish-tailed sea-horse. When the rescuer himself falls through, it sounds like "the snapping of bones," and he and the horse are on their way toward a conjoining and radical reconfiguring of their very bodies. In the blurred struggle, the violent baptism, one and then the other goes under. The man at first hangs "bodiless" (that is, still awaiting his new body), and then the horse comes up under him, and "what [they now] were lunged hard, broke/ to the air, to the wind turning [them] scaly/ with water." They "broke by inches the black shell/ of water" and "roared" (not "yelled" or "whinnied," "screamed" or "snorted," but "roared") "till the night/ cracked like an egg shattered in the storm/ of two beasts becoming one,/ or one beast being born." This roaring creature with feathers and scales, with the body of a horse and the body of a man — this fusion of the human, the natural, and the at least poetically evoked supernatural — surpasses perhaps even the action of the "dwarfed transfiguring angels" in "Under the Vulture-Tree" in its affirmation of securely placed and meaningful human life.

"An Old Voice Crying Up from the Swamps of Our Brains": Darwin Evolving

Just as with the handling of resurrection and related motifs, the handling of ideas having to do with Darwinian evolution begins in something of a darker vein. At first religion's angels are not angels but old men, and men are not much different from hunting dogs and tormented rats. "Hiking Toward Laughing Gull Point" even describes humans as being like a plunging gull the speaker once saw caught by its beak, mid-air, on a baited hook. And in "Watching Gators at Ray Boone's Reptile Farm" (one of a number of poems fascinated with our evolutionary connection to the reptilian) the visitor senses in alligators "an old voice crying up from the swamps of our brains," "crying now through our common memory,/ the answer to all the animal inside us." There is a comic, even indulgent, depiction of this animal in "Crawling Out at Parties," which describes a creature of evolution's old reptile brain — located at the base of the later, larger human brain — as being released by Scotch from "the ancient swamps" and literally crawling about the floor of someone's tastefully decorated twentieth-century living room.

But even in the earliest sections of *Armored Hearts* some of the more positive implications to be drawn from the notion of evolution may be found. In "Calling Across Water at Lion Country Safari" a silverback gorilla is described by a visitor as "calling [him]/ across water, the only thing he [the gorilla] believes is really between [them]," and the motorist who stops to save a tossed-aside fish in "The Catfish" sees the animal as "swimming on the sidewalk/ ... like a document on evolution": a fellow creature, but one still quivering in its "pre-crawling" stage. He takes the time to return it to the water and the "current of our breathable past." In actual practice, we may have lost some of our former adaptability and become (like the snagged and nearly drowning husband in "Under the Boathouse") hardly more than a "curiosity among fishes," but in that all-important manner of speaking it is our breathable past, the past from which we have all evolved.

There may be a few poems which see the universe as a frighteningly vast and indifferent place (the "infinite/ and indiscriminate creation" of the poem "Appearances") or at the very least as an impenetrably mysterious place (like the watery depths in "Sounding Harvey Creek" from which an "infinite variety of oddities / [comes] crawling out ... / to reveal nothing"), but there are many more which can find a sense of closeness, kinship, even oneness with the world and all the life in it. The fisherman in "The Copperhead" imagines himself entering snake-like and wholly into the natural world, "pulling [him]self down a fallen branch toward the trunk / where [the copperhead] lay quiet and dangerous and unafraid, / all spine and nerve." The fisherman in "Rats at Allatoona" even imagines himself going to sleep among another group of our vertebrate relatives, the scavenging rats, and waking to find himself among the "shreds of their sacrament," waking to "what [he is] in [his] dream," his Christ-like "body whole/ and broken, having taken from the feast / and given to it."

As "Rest at the Mercy House" has it, it may be that "nature doesn't specialize / in mercy," and like the naturalist John Muir in "Sierra Bear" we may be guilty of "rude behavior," may sometimes not exercise the "'right manners of the wilderness,'" but the poems of *Armored Hearts* do ultimately find comfort and meaning in our life here.

In the final section, among the new poems rounding out what has more and more clearly come to suggest the working out of an emblematic twentieth-century spiritual life, the sense of union with the world and with all of evolved life is so profound that in "My Perfect Night," the penultimate poem — a poem set up very much like a little creation story — the speaker/poet/creator can imagine "clos[ing] the door on a dark house/ and walk[ing] out into [himself]": all of dying and yet ever-renewed creation. And responding to the call of the natural world in the concluding poem, "Allatoona Evening," a boatman allows himself to consider the possibility that there is "no better place" and nothing "more beautiful" than this emptying himself of his ego and anger and peacefully giving himself up to his sense of connection to the world, to the dark lake, and the trinity of stars just coming into sight, "soaking up twilight."

If traditional religion has finally not quite worked out for them, the poet and his *Armored Hearts* speakers seem to have come to full appreciation of nature's own transfiguring power (nature with "mercy enough to ... give us wings"), to full appreciation of the wondrously transforming power of human regard for other creatures, and of the comfort of recognizing that the evolved world is not just our home but what we are, all of us sharing our one "breathable past." Bottoms' speakers so often seem the same speaker that readers might be tempted to try to piece together for themselves an individual poet's autobiography (childhood, disillusioned youth, a marriage, a break-up, another marriage, the birth of a daughter, etc.), but the concerns of *Armored Hearts* are greater than that. They and we are always our separate selves — sometimes isolated, sometimes with others — but we learn to "empathize with everything." In "In the Kitchen, Late," a poem near the beginning of the final section, even the lowly roaches are described by a solitary midnight snacker as "bring[ing] back/ in perfect innocence through the veins of the house/ their own small portion/ of the night," and Bottoms somehow makes it seem a good night, a "pure loneliness," a "darkness/ you feel somehow you['ve] miss[ed]." We can know the night, and along with the back-yard camper in a much earlier poem called "The Tent Astronomer," we can remain anchored in the natural world and also let the "lens and mirror" of our consciousness lift us "up toward light."

Works Cited

Bottoms, David. *Armored Hearts: Selected and New Poems*. Port Townsend, WA: Copper Canyon Press, 1995.

The Onion's Dark Core
Ernest Suarez

This interview took place in Bottoms' pickup truck on April 7–8, 1996, as Bottoms and Suarez traveled from Atlanta to Macon to visit the Big House, the legendary domain of the Allman Bothers Band.

Suarez: You won the Walt Whitman Award in 1979. What were you doing then?

Bottoms: I'd been teaching high school for four or five years in Douglas County, Georgia. It hadn't been a good situation, and I was thinking about going back to school to work on a doctorate. Also, for several years I'd been writing poems and trying to place them in the magazines. I'd racked up around sixty since 1973, when I finished my M.A.—some in pretty good places, such as *Harper's* and *Poetry*—and I'd chosen the best thirty or so and put together a manuscript. I sent it around to a few university presses, the University of Georgia Press and LSU, and it was rejected. Then a friend of mine, Gerald Duff, phoned and told me about the Walt Whitman Award, which is a first-book competition sponsored by the Academy of American Poets. He suggested I send my book because Robert Penn Warren was the judge that year. I thought it would be great if Warren just read my poems. I fiddled with it some and changed the title to *Shooting Rats at the Bibb County Dump*, after a poem that had appeared in *Harper's*—the original title was "All Systems Break Down"—and I sent it off. A few months later I got a phone call from a very nice lady, Mrs. Marie Bullock. She introduced herself as the president of the Academy of America Poets and asked if I was sitting down. I said, "No ma'am, but I can sit down." And I did—on the side of the bed, as I recall. Then she said that Robert Penn Warren had chosen my book as winner of the Whitman Award. I was literally stunned with elation. I really don't remember anything else about the call. Later on Warren wrote me a nice note about the book. He also wrote a very generous comment for the jacket. It was a hard decision for him, I think. There were several good entries, and well over thirteen hundred in all.

And Morrow published it the following year?

Yes. At that time the Whitman book rotated between four publishers. It was William Morrow's year. I was very excited about having a first book, an award, and a New York publisher. The award included a $1,000 cash prize. I don't think Warren really knew what all of that meant to me at the time. The real prize was the boost it gave me out of my situation. I was unhappy with my life and in a rut I feared would only get deeper. On the strength of the prize and a first book, I was offered a fellowship to pursue my doctorate at Florida State, which is what I did.

Is the manuscript that won the Whitman Award essentially the same as Shooting Rats at the Bibb County Dump?

Yes. There are a few minor changes. I added a poem called "The Copperhead," which had come out in the *Atlantic*. I asked Warren if I could include it, and he was agreeable, of course. I think I made a few minor changes to a couple of poems in the last section. Nothing serious. So it was basically the same book that Warren selected.

Did you ever get to know Warren?

Not really, no. We only exchanged two or three letters, though he was very generous with young writers. I remember sending him a copy of a poem called "Under the Boathouse," and he made a good suggestion. But that's the only time I ever did anything like that. I didn't want to annoy him with a lot of correspondence I knew he didn't have time to answer. Later on, though, I did ask him for some poems when I was gathering a few for *Atlanta Magazine*, and he sent four or five good ones. "First Time" is the one I remember because I framed the signed manuscript and hung it in my office. Ironically, we only published one of the bunch before the whole staff was fired and I had to return them. A few months later a couple of them came out in the *New Yorker* and the *Georgia Review*.

You never met?

No. I had two opportunities to meet him, but they both fell through. The first was in the early eighties at Bennington, where I was doing a reading. Dave Smith had arranged to drive me over to Warren's house, which was fairly close by, but as it turned out Warren was too sick. Several years later, Warren invited me to read at the Library of Congress. He was poet laureate then, the first actually. He was going to do the introduction, but he got sick again and couldn't travel. He sent his introduction along, and one of the librarians read it. So I never got to meet him. That was a real disappointment.

Go back to "Under the Boathouse." Do you recall the change that Warren suggested?
   It had to do with point of view. The poem is about a fellow who dives into a pond and goes all the way down to the bottom, where he gets his hand caught on a fishhook that's attached to something down there. Anyway, he's caught and can't tear loose, sort of hanging "Halfway between the bottom of the lake/and the bottom of the sky." The line Warren suggested I change had to do with the moment when he's somewhat mysteriously freed. I'd written something like "In the lung-ache,/in the blue pulsing of temples," and he pointed out that the swimmer wouldn't be able to see his own temples. True enough, though I hadn't intended it exactly that way. Still, I didn't argue. I changed it to "loud pulsing of temples."

You and James Dickey were friends for many years. He passed away recently. How would you assess his career and his significance to you as a poet?
   I had a long phone conversation with Jim a few days before he died. He told me he was dying. He'd told me that before, but this time I sensed it would be soon. He was very concerned with my opinion about his place in American poetry. I told him what I'd always told him. Simply that he was the champ. He liked the sports metaphor, and, as always, I said that with a clear conscience. He was a giant in American poetry. The attention he continues to draw will probably depend on the political fads of the critics. But from my perspective he was the finest poet to come out of the American South. His combination of narrative gift and lyricism seems to me unequaled. Others might argue for Warren, and they'd have some powerful ammo to shoot. Ultimately, it's probably a matter of sensibility and silly to weigh them against each other. They're both extraordinary. But Dickey's poetry, I think, has most influenced my own—his early work especially, and most especially in terms of the things he chose to write about. We had many of the same interest—fishing, hunting, bluegrass,

and old-time country music — and we came from the same part of the country. He showed me the poetic possibilities of the region we come from. But I don't think I write very much like Jim. Fred Chappell said once that in terms of style, Dickey and I were just about as far apart as two writers could get. Dickey's power, he said, was expansion and mine was compression. I think that's a fair assessment. If you look at poems that are uniquely Dickey — say "The Firebombing," "Falling," "May Day Sermon," "The Zodiac" — you see that expansive imagination fiercely at work. It's almost as though the fullest degree of intensity must be wrung from each moment of the narrative. My best poems, I think — poems such as "Under the Vulture-Tree" or "White Shrouds" — tend to focus and compress the experience. My method, to me, seems closer to the method of James Wright in *The Branch Will Not Break*, which is still one of my favorite books — I'm thinking here of poems such as "A Blessing" or "A Dream of Burial" — or maybe to the Theodore Roethke of "The Meadow Mouse," "Slug," "The Pike." Ironically, though, what I really love of Roethke's is "The North American Sequence," which may be built out of a sensibility closer to Dickey's. I'm talking about that openness, that ability to touch every detail.

But occasionally you've experimented with longer poems.

Yes, but my poems still tend to depend on focus and compression. If you look at *Armored Hearts*, you'll find very few poems that run over sixty lines. And those are usually broken up into parts — for instance, "In a U-Haul North of Damascus." This is essentially a strategy for controlling the narrative, for reining it in, so I think Fred is probably right. Mine is ultimately a sensibility that leans toward compression, the illuminated moment. Though Dickey wrote some beautiful shorter poems — "The Performance," "Buckdancer's Choice," "Heaven of Animals," and I could go into a very long list — his imagination and lyric gift were such that he could sustain the intensity of the poem for pages. My mind just doesn't work that way, and I may be fortunate that it doesn't. His talent simply dwarfed so many southern poets, particularly those of his own generation.

In what ways? Can you give us some specifics?

Well, it's not uncommon to hear southern poets say that they've always felt like they were standing in Dickey's shadow. This is understandable. He threw a wide and tall one, and it must have been a dark place to find yourself. I remember hearing Van Brock, my old professor at Florida State, say that when he first stated writing poetry his approach was very similar to Dickey's, but Dickey's voice was so powerful that he felt he had to alter his own. Now think about that. His natural inclination was to go at the poem much as Jim did, but Dickey did it so much better that he felt he had to change. This denial of one's own sensibility, one's own natural way of writing, has to be something like creative suicide. I remember hearing a musician friend of mine, a pianist, say that after she heard Horowitz in concert, she felt like going home and taking a hammer to her fingers. That was something like the effect Dickey's work had on other southern poets.

Let's push off that for a moment and talk about method. Can you describe what you try to accomplish in a poem?

In the introduction Warren wrote for the Library of Congress, he said that the world is always trying to tell us something. Or something to that effect.

I'll read that to you. I have it here on the jacket of Under the Vulture-Tree. *He says, "Underlying all his work is the simple and unusual conviction that the world we see is trying to tell us something." What does he mean by that?*

Simply that the world tries to tell us its secrets through the poem. The poem can reveal something about the hidden things of the world, the vague or shadowy relationships and connections that exist just below the surface of our daily lives. Or to say it another way, poetry can provide an artistic and emotional connection to the less obvious undercurrents of the world. I like that. I like to see poetry as a self-exploration of the personal that reveals through language the general patterns of human experience. I spend a lot of time in my classes discussing creativity and sensibility. I'm careful to tell my students that every writer who comes to class brings his or her own bag of prejudices. I have mine. Poetry, of course, means a lot of different things to different people, but for a long time I've been interested primarily in the way the poem works figuratively to reveal the universal through the personal. The meaning of the poem is always more than the sum off the literal meanings of all the words. We talk about the DHM—the deep hidden meaning—and how to get there through language. One element I emphasize from the start is narrative, what narrative can do for a poem simply because of what it is, simply because it carries with it so many of the basic elements of good writing. I like to use a little story about going out and buying a truck. A couple of years ago I bought a GMC pickup, and it didn't have a radio in it. Radios aren't standard equipment anymore. Well, that's a drag. Narrative in the poem is like buying a truck with everything on it. You get a package — radio, air conditioner, power windows, all at the same time. If you buy the narrative package you get a lot of good stuff. You at least get some degree of clarity, some sense of time and space. This is no small thing. It forces an attention to physical detail, the concrete, and so provides a greater sense of immediacy. It also provides what I call a concrete level of meaning, a narrative surface. Students always want their poems to be deep, and I say, "Well, in order to have a deeper meaning, you at least have to have one meaning for it to be deeper than. Right?" That's the narrative surface. In the narrative surface a good writer can embed various devices to spring the poem into the figurative, the DHM.

And this is done through language?

Yes, through figurative devices: metaphor, simile, word-play, association, whatever. But oddly enough there's at least one other way this can happen, and that's when the narrative itself becomes figurative, when the narrative structure of the poem begins to mirror archetypal patterns and myth. I talk a good deal about Carl Jung's notions of archetype and the collective unconscious — this really fascinated me — and try to relate it to poetry. Take that poem "Under the Boathouse." As I said, this fellow jumps into a lake and goes all the way down to the bottom, where he gets his hand caught on a hook and he can't get loose. He looks up and sees his wife's shadow floating on the surface "like an angel/quivering in a deadman's float." Then, miraculously, he does tear loose and floats back up to the surface. So what you have mirrored here is simply an archetypal pattern — submersion, symbolic death, ascension, and rebirth. This pattern is what Jung calls the myth of the night journey, one of the oldest and most common patterns in Western cultural. He cites as an example the *Old Testament* story of Jonah and the whale. We all know what happens there. God says to Jonah, "Go over here to Nineveh and preach to these bad people." And Jonah says to God, "Well, you know these people over there are mean, and they don't really like me. I was sort of thinking about taking a cruise." So Jonah tries to sail away from God, and the big storm comes up on the water. The crew treats Jonah to a swim, the big fish eats him, and he goes all the way down to the bottom of the sea, a symbolic death. Jonah begins to see then that Nineveh isn't such a terrible place after all. He has a change of heart. Then the great fish rises and spits him out on the other side, and he's a new Jonah. Descent, death, ascent, rebirth — that's just one of a number of narrative patterns that keep repeating themselves in the literatures of the world. Students are amazed when they're confronted with this, and soon enough they begin to see how the narrative structures of their own poems reverberate in odd ways because they bang up against archetypes.

How much of this mirroring of the archetypal is a conscious part of the poet's strategy?
    A good deal, I think. But fortunate things happens unconsciously too. Most everyone reading this will be familiar with Seamus Heaney's notion of the poem as dig, the poem as a type of personal archaeology. He talks about this best in an essay called "Feeling into Words," where he says that the first time he ever wrote a poem he really liked, he felt as though he'd let a shaft of light down into himself. Well, the process of writing can produce some surprising and often intriguing discoveries. But the best things that can happen for me is when the seed of the poem, the initial idea, is also the figurative device. I'll give you an example. When I was writing "Under the Vulture-Tree" the first line that came to me was the last line of the poem, "with mercy enough to consume us all and give us wings." I'd had a memory about an encounter with some vultures — on a fishing trip in north Florida — and I suddenly conceived them as these "dwarfed transfiguring angels," an odd way to look at a vulture, but with it the came the figurative device, the play of words *consume* and *wings*. The rest of the poem is simply a narrative architecture supporting that line. For me, that one line is what makes the poem work. In "Sign for My Father, Who Stressed the Bunt" the same thing happened. That last line of the poem, "I'm getting a grip on the sacrifice," was the first to occur to me. The play on the word *sacrifice* in the dual contexts of a baseball game and a father's relationship to his son was the original idea for the poem. In my best poems, at least the shorter ones, this is what happens. The seed of the poem, the engendering idea, is the figurative device. About the worst thing that can happen is when I feel I want to write a poem about something and I don't have that device. I must have hundreds of drafts that are interesting narratives in themselves but fail to make that figurative leap, to reveal the connections operating under the surface. So I'm always careful to tell my students that as important as narrative is to poetry, it is not everything required to make a good poem. We're in a period now where narrative is hot again, perhaps fashionable as the new formalism, but it can be equally as superficial. You can open up just about any mag-

azine and find poems that are simply little stories broken up into twenty-fie or thirty lines. They just lie there and never get beyond the literal. Perhaps this is why many poets — and some good southern ones such as Ellen Voigt and Charles Wright — are suspicious of the narrative.

Would you go back for a moment to "Under the Vulture-Tree." I heard you say at a reading that it was typical of the way poems come to you. Could you describe in more detail how that poem came to you?

I was living in Tallahassee. This was around 1980 or so, when I was doing my doctorate at FSU. One of my favorite pastimes was fishing, and there were some really beautiful rivers around Tallahassee. My favorite was the Wakulla. You'll know exactly what it looked like if I tell you that back in the forties two of those old Johnny Weissmuller Tarzan movies were made there, along with a movie called *The Creature from the Black Lagoon*. It was almost like a jungle, this slow tranquil river flowing through a jungle. Anyway, I was out there very early one morning, just about dawn, I think, and I was in a little aluminum boat. Then I came into a bend and on the far bank the jungle opened up into a small clearing. It was very odd because right in the middle of this clearing stood one giant black tree, so black you couldn't see light through it. It looked as though someone had taken a piece of black construction paper and cut out the silhouette of an oak tree and pasted it there. Well, it gave me a strange feeling, so I drifted in a little closer. Then the strangeness intensified because I could see that it was a fruit tree. It was speckled all over with tiny pink fruit. As I got even closer the feeling turned eerie. These things weren't really fruit at all — they were heads, the heads of vultures. I'd come on a buzzard roost, and they were literally crammed into this tree shoulder to shoulder. Well, there's some material. Years later, maybe four or five, I was living in Marietta, Georgia, and something jarred that memory. As I said, for some reason the notion of these vultures as odd angels came to me, and with that the worldplay on "consume" and "wings," which fell into the last line.

Many of your poems are filled with wildlife.

Animals fascinate me because the real world is the wilderness. Everything else is artifice. By virtue of our consciousness we've separated ourselves from the natural world. No matter how many rivers we canoe down or how long we stay out in the woods, self-consciousness is still an act of separation. We've lost our instincts and must depend on our rational faculties. Few other people care much about this, but poets and other artists often feel intensely the need to get back to some notion of the natural state. James Wright has his encounters with horses. James Dickey has his animals and violence. Think about that great poem, "The Sheep Child." Talk about a unique point of view. In the woolly baby, the sheep child, Dickey achieves this amazing reunion of the two halves of human nature — the rational and the instinctive — and, of course, the irony lies in the fact that this is so horribly unnatural the sheep child dies immediately. What a great line, "My hoof and my hand clasp each other." Anyway, to put it simply, like many other poets, I see animals as a conduit into the real world. Several of my very early poems deal with that. I'll give you an example. I've always been fascinated with the notion of the triune brain, a concept I ran across in a Carl Sagan book called *The Dragons of Eden*. I forget who actually pioneered this research, but Sagan distilled it for the common guy, a thing he was very good at doing. Anyway, it's the concept that the brain actually developed as three different brains, all of which are still there. The first is that little mass of tissue at the top of the spine, the R Complex or the reptile brain, which supposedly controls eating, sex, and ritual, and then on top of that formed the limbic or mammal brain, which controls emotions, and finally on top of that, the neocortex, huge in comparison, which accounts for abstract thought and differentiates us form other creatures, which perhaps isn't considered to be quite true any longer. Aren't they figuring out that in some small way apes can actually abstract? At any rate, thus the attraction we often have for certain animals and the vague sense of recognition or affinity we may feel. It's interesting to think that the attraction D.H. Lawrence feels for his snake at the water trough may have not only a mythological basis — he calls him "king in exile, uncrowned in the underworld" — but a physiological one as well. Jung talks about the serpent in our abdomen. True, and we also have one in our brain. Seeing the snake jars some kinship in the R Complex, the reptile brain. The same thing happens to the persona in my poem "The Copperhead." He becomes fascinated by this snake sitting out on a tree limb that's fallen into a pond. He just wants to get closer and closer because something in him is drawing him to it, just as in the Lawrence poem the tension arises between his fear, a product of his "human education," as he says, and a deeply felt affinity.

So this is where those poems in Shooting Rats *come from?*
    Yes, the poems in the section called "All the Animal Inside Us" —

"Crawling Out at Parties," "The Copperhead," "Watching Gators at Ray Boone's Reptile Farm," and the rest. But the reptile brain is still essential to me, literally a part of me, and everyone else. Occasionally it still creeps out of the shadows when it recognizes a distant relative in the real world—most recently, perhaps in the poem "In a Kitchen, Late," which is in the new section of *Armored Hearts*. The conduit into the wilderness there is a cockroach. The persona is sitting at the kitchen table snacking on chicken, and he feels a cockroach in the hairs of his leg. Disgusting, true. But it becomes for him an odd connection to the darkness and the woods outside, to something he feels he's lost.

What creatures serve as the most effective conduits for you?

Snakes, turtles, alligators, rats, vultures. I tend not to be as fascinated by the nobler animals, say Warren' eagles or even James Wright's horses, but I tend to run with the lower order. Neruda says, "It has never occurred to me to speak/with the genteel animals." He wanted to speak with the serpents. I feel the same way. That same sensibility is developed much further in Roethke, and this must have been where I first encountered it. He loved what he called the "minimal," the elemental, and in his greenhouse poems he even extends it into the plant world. But he has his animals too—slugs, mice, lizards, fish. His little poem "The Meadow Mouse" has always been one of my favorites. He calls it "My thumb of a child that nuzzled in my palm."

Do you see any connection between Roethke's meadow mouse and your rats of "Shooting Rats at the Bibb County Dump"?

Indirectly, yes. That aspect of Roethke probably made a poem like "Shooting Rats" possible. But my approach in "Shooting Rats" is not typical of the animal poems we've been taking about, which take an approach similar to Roethke, an approach through affinity, or in the case of "The Meadow Mouse" we might even say affection. This stance is a little more enlightened than the persona of "Shooting Rats," who doesn't see anything particularly cuddly about these rats at the garbage dump and feels only a vague and perverse similarity of fate. Nevertheless, Dickey told me once that I'd created about as much sympathy for a rat as anyone could hope to create. But this is reader sympathy, at the persona's expense. Roethke's attitude toward this meadow mouse is a recognition of kinship. In that recognition lie his connections with the spiritual undercurrents.

You see poetry as a means of reaccessing the primal.
　Certainly, but not only the primal world, the primal self, in the sense that poetry is self-exploration, a journey into the darker and more dangerous coves of one's own psyche.

What do you mean by "dangerous" here?
　Well, poetry can be dangerous in the sense that the poet often has to confront things about himself or herself—fears, impulses, desires, repressed memories—that may not be exactly pleasant. In fact, they may be ugly, troubling, and even very frightening. Let me explain that with a metaphor. Fishing provides a good one for writing this kind of poem. You're out there alone in some cove in the little poetry boat, throwing out your lure— a good word here—and you're casting down into the depths, the psychic depths. Of course, you're going for the little creative impulse, the stuff of the great poem—on our metaphor, you're going for the seven-pound bass—but you don't know what's down there. You just have to be willing to cast out that Jitterbug or that Mirr-O-Lure or that Rooster Tail and take whatever hits the line. I see all of this again in relation to an idea Jung had about creativity, that the seeds of creativity are mixed into what he calls "slime from the depth," that psychic slime where the ugliest and most animalistic aspects of our personalities reside. These are all those fearful things we've confined, repressed into our subconscious. But if you're after the creative impulse, you have to be willing to wallow around in that. Or, coming back to our metaphor, you have to be willing to drag up whatever hits your lure—gar, copperhead, water moccasin, alligator. When we confront the lower beasts of our psyche, we can be in for a dangerous encounter.

Your themes don't seem to have changed much over the course of your career. If anything the poems may have gotten somewhat darker. I know that you are happily married now and have a beautiful five-year-old daughter. How do you account for that bleakness of vision?
　My friend Dave Smith wrote an essay somewhere that all poems are about two things—life and death. I wrote a little piece a few years later and said that he was at least half right—all poems are really about death. We talk about this a lot in my classes, and one thing I like to point out to students is a book that turns up in Woody Allen's movie *Annie Hall*. Woody Allen and Diane Keaton are working on a relationship, a problem since he's the typical neurotic New Yorker and she's so sunny she wears flowers

on her hat. Well, they walk into this bookstore. He's just met her and wants to impress her, cue her in on everything that's important to him and such, so he takes her over to the psychology section. He reaches up and pulls a book off the shelf and camera zooms in. It's Ernest Becker's *The Denial of Death*. Of course, it's a pretty funny moment, but the first time I saw the movie, I was startled by that because I'd just finished reading *The Denial of Death*—a great book. Becker's premise is that the only real truth in our lives is our death. It's our one undeniable fact, nothing we can do about it, and Becker says that all the other aspects of our personalities are geared to deny it. They're all lies. Of course, they're very healthy and necessary lies. Otherwise we'd just step out in front of some truck. One of the best metaphors Becker uses to illustrate the nature of the personality is an onion. This onion represents the whole of your personality. You take it, put it down on the table, and slice it in half. The core is your death — the fact at the center-and all the layers built up around it are the various layers of your personality, all of your interests, your ambitions, the things you involve yourself in — I'm going to be a great poet, I'm going to be a great pianist, I'm going to be a great painter — the stuff that makes you believe in a future. Well, these things are only distractions, denials, lies. As life-affirming as they may be, they won't save us from out one undeniable fact. Where are Whitman and Emily Dickinson? Where's Vladimir Horowitz? Where are Gauguin, Matisse, Picasso? But here's the point. These things, even though they are lies, are the material out of which we create art. This is the stuff from which we make poems and stories. So, in that sense, all poems are about death. At the heart, at the core, there's always that fundamental truth. Even the sunniest person has this kind of death shadow, this dark spot at the core.

In a recent review, Benjamin Griffith points out that many of the new poems in Armored Hearts *are more openly Christian in their themes than your previous work. Could you comment on that?*

    Yes, I suppose he's right about that. I've been concerned over the last few years, maybe since the birth of my daughter, with the possibility of living a Christian life in our culture. So much in American life, at least in the popular culture, seems to mitigate against it. Perhaps this was always the case, but at forty-seven I seem to be getting more perspective on it. No, I don't actually believe that. I don't believe it was always the case. Things that were once relegated to the underworld are now mainstream virtues of pop culture. We've generally lost our ethical foundations. You don't have to look further than the local movie theatre or music store to see what virtues our culture holds in high esteem — violence, murder, rape, drugs, promiscuity, the general abuse of women. Of course, this view is very simplistic because I'm speaking so generally. Ours is a complex culture. Not everyone in America holds those values. But a significant number of people have developed a frightening tolerance of them, more than is healthy, and they generally have the advantage of fashion and fad. To make the situation even more perverse, among some folks — including many academics — traditional values are now thought to be deviant. The problem of the Christian in our culture no longer seems to be the task of converting the masses, which has become overwhelming, but the problem of survival without withdrawing entirely from the world.

How do these things relate to poetry today?

Well, poetry is individual vision. Pure art has no moral responsibility or agenda. But, generally speaking, poetry seems to me an antidote of sorts against much of our trouble — at least to the extent that it seeks to put us all in touch with our common humanity. Jung believed that in our rush to technology, Western societies lost touch with myth, and thus we lost our souls. I like to think of poetry, and all art, as the act of getting back in touch with the soul. The great difficulty in America is getting people to listen. Most folks are numb to the spiritual possibilities in their lives. As Ed Hirsch says in his poems "For the Sleepwalkers," "We have to drink the stupefying cup of darkness/and wake up to ourselves, nourished and surprised." This is no easy task, but there are a significant number of people in this country who have not been totally dulled by television and Hollywood. Here's an interesting irony. Over the last few years, what has probably generated the most public interest in poetry is not a poem or a book of poems, but a film. I'm speaking of *Il Postino*, the film about Pablo Neruda exiled on a Greek Island. It's marvelous to see how this semiliterate postman's encounter with Neruda opens up his life to the possibility of beauty and meaning. I'll bet Neruda's book sales have gone through the roof because of that movie. I hope so. I'd like to think that this could be the first step for many people who are thoughtful but still strangers to poetry. You'll note, though, that it's a foreign film. It was not made in Hollywood. American pop culture generally refuses to make its audience think, to confront meaningful issues such as values and faith. Oh, occasionally you'll see a TV sitcom deal with some current social issue — gay rights or interracial issues, the juicier the better — but how many prime-time programs have ever dealt with the problems of religious faith? Or have even suggested that anyone should think twice about such? Unfortunately, not many of our so-called serious writers even seem willing to deal with these questions, as though they were conveniently no longer relevant. The Greek poet C.P. Cavafy has a wonderful little poem called "The First Step" where he calls all poets "citizens of the city of ideas." I like that. But we need to remember also that there is good citizenship and bad citizenship. To be a good citizen of the "city of ideas" a writer must act in a responsible manner. This requires honesty of sentiment and approach. It also requires that a writer not trivialize, not turn his or her face from the important questions.

Let's use that to dig back into your own poetry. I remember in an early poem called "The Boy Shepherd's Simile" you talk about a time when "believing was an easy thing." Can you say something about the origins of that poem and what it tries to accomplish?

I was raised in Canton, Georgia, a small town about fifty miles north of Atlanta, and got my religious education at the Canton First Baptist Church. In the late fifties — when I was six, seven, and eight — my mother was superintendent of the Primary Department of the Sunday School. Every year, of course, they'd have the annual Christmas pageant — a manger scene on the front lawn — and when she couldn't recruit enough boys to play the parts of Joseph and the shepherds, which was always a problem, she didn't hesitate to draft me into service. For a boy that age, this meant a large dose of embarrassment — the indignity of being dressed in an old sheet, of having to hold a crooked stick and stand out in the cold beside a cow or goat, whatever animal could be dredged up off a farm, and also the horror of having all my friends come around with their Polaroids to take pictures that might be passed out at school. Children can find terror in the most innocent things. Anyway, the poem is spoken by one of these boy shepherds who is grown now and remembering those scenes. He's simply asking why anyone would go through that. He says, "This was not a child or king,/but Mary Sosebee's Christmas doll a year ago." Just a doll. So what does this have to do with adoration and devotion? What does it have to do with worship? The answer comes then in the simile, "But it was like a king." Whether or not the simile has any meaning depends, I suppose, on faith.

But you imply a contrast between the relative ease of a child's faith as opposed to the more difficult faith of an adult. For the culture as a whole, is faith a more difficult question in the nineties than it was in the fifties?

Probably. These times are less childlike, more cynical, more permissive. But faith has always been difficult. Most everything in the world argues against it. Just take history. How could God have permitted the Holocaust? Or slavery? Or the slaughter of the Jews during the Roman occupation of Jerusalem? According to Josephus, during the first Roman-Jewish war, over three thousand Jews were crucified in one day. Our times, at least in this country, are not so generally bloody. But yes, faith is a difficult matter, and coming to terms with human violence is far from the only threat. Our current myth is science, and science denies completely the ability to know except through the methods of science. We don't often talk about tension or conflict in poetry, at least not to the degree we discuss it in fiction, but conflict is important for creating intrigue in all art. What interests me very much are the poetic possibilities in the tension between the spiritual and the secular, what happens when these two realms collide, and the survival strategies faith seeks to employ. I tried to get at some of that in several of the new poems in *Armored Hearts*.

Is "The Blue Mountain" an example of that collision?

Yes. That poem comes from a story about my wife's family. She's from western Montana and was raised in a fairly strict fundamentalist church. The poem is about her niece and her niece's husband, who also belonged to a fundamentalist denomination. Anyway, one night a deacon in their church had a dream that God was going to burn Portland because of sinful doings. This was supposed to happen at a certain time, and so when the date got close this woman and her husband gathered their two year old, packed whatever they could into a van, and literally headed for the hills. Of course, Portland didn't burn. God apparently spared it. Well, when I heard about this, I couldn't believe it. How stupid, I thought, for these two kids — they were both very young — to leave their home and jobs and cart their baby off to the mountains. All to flee a nightmare sparked by someone's bad Mexican dinner. But then as I started to write a poem, as I started to involve myself in the situation, I had a change of heart. The more I got into the thing, the more I liked them. Eventually, I started thinking, "Now, that's real faith. I wish I had a faith like that." I came to see it as a faith one could put to some literal use in the world. The poem ends, though, on a note of ambiguity, and I wanted that. In the last few lines they seem reluctant to talk about what appears to have been their folly, but they've discovered something too. What they like to talk about instead are the owls they heard in the mountains during the boat trip they took. What they've experienced, of course, can be read as metaphor. The owls in the distance are heralding out those narrow passes.

Griffith writes in his essay that your attention to "emptiness" reminds him of a concept Flannery O'Connor was attracted to in the work of Pierre Teilhard de Chardin, namely "passive diminishment" or as Griffith says, "the serene acceptance of inevitable loss." Would you comment on this in relation to the later poems?

I believe he talking about that poem "Allatoona Evening," which I put at the end of the book. But what he says generally holds true for my later poems. I think what many are trying to do, especially in the last half of *Armored Hearts*, is find a gradual sort of working toward resignation and peace. Elizabeth Bishop says, "The art of losing isn't hard to master," but we all feel the tragic irony there. Christianity provides some help, of course, through a shedding of false ambition, which only creates in us anger and frustration. Poetry helps here also. That's what "Allatoona Evening" is about. It's an important poem for me in many ways, a poem that came out of many frustrations—about writing and teaching and other things—and I think the key lines of the poem are the ones that equate anger and ambition. The persona is out beside this lake at evening—he's going fishing—and it's a very peaceful scene, and suddenly he senses that the whippoorwills and the bats are telling him to lay down all his anger. "Lay it down, they say, your ambition,/which is only anger,/which sated could bring you to no better place." That's a powerful healing thought for me. Even if all our ambitions, which are generally misplaced anyway, were realized, they could bring us to no better spiritual place than this one moment beside this lake with "these three stars soaking up twilight." I like the ending of that poem as much as any I've ever written.

You said poetry helps us achieve this resignation. How does it help?

Well, in a number of ways. For one, it helps us ask the right questions about our lives. Literature never solves any of the great problems, of course, but it helps us define the significant questions and, in this way, provides a focus that helps us avoid the temptations of the superficial. I don't think that can be said about American culture in general, pop art, I mean. I'll give you one other way poetry can help too. Our whole lives are extended exercises in learning to accept loss. But as I've said before, literature can achieve a curious emotional bargain with death. Not that death negotiates very much. Still, a deal can be struck, good things may be wrenched from despair. Out of a good poem we can get understanding, resignation, empathy, even beauty. Occasionally in really fine poetry we may even find an aesthetic or emotional affirmation and transcendence.

What do you mean by that? Could you give us an example?

Sure. I love a little poem by Warren called "After the Dinner Party." The narrative runs something like this. An old couple is sitting around their table late at night. The dinner party is over, the guests are gone, the fire is burning down in the fireplace. Everything about the scene suggests an ending of things. They talk of the past for a while, of their children who are away and building their own lives. It's painfully clear that they understand the past is gone and that they can expect no real future. The woman snuffs out the candles, and they sit quietly in the last light of the fire. Then Warren writes: "Soon the old stairs/Will creak to a briefness of light, then true weight of darkness, and then/That heart-dimness in which neither joy nor sorrow counts." Now what could be darker than that? What could be bleaker and more honest? No joy in the past or the future, no sorrow, no human emotion will stop their inevitable separation. Then the last line, "Even so, one hand gropes out for another, again." An amazing affirmation — not of the past or the future, but of the only thing left, the moment. This is what real poetry can do, even against the inevitability of death. It can take the terrible, the frightening, the tragic, and transform it into something positive, something we might even call beautiful. Yes, I think that is a powerful help.

To Own My Father's Name: Not Hiding the Masculine

JANE HILL

Born in 1949, David Bottoms can be read as an archetypal baby-boomer poet, though to limit any writer's career to the historical function of being a spokesperson for his or her generation is inherently unfair.[1] Yet, as a male poet who came of age during the Vietnam era and the heyday of the contemporary women's movement, Bottoms both records and critiques the ideologies or, we might say, the baggage that comes with that particular journey. As a southern poet whose coming-of-age also coincides with the modern civil rights era, Bottoms becomes a cultural "three-fer"—a barometer by which we can assess who we are and how we have evolved during history's most instantaneously recorded and analyzed era of change.

In my reading of David Bottoms' poetry, I proceed with the supposition that he has relied primarily upon a single poetic persona throughout his career, and that we can trace the evolution of that persona—the first-person speaker of so many of his poems—from his early work of the 1970s up through *Vagrant Grace* (1999). In watching the shifts in that character's conception of his role as a man living within the specific current of history that distinguishes him from men of other times and places, we begin to see the poet's gradual yet steady (re)alignment with the traditional image of southern maleness even as we also note how he modifies and expands that image. In analyzing Bottoms' poetry, Ernest Suarez has cited Robert Penn Warren, who describes the poetic process as "a certain kind of freedom and lack of dogmatism under some notion of a shaping process" (73). Seeing him as being rooted firmly in this aesthetic tradition, Suarez argues that "Bottoms emphasizes the individual and universal instead of the social and topical" (74). But I want to depart slightly from this view of Bottoms' work, focusing instead on Warren's concept of the shaping process that works throughout a poet's career as well as in the genesis of individual works. The process by which Bottoms' career has been shaped, largely by coincidence of his birth date, makes any clear-cut separation of the individual and universal from the social and topical nearly impossible. Even if such ahistorical attention to this work were possible, omitting the questions posed by the poet's relationship to the social changes going on around him from an analysis of his work would undermine the richly complex interweaving of the individual and the social that is integral to Bottoms' poetry, and would create a somewhat misleading, even artificial, dichotomy.[2]

The basic questions that I want to pose concerning Bottoms' poetry are these: How and why does his poetic persona undergo this shift? And what are the particular gifts that the masculinity that ultimately presents itself within the context of his work offers its readers?[3] In pursuing these questions, I have found it helpful to organize the poems into four stages of Bottoms' experience as a baby-boomer male: boyhood foundations, adolescent rebellion, adult reconciliation, and fatherhood.

In 1979, Herb Goldberg articulated the dilemma of men living in an atmosphere of change regarding gender identity: "The masculine imperative, the pressure and compulsion to perform, to prove himself, to dominate, to live up to the 'masculine ideal'—in short, to 'be a man'—supersedes the instinct to survive" (1). Mark Gerzon, writing five years later, continues the same line of argument regarding masculine identity: "we want to be seen as real men, whatever that may mean to us. This need is so strong, so primitive, that some of us will risk anything to satisfy it" (2-3). Gerzon goes on to suggest that contemporary males struggling with their identity as males often find themselves misled by the models they adopt: "Thus men today consume certain images of manhood even though the world from which they are derived may have disappeared—if it ever existed" (5). In the turmoil of such social change and the ready availability of obsolete models, Gerzon argues that "true heroism" consists of "the courage to explore oneself deeply and to act with self-awareness" (6).

It is precisely such courage that I believe Bottoms displays in his poems. For *Armored Hearts: Selected and New Poems* (1995),[4] Bottoms takes as one of his epigraphs a passage from Saint Augustine: "My soul is like a house, small for you to enter, but I pray you to enlarge it. It is in ruins, but I ask you to remake it. It contains much that you will not be pleased to see: this I know and do not hide." If we read Bottoms' poetry as a reflection of his speaker's soul, we receive in this epigraph fair warning that all we encounter here might not be to our liking. Considering that three-fourths of this volume's contents come from earlier books, that the poems voiced by those "previous" selves inevitably will run afoul of latter-day notions about gender roles and other social expectations, we enter this poetic house armed with the poet's own proclamation about our possible and possibly negative responses and with his public affirmation of a decision that could have remained private, or at least unnoted in the volume's editorial apparatus: the poet has chosen not to hide. He will, rather, stand before us, warts (political or sociological) and all. He will even ask us to take note of the imperfections and, if our own abilities permit, to participate in the act of remaking them, of enlarging our sense of who and what a man such as this speaker was, is, and will become.[5]

Boyhood Foundations

In "Last Nickel Ranch: Plains, Montana," Bottoms sets a scene involving the family "of the woman / I love..." (AH 124); the patriarch, the woman's father, has called for the family to join in a huddle for prayer. The speaker, still an outsider here, knows in this situation some of the tension created between males that Michael Kimmel identifies in *Manhood in America: A Cultural History*: "the evaluative eyes of other men are always upon us, watching, judging" (7). When he is summoned to join the family circled in a hug, he ponders "the humility necessary for prayer," in effect acknowledging that he too is watching, judging, this man, the other male figure in the life of the woman he loves. Though the poem does not reveal whether the speaker joins the group, he does assert a strong confidence in his own moral system: "I know what I've valued" (AH 124).

This assertion comes from an adult version of the Bottoms persona, one who has passed through almost all the evolutionary stages I want to consider, with the exception of fatherhood. But the knowledge that he asserts here originates in a place familiar to anyone who has read this poet's work. What he has valued resides in the world of his boyhood, a space defined by the family, the churches, and the life of Canton, Georgia, during the 1950s and '60s.

If we grant that identity formation and values acquisition begin in the home, we can look to Bottoms' representations of his parents and other members of his extended family to begin defining what he has valued. In "The Christmas Rifle," Bottoms describes what is, for rural boys, an almost formalized rite of passage. With his father, he takes his first gun into the woods to learn the ways of hunting. Their ostensible target a squirrel, Bottoms and his father are really seeking through this male initiation ritual a bond that will mark their relationship for life. Looking back on this experience from adulthood, the speaker recalls two particularly vivid images: one is the dead squirrel itself, remembered in precisely the sort of sensory detail that foreshadows a poet's life, but the other and, I would argue, the far more significant image in terms of what this poet will grow up to value is the touch that signifies the father's unspoken praise for the child's success: "Just behind me, my father is walking on needles, / the weight of his hand comes down on my shoulder" (AH 50). Through the paradox of the fragility and tentativeness evoked by "walking on needles" and the sturdy, solid weight of the father's hand on his shoulder, Bottoms evokes much about the mysteries of parenting in the world that he grew up in.

The parallel poem to establish the place of Bottoms' mother during these formative years is "The Boy Shepherds' Simile.'" Taught the Christ story as a child, Bottoms recounts how even from "an early age I understood the problems this story presented and wrestled with them in my own ways, which I touched on years later in ... 'The Boy Shepherds' Simile'" ("Turn Your Radio On" 87). He goes on to provide background information on his mother's role as superintendent of the Sunday school and as organizer of the annual nativity scene performed on the church lawn. Because of his mother's role within the church (and hence the community), Bottoms found himself regularly installed in these productions (87). Thus, we can assume that it is, at least in part, for his mother and in recognition of the values that she represents that the young shepherd served and that the older man looking back at that service can endorse it:

> This was not a child wrapped in the straw
> and the ragged sheet, but since believing was an easy thing
> we believed it was like a child,
> a king who lived in the stories we were told.
> For this we shivered in adoration. We bore the cold [AH 40].

Here again, the closing image is one of weight, of tangible physical presence. The child shepherds bear the cold, but, in so doing, they experience acceptance from the parent figure who has placed them in this display The fragility in this dynamic is more complicated in some ways than the fragility of walking on needles in "The Christmas Rifle," for here the point of delicacy is an issue of imaginative understanding, of the children's (perhaps innate) ability to understand the figurative as a means of understanding something deeper, more mysterious, and finally "unconfirmable" ("Turn Your Radio On" 86).

By setting each of these parent poems in the context of the Christmas season, Bottoms establishes links between the narrative of his life — its nativity — and the broader implications of the Christian narrative (especially as rendered by Southern Baptists: "the stories we were told"). In a poem about another of his family mentors, his grandfather, Bottoms solidifies our sense of how his life has been measured against that particular narrative. In "A Tent Beside the River," the speaker and a group of children who are his cousins (because Bottoms is an only child and all the children represented have a grandfather in common, I am calling them cousins) spend the last hours of their grandfather's life holding their own church service in a tent outside the house where their relative lies dying. By lantern light they congregate "to call into play [their] own miracle," singing what they can remember of the church hymns they've grown up with, hoping "to be heard / only by the One we wanted to hear" (AH 97). While the capitalization of *One* asks us to read the antecedent as God (or Christ) — the ultimate patriarch — the poem also invites us, through the children's naive perspective, to read the antecedent as the grandfather, who would have taught them the context into which they are now trying to place the incomprehensible fact of his impending death. The speaker, the best reader among the children, reads from the Bible as they ponder their grandfather's contemplation of his passage across the River Jordan (again, Bottoms references the stories any Southern Baptist would have grown up with).

When morning comes, the children's parents find them "huddled / in a ball like a litter of strays" (97–98) and urge them back to the "real" world, in which children are incapable of comprehending, much less facilitating, the safe passage of a dying man. The speaker, however, makes clear that these parents are mistaken; these children have experienced a transcendent moment during their makeshift revival:

> each of us saw him in a special way.
> Then the owl came down to find us, whistled
> a note of departure, and we remembered,
> real or not, a shadow drifting over the roof [98].

Even from the perspective of adult memory — the poem's first word is "Remembering" — the speaker authenticates the child's belief, an affirmation of the grandfather's value system, whether the shadow seen was or was not "real."

In "Sermon of the Fallen," an unspecified patriarchal figure tells the alert young speaker a story about death as the older man works over a "walnut box." The story might be the teller's version of William Cullen Bryant's "Thanatopsis," an account somehow both scientific and romantic of what happens to matter, including human bodies, at death. Because the Bottoms persona is mentored by Baptists rather than American Romantics, however, the story somehow takes a Puritan twist at the end: "So, he said, you had come to fall." Again, in his adult memory of the child's response, Bottoms provides a clue as to the value system that shaped him: "Even as a boy, I could feel the trembling in us all" (AH 41).

Although this moral system has as a foundational element a certain sternness, for the believer it also provides a longed-for comfort. In "Zion Hill," a self-ostracized speaker imagines "the elect of [his] family drenc[ing] themselves to the soul" while he sits alone, refusing to seek the revival embraced by the others. But he shows no sense of rejecting their goal: "who could ever stop desiring / that serenity? Even if it's less out of devotion / than despair." Nor does the speaker suggest that he is no longer a seeker or that he has found a surer path to such serenity:

> it's not because I'm someone
> who wants to be unremembered in his troubles,
> or considers himself a physician
> equal to his own heart [AH 133].

Unable to feel with conviction what those elect of his family feel, the speaker nonetheless endorses their value system. In "Free Grace at Rose Hill," the speaker remembers a Sunday walk undertaken

> to hear the many tongues rendering into one
> the promise of an old hymn
> and [feel] yourself listening suddenly
> with your heart...

—but this still unevolved male figure can only recognize his limitations: "I listened / my whole boyhood / and my listening couldn't save me." The poem's closing lines link his status as unelect directly to the concept of grace: "If it touches us, / it touches us" (AH 132), a recognition that can—

and, in the subsequent stage of our male protagonists development, does — create a period of rebellion, of rejection of the patriarchy from which one springs.

In three early (and related) poems — "Jamming with the Band at the VFW," "Writing on Napkins at the Sunshine Grill," and "In Jimmy's Grill" — although the speaker is chronologically an adult, he still appears to be seeking to make his way in the secular world according to the standards and values of his father's and grandfather's generations. In "Jamming," the speaker chooses to identify with "all men turning gray who dream of having died / at Anzio, Midway, Guadalcanal" and wants to dance with one of "their" women. Because the text of "Writing on Napkins" specifies the time and place of its composition — "Macon, Georgia, 1970" — we can assume that the speaker is twenty, perhaps twenty-one, and a college student. He sees himself as a struggling young artist who feels usurped, made extraneous by the poets of a jukebox featuring "nothing recorded since 1950." These artistic forebears create within the speaker a classic case of the anxiety of influence; as "father" figures, they make him feel small. In "Jimmy's Grill," the speaker and a male companion consciously choose "the back of the room / where a beer gut rolls like a melon on the green pool table" over "The girl in blue jean shorts" because connecting with the female would necessitate "buying a few beers / or telling a lie about the money we made last year" (AH 17). Because this version of the Bottoms persona measures himself against the values of earlier generations and finds himself wanting, he retreats into something close to melancholy self-pity.

Adolescent Rebellion

Not all adolescent rebellions actually occur during adolescence, of course. Sometimes an adult, measured chronologically, reverts to adolescent behavior for any number of reasons. Sometimes a young adult who has grown up in a sheltered, relatively conservative environment finds him or herself ready to rebel the moment he or she leaves home.

Representing rebellion against authority is hardly territory Bottoms can claim as exclusive, but Joe L. Dubbert argues that men growing up in post World War II America found themselves constrained in particular ways that often led to a kind of hyper-rebellion, an overcompensation for the standardization of middle-class American life in that era. Dubbert reports that Edward Strecker, a psychiatrist at the University of Pennsylvania, blamed the "progressive" education movement of the post–war era as "[militating] against a basic masculine instinct of wanting to be aggressive and dominant." Strecker believed that men so schooled "were unprepared for the rigors of the real world.... The result was immaturity and, frequently, a behavior pattern of overcompensation for a felt lack of masculinity" (240–41).

Another factor in Dubbert's analysis of the post–war male mentality is the company man of the 1950s, a figure captured by the image of the man in the gray-flannel suit, a victim of regimentation and rigid social norms that promised, in return, through corporate "pronouncements about togetherness," a new "security and contentment for all" (243). Quoting David Cohn, Dubbert describes the not unsurprising male reaction to this dynamic: "To feel manly, men had to go off to the club, drink, and tell off-color stories 'on the theory [that] this is virile'" (252). Kimmel agrees that, for men of this post–war generation, "Becoming a 'bad boy' [became] a positive goal with important social consequences" (228).

Dubbert reads Norman Mailer's representations of the male figure as indicative of this mindset. He says of Mailer's males, "The real male is a truly virile male, the hunter of animal flesh and the pursuer of sex. To do both well is to achieve and fulfill the American success story, the success of grace and salvation in finding one's manhood" (264). Dubbert goes on to list "the very attributes that ... come to be associated with the most red-blooded masculine men"; these men are "individualistic, anti–authority, and cunning" (259).

When Alice Friman and Bruce Gentry ask Bottoms about the use of crime as a recurrent trope in his work, both fiction and poetry, Bottoms makes an immediate link to common "impulses in our lives, these notions that we as individuals are really more significant than any imposed authority" (102), an observation that both links Bottoms to the mindset described by these social scientists and separates him, at least temporarily, from the value system of his fathers (and his Father, if we accept his statement to Friman and Gentry that "In the poems religion is ... personal and substantial, important in a ... direct way.... It's fundamental to the poems" [104]).

Although certainly not the most vivid example of the impulse to rebel in the Bottoms persona, "The Window" provides evidence of consciously risky behavior during the speaker's high-school years. He and his friends, "After school, newly licensed / by the state" and thus authorized, in one way, drive in "reckless" carloads to observe a mythic, perhaps ghostly, female figure who is reputed to sit in a certain window in a certain house. In this teen boy's fantasy of encountering the female, the speaker points out that element of the experience that is its rebellion: in their effort to validate their sighting, they swear "no matter what speed we tore from the wheels / of our fathers" that they have seen the woman. Eventually, a teen driver risks too much and dies at the curve where the house sits. The speaker confesses that this rebellion took place "half my life ago" and informs us that he hasn't "swerved since / into the wrong lane of any curve" (AH 103).

But any number of other Bottoms poems in the volumes published by Copper Canyon tells us that the speaker's rebellion against the authority of family and church did not stop with high-school reckless driving. Of those poems in *Armored Hearts* that Bottoms selected from *Shooting Rats at the Bibb County Dump*, his first book, originally published in 1980, the first six — "Wrestling Angels" (3), "Smoking in an Open Grave" (4), "Shooting Rats at the Bibb County Dump" (5), "The Drunk Hunter" (6), "Below Freezing on Pinelog Mountain" (7), and "Cockfight in a Loxahatchee Grove" (8) — deal with activities that are not only rebellious but also sometimes illegal. These poems feature cemetery vandals, dope smokers who profane graves, drunks shooting rats in a garbage dump, drunken hunters, and cockfighters. Surely, this is Bottoms' southern version of Mailer's men.

It is also these poems that have been most persistently claimed as the essence of David Bottoms' work. When Georgia Governor Roy Barnes named Bottoms the state's poet laureate in May 2000, he cited the way that "Shooting Rats" evoked the realities of his own boyhood as one of the reasons he connected with the poetry. Barnes, himself only a few years older than Bottoms, believes that he and the poet share a vision of what growing up male in the Deep South was like forty or fifty years ago. Commenting as recently as 1997 about his response to the first review of *Shooting Rats* that he read, Bottoms recalls an illustration that accompanied the *Atlanta Journal-Constitution*'s lead review: the drawing featured "a young man leaning against the fender of a '57 Chevy in the background," Bottoms reports, "a gigantic bottle of Jim Beam stood like a monument to male adolescence.... I was cast for all time into the pit of southern male chauvinism with the likes of Harry Crews and James Dickey" ("Turn Your Radio On" 85). Robert Hill has noted the same phenomenon in relation to response to Bottoms' work. He says, "Early in David Bottoms' career, it was easy but wrong to identify him as a shit-kicking would-be cowboy ... a mimic of James Dickey ... a picaroon" (80). Michael Skube, in profiling Bottoms upon the occasion of his laureateship, says, "You don't have to be around Bottoms long to know what revs his engine. A sweet-running pickup, bluegrass the way it's supposed to be played, old tapes of the late Duane Allman's guitar riffs, a cut of beef at Longhorn Steakhouse, poetry that hears the deep truths the world is trying to tell us" (F1). Skube also notes the irony of the country boy's residing in fashionable East Cobb County, one of metropolitan Atlanta's pricey suburbs, suggesting that the poet's "groundedness" comes more from his "simple upbringing in Canton than [from] his upscale neighborhood" (F2).[6] In repeated ways, critics and others have cast Bottoms as a poet and a thinker defined primarily, if not exclusively, by a very small and generally quite early sampling of his increasingly deep and broad body of work.

Both Don Russ and Ernest Suarez have named part of what is happening in these poems as what Russ calls "directly, if somewhat meditatively, mocking the trappings of conventional religion" (66). Suarez says of the group vandalizing the cemetery in "Wrestling Angels" that "They ravage whatever reminds them of the metaphysical because they dread it and want to affirm their secular perspective" (77). While both critics are right to place the acts of rebellion in this and other similar poems from this period in the context of a rebellion against religion per se, I believe we can also read the aberrant behavior as part of the speaker's rebellion against those father figures of previously cited poems against whose experience he has measured himself and come up short. The only advantage he has to wield against these perceived adversaries is his youth, so the vandals in "Wrestling Angels" transform the angels into "old men lamenting their age." While in an earlier era such angels might have had the cultural strength to prevent "needless" vandalism, they "have grown / too weak to wrestle," and the vandals' stated purpose is to use their "crowbars and drag chains"— images that evoke the James Dean/Marlon Brando stereotype of the masculine —"to salvage from the dead" (3). On a literal level, the dead are those who lie in the graves being scavenged; metaphorically (and ironically, because this behavior is, among other things, an avoidance of direct confrontation with the antagonist), the dead become the strong (and obviously still living) images of the father that the speaker has internalized.[7]

The speaker in "Coasting Toward Midnight at the Southeastern Fair" assumes that his resistance to authority and boundaries is, if not universal, at least common to those of his generation:

> We all want to break our orbits
> . . .
> run the risk of disintegration.
> We all want to take our lives in our hands
> and hurl them out among the stars [AH 9].

While Robert Hill has called it "ludicrous to think of Bottoms' even considering to write something as thunderously challenging to created heavens as Dickey's *The Zodiac*" (81), his thinking applies primarily to the later poems of suburban life. In this image from a much earlier poem, while the speaker doesn't evoke a Dickeyesque challenge to the Creator in the form he chooses for voicing this desire, he does suggest that his rebellion includes something of a desire that Dickey surely would recognize.

In "Black Camaro," the speaker sets out to steal the car of Billy Parker, whose life, as the speaker perceives it, is the opposite of the orbit-breaking defiance desired in "Coasting Toward Midnight at the Southeastern Fair." Instead of breaking free, Billy Parker finds himself digging deeper and deeper into the traditions of middle-class domestic life:

> and I could hear through the cricket chatter
> the rockers on Billy Parker's chair
> grinding ridges into his living room floor,
> worry working on him like hard time [AH 47].

By comparing the consequences of Parker's choices to hard time, Bottoms' speaker suggests that he's running no greater risk in stealing a car than does the man who sits

> rocking in his chair,
> studying his coverage, his bank account,
> his layoff at Lockheed, his wife laboring
> in the maternity ward [47].

Crime exacts no higher penalty than does ordinary life; therefore, a man might just as well enjoy the risk and excitement of life beyond quotidian boundaries.[8]

Several poems from Bottoms' second book, *In a U-Haul North of Damascus*, capture the male tendency to incorporate elements of resistance to the civilizing, or limiting, nature of middle-class life within that life itself. In both "Neighbors, Throwing Knives" and "Local Quarrels," men seek to recreate something of the male wilderness experience in their suburban environments. In "Neighbors," the speaker and his knife-throwing companions use the sport of throwing at "Magic Marker images" of various beasts to "gauge the fine balance / between what is real and what is imagined," to "whet [their] aim" in their world of "boxwoods manicured by wives" (AH 33). "Local Quarrels" describes a suburban cocktail party turned into a duel for a group of men who exit the gathering to watch their "principals" settle a quarrel "[a]s though the nineteenth century hadn't crumbled / and polite society still made pretensions / about honor" (35). Although neither of the principals falls as a result of the exchange of gunfire, their effort to dramatize their differences in this manner that harkens back to an earlier code of male behavior makes them typical of a tension in many of Bottoms' rebellious males. They often seek to solve contemporary problems according to codes of male behavior from a less ambiguous time.

In another of the poems most often cited to establish Bottoms' "bad boy" persona, "Crawling Out at Parties," the speaker takes the movement backward in time even further. He sees his "natural" self, what we might call his truly masculine self, as caged by modern social expectations, and praises the Scotch that frees him from those inhibitions and allows this other self to (re)emerge. This "old reptile" self enjoys particularly encounters with "tight-skirted girls," further emphasizing the connections between the speaker's conception of self and issues of gender identity and interaction. The irony, however, of the temporary freedom that the Scotch allows this aspect of the speaker's self is that, in his contemporary world, this self is "out of date" and "moves awkwardly." Apparently rebuffed by the women he approaches, he finds himself out of options, "so slides back always to his antique home, / the stagnant, sobering water" (AH 22).

As in "In Jimmy's Grill," the speaker here chooses not to pursue interaction with the female because of limitations he sees within himself. Sometimes Bottoms names his speaker's limitations as economic, as in "A Home Buyer Watches the Moon":

And I,
who can no longer afford to live
in my two-story, have come out into the street
to stare past the mailboxes at an abrupt dead end [AH 34].

Here, the conception of the masculine is clear: if one cannot be a provider of a certain sort, one is not a man and faces only a dead end. No other future is imaginable. Yet, in later poems, such as "In Heritage Farms, Settled," the speaker continues to live that life he cannot really afford, watches "the Volvos crawl through the streets ... and neighbors / ... water / the same pink rose for an hour" (AH 82), and he laments the very condition that has defined successful masculinity in "A Home Buyer Watches the Moon":

> What worries me most is this constant settling,
> my dog refusing to bark at joggers, content to stalk
> to the edge of the porch, whimper back
> to his nap, his muscles breathing [34].

Torn between the fear of becoming Billy Parker, rocking himself into the deadly groove of middle-class responsibility in "Black Camaro," and the panic of not being able to pay for exactly those things Parker sits calculating his ability to pay, the speaker projects his fears onto his dog. Even a beast finds his natural impulses deadened, his will to assert his dog masculinity undercut by the life being lived in Heritage Farms. The name of the subdivision, then, becomes ironic because the narrator has moved to the contemporary rendering of his rural past, only to find himself still not measuring up to the males of the preceding generation in terms of being a provider and maintaining his sense of himself as a man. In "The Catfish," the speaker stops on the bridge at St. Simons, Georgia, to "rescue" a catfish abandoned there by the fisherman who caught him and deemed him "too small to keep." The narrator identifies with the fish's dilemma and tenderly picks him up with a towel and throws him high over the bridge's rail so that the fish might reconnect with his natural habitat, a place where he is an acceptable creature of acceptable size. Metaphorically, the narrator sees himself sending the fish out of water "back to the current of our breathable past" (AH 23).

Just such a return to a "breathable past" is what the rebellious Bottoms comes to long for more than anything else. In the poem that suggests the speaker's involvement in the most dramatic illegal activity rendered in *Armored Hearts*, the narrator in "Rendezvous: Belle Glade" finds himself participating in a Florida drug drop. As he waits for the plane bearing "wrapped bales" that will hit "between the strands of light" (43), he thinks not so much of the present reality and what it says about him and his life as about a British soldier stationed in Burma in a much earlier era. That legitimate military man from the breathable past might have used the pawnshop gun that the speaker now holds. By connecting psychologically to the British soldier's fears and jumpiness in a combat environment, the speaker seeks imaginatively to legitimize his illegitimate activity. He seeks to be a soldier like the soldier his father (literal or metaphoric) had been, but he knows that he pursues a course of action that will not lead to such a resolution.

In "Hiking Toward Laughing Gull Point," the aging speaker enacts an annual ritual walk but realizes that he is reaching a point of no return, that the options open to him diminish year by year, just as his hairline recedes:

> I think how the point
> keeps drifting farther away
> like some water-mirage
> or a piece of land in a speculator's dream.
> How each summer I search for my dream
> vacation, only to find myself feeling more like some gull
> climbing toward the edge of an island,
> a hook, the end of the line [AH 32].

Perhaps no poem from his early work captures the struggle within Bottoms' persona to reconcile his impulse to rebel with his desire to deserve his father's name, to be a rightful inheritor of the mantle of the patriarch's experience, than does "Light of the Sacred Harp." Beginning as a classic rebellion poem in the manner of "Wrestling Angels" or "Shooting Rats," "Light" depicts the speaker and a group of fellow drunks as they find their way to a rural church, where, for warmth, they proceed to set hymnals afire in a trash can. They see themselves as transforming "God's old house" through the "good new warmth" generated by their bottle; they too are transformed through "the plasma of visionaries and hunters" (AH 44). Eventually their fire gets out of control — along with the hymnals, they toss in withered altar flowers and funeral-home fans that picture Jesus in various scenes from scripture — until ultimately the pulpit itself catches fire. This cleansing blaze causes them to "kneel / for drunkenness and joy," to hear the pure spirit

> of voices returning in the joyful noise
> of the Sacred Harp, singing over and over

> the good gospel news that men do rise from dust
> and ashes [AH 45].

Here, the speaker takes a sudden, dramatic turn back to the boyhood values that are the essence of his identity, and he longs to believe that, for him, there is still time to rise from the ashes of the dead ends and the destructive desires that have dominated his experience during his period of rebellion. He longs to believe that he still might become a man.

By understanding that the poems in *Armored Hearts* are arranged in four sections, presented chronologically, readers can see that the phases of development that I am suggesting in the Bottoms speaker are not part of a clear-cut, linear progression, but that these aspects of the speaker's psyche rise up and recede periodically throughout this character's development. It is possible, however, to see in each of the book's four sections an emphasis on a specific phase; in that way, there is something of a chronology to the progression of the narrative persona. "Sign for My Father, Who Stressed the Bunt" comes roughly one-third of the way through Part II of *Armored Hearts*, included with the selections taken from the poet's second book, *In a U-Haul North of Damascus*. This poem, which clearly harkens back to the speaker's boyhood and which pairs nicely with "The Christmas Rifle" as an initiation poem of sorts, again suggests that the speaker's childhood was one typical for male children of the post–war generation. The men of that generation, according to Gerzon, turned the baseball diamond into "a gymnasium of American virtues." "Behind the Chrysler factory," he says, "were the baseball diamonds. Inside the factory, men shaped auto bodies. On the diamonds, men shaped [their sons]" (155). What was true in Detroit was also true in Canton, Georgia, where the speaker's father's hand cuts a "rough diamond, / ... below the dog lot and barn," where he rehearses his son in "the strict technique / of bunting." Although the father is an excellent bunter with control and skill to envy, the son cannot keep his "eyes off the bank / that served as our center-field fence" (AH 39). The father is trying to teach a controlled, responsible, workable path to success; the son longs to let one fly over the center-field fence as a visible sign of his power, his personal sense of the masculine.

In this baseball metaphor, Bottoms evokes perfectly the essential conflict between father and son, between the World War II generation and their baby-boomer offspring. Contrary to well-entrenched stereotypes of the war generation, "individual accomplishment and being a hero were," according to Dubbert, "secondary to the vast majority of soldiers, who fought more for self-protection rather than for personal glory or adventure, the kind of quest for action that had characterized a Hemingway and Dos Passos in 1917" (234). Thus the bunt is the perfect skill for such a father to pass on, but his child, consumed perhaps by images manufactured by Hollywood or other elements of the cultural myth-making machinery, seeks a more heroic model than that implied by the bunter. Even as the son passes through "three leagues of organized ball" and finds himself able to "homer / into the garden behind the bank, / into the leftfield lot of Carmichael Motors," still the father keeps stressing the bunt, "the same technique, / the crouch and spring, the arm absorbing / just enough impact." And still the son resists: "That whole tiresome pitch / about basics never changing, / and I never learned what you were laying down" (AH 39).

The father wants to teach his son something far more important than the bunt, something of greater significance than baseball. Like those Chrysler fathers, he is trying to teach his son to be a man; the baseball diamond and the bunt are merely tools for the work of fathering. The adult son who looks back through this poem is a person just now beginning to absorb the metaphor that defines his relationship with his father. In adulthood, he can say, through his own metaphor of the poem, that he is finally receiving the message: "Like a hand brushed across the bill of a cap / let this be a sign / I'm getting a grip on the sacrifice" (AH 39).

If this poem about baseball can be seen as a defining statement about the links between the speaker's childhood and the path that he ultimately will take to male adulthood, a poem from near the end of Part II of *Armored Hearts*—the title poem from Bottoms' second book, "In a U-Haul North of Damascus"—serves as an equally helpful marker by which to gauge the poetic persona's recognition that rebellion in and of itself is truly the dead end of "A Home Buyer Watches the Moon," the hook that awaits the gull in "Hiking Toward Laughing Gull Point." The poem that precedes "U-haul" in *Armored Hearts*, "In a Pasture Under a Cradled Moon," links the loss of a child to miscarriage with a hard-gained knowledge about adult love and loss. "U-haul" picks up the life-altering event of the miscarriage ("that morning long ago / just before I watched the future miscarried" [641] and connects that loss to the impending loss of the marriage within which the lost child was conceived.

In leaving his marriage, the speaker seems to take with him only items that define his rebellious self, possessions that mark him as male:

> So the jon boat muscled up the ramp,
> the Johnson outboard, the bent frame of the wrecked Harley
> chained for so long to the back fence,
> the scarred desk, the bookcases and books,
> the mattress and box springs,
> a broken turntable, a Pioneer amp, a pair
> of three-way speakers, everything mine
> I intended to keep. Everything else abandon [63–64].

Among the things abandoned are his failures within the environment of the marriage:

> Lord, what are the sins
> I have tried to leave behind me? The bad checks,
> the workless days, the Scotch bottles thrown across the fence
> and into the woods, the cruelty of silence,
> the cruelty of lies, the jealousy,
> the indifference? [63]

Thus a "bad boy" seeks to drive away from his failed adult-male experience, packs emblems of what he has perceived his male identity to be shaped from, and rides away in a rented truck, thinking his sins can be abandoned along with his marriage, his failed self.

But awakening in the morning sun of a vacant field "on Georgia 54 / a few miles north of Damascus" (AH 63), the speaker finds himself taking cues from nature that suggest that "the world really could be clean again" (64). From the biblical associations of the name of the town near which he finds himself, the speaker generates a series of questions to suggest that he will become someone who understands, at long last, the lessons of his fathers, both literal and biblical:

> Could I be just another sinner who needs to be blinded
> before he can see grace? Lord, is it possible to fall
> toward grace? Could I be moved
> to believe in new beginnings? Could I be moved? [64–65]

The poems that comprise the third and fourth phases in the evolution of Bottoms' poetic persona suggest that the answer to all four of these questions is yes: he will be moved toward embracing the very values he rebelled against. His new beginning will, in fact, be a return to his original identity: he will finally come to own his father's name, which is his own as well.

Adult Reconciliation

Despite the emphasis in discussions of Bottoms' work on poems pertinent to the first two phases of development as outlined above, more poems focus on issues of adult reconciliation, including the culminating stage of the speaker's own fatherhood, than on these earlier developmental stages. Thus mine is partly a task of redirecting attention toward this work somewhat different in tone and emphasis with the end of establishing a more balanced and complete understanding of Bottoms' speaker and, consequently, of his overriding poetic vision.

In "Sounding Harvey Creek," the speaker acknowledges that, for him, the point of fishing is not fishing itself, in any traditionally masculine sense, but water, the basic element in which fishing takes place. That element, often associated with the feminine rather than the masculine, is to the speaker "mystery, / the something unknowable" that he pursues despite an "ignorance of fishing" and of the instruments that he characterizes as "dull / and virginal Eagle Claws" and an "impotent wealth of jitterbugs." By casting this imagery in sexual terms and imagining the fishing apparatus as "glow[ing] like jewelry" (AH 57) in his tackle box, the speaker begins to complicate the reader's sense of who he is and how he sees himself in relation to traditional conceptions of gender.

Although "In the Ice Pasture" figures the speaker in traditional heroic terms — he runs from his safe suburban home onto the icy but cracking surface of a pond to save a trapped horse — and suggests a mythic solution to the transformation the speaker prays for in "U-Haul," ultimately the heroic self-conception is undercut by the horse's having to save the speaker, who becomes finally only a passenger in the transforming experience. This poem, the first from *Under the Vulture-Tree* in *Armored Hearts*, is followed by "White Shrouds," a poem that recounts a much subtler but ultimately much more significant transformation within the speaker. In this poem, also set during an uncharacteristically cold southern winter, the speaker displays a protective impulse toward his wife that is similar to that directed toward the horse in the previous poem. But here the heroics spring from his willingness to accept the mundane responsibility of turning a single night's worth of wood, burned in a shallow fireplace meant mostly for decoration, into the warmth necessary to sustain the couple during a power outage caused by a freakish ice storm. A sense of responsibility to others, raised to the level of heroism, emerges here and will become central to the character of the "adult" Bottoms. He phrases this new version of heroism in language specifically linked to gender and, more specifically, to the male's role within marriage when he says that the husband stays awake all night, his beard freezing in the den's frigid air, in order "to husband the small logs, two at a time, onto the fire" (74).

Even as the speaker comes to redefine the heroic in this context — he must remain awake enough to husband, essentially — he also recognizes the limitations of male agency within the domestic world of the suburbs. In "The Voice of Wives Dreaming," the speaker imagines a gendered response to the drowning of a neighborhood child. In this scenario, the men are, like the husband in "White Shrouds," wakeful, but they also "[know] / in this we account for nothing." The dreaming wives have a visionary power that takes them beyond what the men can know or do: they "[float] face down / dreaming the voice of a different child" (AH 80). Two other poems suggest a similar male response to the complexities of negotiating a gendered world. In "The Resurrection," the speaker returns to Rose Hill Cemetery (an early Bottoms locale) as a setting, but this time his companion is a woman with whom he debates the question of the afterlife and whom he dares to enter an open grave as a means of settling their differences. He knows that this strategy is flawed, but he also believes in the possibility of renewal if he can make some kind of connection with this "other" who is so clearly different from his earlier cemetery companions.

"Home Maintenance" is even more direct in its assessment of the gulf that separates male and female in the contemporary domestic space. Portraying a scene of domestic violence, including male denial as part of that landscape, the speaker here abandons first-person narration for a generic second-person pronoun, casting the male figure as "you." Through this narrative strategy, Bottoms signals to his readers that certain elements of his portrait of the male are perhaps separate from his own lived experience (or are lived experiences that he is less than willing to claim directly), but more significant perhaps is the suggestion that the limited male ability to "read" female actions is a generic attribute of the gender. He conveys this assessment through standard poetic imagery made ironic by the poem's dramatic situation: "Even now her meaning slips through your fingers / as she raises a glove full of roses" (AH 120).

When this inability to read the signs a woman sends is contrasted with an entirely successful though silent communication between male and female, such as that represented in "Shingling the New Roof," we return to the speaker's need to reconcile himself with the image of his father. In "Shingling," the speaker looks back at another childhood experience: he helps his father and grandfather put on a new roof, an activity that his mother is convinced he is too small to participate in. When the speaker falls, only to be caught by his father, whose face is "whiter than caulk," he remembers vividly "the expression / that passed from [his mother's] face to his [father's]" (AH 99), a look so clear in what it communicates that the speaker spends the rest of the day on the porch with his mother, contemplating the deep bruise created by his father's desperate grip as it emerges on his wrist. Here, not only can he see his mother's message sent and successfully received by his father, but he can also read, in the bruise that now marks him, the power of the commitment that his parents have to each other and to him.

According to Kimmel, after World War II, "It was often as fathers that men sought to anchor their identities as successes as men," and, he goes on to say, "In the increasingly suburban postwar world, fathers embodied masculinity" (226–27). I would suggest that the young speaker in "Shingling the New Roof" reads precisely this message in the brief moment of silent communication between his parents, and I would further argue that the speaker's chief goal in terms of reconciling himself to his adult role is to come to terms with the concept of masculinity embodied in this particular image of his father.

Because it is often easier to deal with surrogates than with the real thing, Bottoms offers a series of poems representing specific male artists as such surrogates. As the speaker comes to terms with each of these "historical" father figures, he prepares himself for the eventual task of coming to terms with his actual father. "Homage to Lester Flatt" takes as its epigraph the telling line, "Troublesome waters I'm fearing no more" and ends by addressing the musician directly: "Lester, singing whatever we want to about the dead / is the easiest thing in the world. / Believing it the hardest" (AH 88). "Face Jugs: Homage to Lanier Meadows" makes even more explicit the speaker's willingness to explore links between himself and his fathers, both literal and metaphoric, in order to find the belief that will carry him past his adolescent doubts. Looking at the shelves holding the sculptor's jugs with faces, the speaker suddenly finds himself among the ceramic faces staring back at him, and, "happy as a man who's found his puzzle's missing piece, / it frightens you to think you might have left him" (89). The gospel banjo of Little Roy Lewis serves as the vehicle of the speaker's return from a three-day fever in "Gospel Banjo: Homage to Little Roy Lewis," a return to reality for which he is grateful, despite the beauty of the music-inspired dream of his fever. In all three of these "homage" poems, we see the speaker honoring a father figure and choosing to deepen his understanding of self and father through the act of voicing his homage.

In "Fiddle Time," the musician father figure has no name, but it is from this unnamed figure in the speaker's past that he takes his first memory of music. This mentor instills in the speaker the true artist's desire, the level of caring necessary to art, and, in memory, these gifts of process are even more significant than those of product — the actual music the fiddler was able to produce:

> The truth is
> he wasn't that smooth a fiddler. But he cared
> for the fiddle, and in memory's raw first music
> I still catch a measure of that care [AH 96].

This level of care is, in essence, an aural rendering of the bruise that is the visual sign of caring in "Shingling the New Roof." As the speaker begins to connect the concerns of such artists with the concerns of living and, more specifically, with the concerns of domestic life, he moves ever closer to adult manhood, as Bottoms will come to define it, and toward fatherhood.

While each of these artist figures is a musician or a visual artist, in "A Canoe," which carries the inscription "remembering James Dickey," Bottoms comes to terms with the figure who has been most often cited as his poetic "father." Written after Dickey's death, this poem finds the speaker contemplating an empty red canoe making its way down a river. He notes its effect — or lack thereof — on three fishermen it passes; they continue to lounge in lawn chairs, waiting for carp to bite. Unlike the speaker, they feel no need to make a metaphor of the empty canoe. But to him — the Bottoms persona — the canoe represents the deepest possible stirring humans could ask for; to him, it is "A metaphor untethered, loose / and retrievable, / but drifting away ..." (VG 62). This crucial acknowledgment that our best efforts to make meaning, achieve knowledge, and come to understanding are ultimately never enough, and can never be adequate to the reality we seek to know and understand, does not mean that we should cease our ultimately doomed attempts to grasp the essence of the father, to shape what we can come to know through metaphor into meaning. But the speaker's reverent representation of the poetic father as a metaphor finally free of our efforts to make him mean is possible largely because that speaker has come to terms, between the earlier homage poems and this one, with the literal father and with his own limited abilities to render the father his due, either through art and/or through the poet's living his own "real" life.

Just as the understanding evidenced in "A Canoe" springs from the speaker's being positioned on the river bank in a way that allows him to see canoe, fishermen, and the relationship between them, most similar recognitions depend upon the perceiver's positioning himself appropriately. While every narrative poem develops (to some extent) a setting within which recognition occurs, the tradition of poetry itself has developed certain standard metaphors for the optimal conditions for poetic perception. In American literature, one of the most famous of those metaphors is wakefulness." Bottoms uses his poem "Awake" to link his poetic persona's character to that tradition. In addition to serving as a call to a general poetic alertness to the world around us, this poem also solidifies Bottoms' connections to another set of images central to American poetry, those of T. S. Eliot's *The Waste Land*.

Beginning in a winter that lingers too long and thereby creates doubts about spring and its promised renewal, "Awake" cautiously embraces "a green tentative feeler" that appears in the yard as evidence that "Underground / something is stirring, climbing through the veins." Like the protagonist of Eliot's epic, Bottoms' protagonist, here again rendered with the second-person pronoun, faces the situation before him by engaging in a cautiously optimistic fishing expedition:

> so you take your rod and tackle box,
> you walk the quarter mile of thickening woods,
> stand in the weedy mire bordering the shallows,
> ease your fly onto the surface [AH 90].

Reading backward from this place in Bottoms' career can place a poem such as "Shooting Rats" in a context somewhat richer than reading it solely as a poem of adolescent rebellion.[9] But I want to read forward from this poem instead, using this image of the patient fisherman, who seems at peace in this place despite its irregularities and inherent insecurities, to serve as a figurative guide in the search for the father and his essence and in the speaker's subsequent effort to use that knowledge to construct his own genuine adult male identity. This fisherman is awake enough to see as the "poetic perceiver" tradition demands that we see.

Another fishing poem, "In Louisiana," sends the speaker stumbling under the burden of his equipment into an early autumn evening in hopes of fishing. He falls and dreams of his father, making of him a mythic savior who reaches into the murk of the swamp and pulls up "the chest and head of a boy, / his fingers still tangled in a knot of roots." This Everyboy, we might call him, is a "gaped mouth drooling sludge…" with "dull fish eyes / wide in the new light / like the stunned eyes of the dying." For the speaker, this boy — obviously characterized as unawake and unfit for the tasks of the real world — becomes all boys, wrested into an awareness of their adult responsibilities by their strong, perhaps even overpowering, dreamed fathers, yet unprepared for the tasks they face, "their dumb, stunned eyes already clouding, / looking for one root, / the corner of a bed sheet, anything in the world to clutch" (AH 104).

The specific biography of Bottoms' father becomes clear in "Naval Photograph: 25 October 1942: What the Hand May Be Saying." In this poem, the speaker's father inhabits the all-male world of the cruiser *Atlanta* in the Pacific. The photograph from which the poem departs underscores the overwhelming maleness of this environment: "a sailor / clowning on a gun turret, barrel straight up between his legs." But the hyper-masculine assertion of this comic image is juxtaposed with a different representation of masculinity when the speaker observes "[his] father … standing with the gunners / … a shadow / in a wide cluster of shadows." Because history's infallible hindsight allows the speaker to know the men's futures, he seeks meaning in the sign of his father's wave (just as he would later and belatedly see the sign of his father's message to him in the bunting lessons of "Sign for My Father, Who Stressed the Bunt"); but this more mature speaker is also acutely conscious that the men who wave, including his father, do not know the future but wave only "for all the reasons anyone / waves" (AH 105). They are, he understands, both ordinary and extraordinary, and it is the job of his adult life to learn how to relate to both those identities that are his father.

"The Anniversary" continues the story of the speaker's father's experience in the Pacific. As an annual ritual, the adult son performs a commemoration of his father being wounded in the Japanese attack on the

Atlanta. He drinks alone in a room without lights so that he might understand the darkness his father faced a generation earlier. He also denies himself the music that might accompany his drinking on any other night of the year. In other words, he seeks to live, as closely as he can through his imagination, his father's experience." But he also seeks to partake of his father's lived experience as a means to his own resurrection or renewal, a desire made clear by the speaker's appropriation of the language of the sacrament of holy communion: "This is your blood in remembrance of you, / who died one night at sea and lived" (AH 107). The explicit linking of the father figure with Christ and the speaker's ritual of imbibing the father via the metaphor of communion create the possibility of the speaker's rebirth as an adult male.

Yet this post–war baby-boom child is unable to escape the irony of his imaginative engagement with a terrifying reality that his father was forced, by history, to encounter literally his father, fished from the Pacific and taken for dead by the sailors who rescue him, was, according to the speaker,

> dead as any drunk in any armchair
> who trembles at the horror of his thoughts
> and learns, as he learns every year
> that the power in the blood to terrify
> is sometimes the power of love [AH 106]

The struggle to identify with the father leads the speaker to his desk, from which he takes not the poet's pen to record his experience but a small knife with which to touch an old scar. He wants to encounter his father's truth in a physical way, but the ultimate act of the poem itself suggests that he moves beyond the knife to the pen eventually, an acceptance of the essential irony of his position vis-à-vis the father.

Several poems in *Vagrant Grace* reiterate the adult speaker's realignment with his father, suggesting that the paternal relationship remains a theme central to this speaker's evolution. The best example is "A Family Parade" (11–14), in which the speaker recreates his father's participation in a small-town parade by clowning and doing tricks on a bicycle for the kids, including his own daughter, in his suburban subdivision. Through this recreation, he comes to understand his place within the family constellation and the adult male's place within the social order:

> Finally, yes, I know this is about eternity,
> this circling, this following
> . . .
> the way my father leads.

Then he solidifies his new understanding by evoking his father's superior performance in this clown's role as well: "Yes, here he comes again, noble // And father, clutching / And revving, making his circle" (13).[10]

"The Desk," which follows "The Anniversary" in *Armored Hearts*, is the poem in which the speaker most directly names the dilemma he faces in regard to his father. In an action that he identifies as "my first crime," the speaker, with a kind of desperate frenzy, enters the school in Canton where his father as a student had carved his name into a desk. The entry into forbidden territory, belonging to patriarchal figures that we might label the enemy here ("the city, the county, / the state, whatever government claimed dominion" [109]), becomes an approximation for the speaker of the dangers of battle that he knows his father to have endured. Yet, as in other poems on this theme, there is an acute consciousness of the irony involved in such an imaginative association. The speaker has first encountered this marked desk in his own years as student, when he must literally follow in his father's footsteps; finding it again years later on his illicit mission, he uses the carved name in the wooden desk to trigger a genuine adult effort to know and understand his father:

> and [I] wondered at the dreams he must have lived
> as his eyes ran back and forth
> from the cinder yard below the window
> to the empty practice field
> to the blade of his pocket knife etching carefully
> the long, angular lines of his name,
> the dreams he must have laid out one behind another
> like yard lines, in the dull, pre–practice afternoons
> of geography and civics, before he ever dreamed
> of Savo Sound and Guadalcanal [108–09].

Because he grasps that his father might have dreamed a life different than the life he has led and because he, in this late transition into adult maleness, in fact bears his father's name, the speaker steals the desk. Having been given the name at birth, he now feels compelled to take it, by his own choice, and to rest easy in his possession, despite the irregularities inherent in the process he uses to accomplish his goal: "And rarely do I fret when I see that oak scar leaning / against my basement wall, though I wonder what it means / to own my father's name" (109).

The conclusion here, I would argue, is another prime example of Bottoms' particular brand of irony. The continued posture of not quite grasping the import of his relationship with his father is in part homage to the man he clearly perceives to be the better man and partly a diminishing of his own growing understanding and his clearly superior abilities to express himself. Not only does the speaker use this irony to underplay his abilities to express himself, but he also allows the irony to intensify the homage to the father by underplaying the son's growing ability to express his perceptions regarding his father's heroism. He uses irony to maintain the superiority of the father's actions in relation to the poet's expressive abilities. Through his expression, however, the speaker makes abundantly clear that he does know what it means to own that name-in both this poem and many of the others I've discussed. Another element of this irony, however, emerges in the gap between where the speaker is at this stage in his development and the even greater understanding of what it means to own his father's name that emerges in those poems devoted to his own experience as a father. In one sense, until he becomes a father, he cannot know fully what his name means.

Coming to terms with the father and accepting one's adult male role, of course, also affect aspects of one's experience and identity not directly related to the paternal relationship. Whether the change is as simple as the substitution of bird watching for movie watching (and other typical drive-in activities)—in "Warbler at Howell's Drive-In," in which the speaker acknowledges that "That was you then. / ... // And this is you now, middle-aged and beyond" (AH 121)—or as profound as the transformed conception of male-female bonds revealed in "Chinese Dragons," in which the speaker and the woman he loves get tattoos to make their connection both tangible and permanent ("our desire for permanence and the permanence / of our desire" [122]), becoming an adult creates different ways of perceiving and of living.

Perhaps the distance that Bottoms' speaker has traveled can best be measured by examining how the ways of perceiving and acting he endorses in "Armored Hearts" differ from his perceptions and actions in "Shooting Rats at the Bibb County Dump." In the earlier poem, the speaker, inextricable from his companions, seeks out the experience of killing rats at the dump. Even if the rats become spiritual cousins of humans, all of us heading toward an eventual darkness, the primary impulse at the time of the shooting grows out of a perception of the rats as fair game in the quest to release male energies and prove masculine prowess. In "Armored Hearts," the speaker consciously and conscientiously separates himself from his neighbor, his ostensible male peer in this scenario, and chooses to assist the turtles that the neighbor sees as fair game in the same way that the younger speaker had perceived the rats. In fact, because the turtles are guilty of killing the neighbor's ducks, they are perhaps fairer game than were the rats in the speaker's ethical terms. The speaker here also needs only to enact his particular brand of protection, even nurturing, rather than claiming public credit for his heroics or creating a direct and public confrontation with the neighbor.[11]

"Allatoona Evening" summarizes nicely the path the speaker has taken to attain his hard-won maturity. He tells the reader about a burden he has carried, an "it," that he intends to discard in the lake's waters. Nature, the master he perceives himself to serve in "Armored Hearts," again takes his side, encourages him to pursue the path he has come to see as his. A choir of crickets calls him

> to lay down
> [his] anger
> ....
> lay it down, they say, on the green stones
> beside this water.

And, in following their advice and laying down the anger that has driven him for years in what finally has proven to be a false direction, he will lose nothing, because that anger sated "could bring you to no better place. / Nothing is more beautiful than your emptiness" (140). That emptiness is, of course, another irony, for it is only of anger that the speaker is empty. Its absence is the thing that has allowed him to acknowledge the presence of so much more — the values that are his values, the identity that is essential to the man he wants to be and has chosen to become.

Bottoms makes clear in "A Morning from the Gospel of St. John" (VG 75) that the man he has chosen to be is not the traditional heroic male figure. Pondering his reflection in the bathroom mirror, the speaker perceives the gap between his body and our culture's conventions of the ideal male:

and pondering myself limp and priestly,
laced with blue veins, I judged nothing threatening.
Sometimes, I admit, I even look at this unremarkable body
which is beautiful only
in design, and feel a laughable joy

Imagining where one might go from this point, the speaker says, "I love to imagine being startled / into innocence, heedless / of the body leaping naked toward God" (VG 75). No longer bound by his body's constraints, no longer defined by personal and cultural expectations of the male form and the actions and beliefs attached to that form, the speaker positions himself for possible transformation, despite the difficulty inherent in that process: "in middle age rebirth isn't such easy work" ("At the Grave of Martha Ellis" [VG 73]).

Fatherhood

Perhaps the central element for Bottoms' speaker in his rebirth is fatherhood. In "Barriers" (AH 123), alone and lonely during a thunderstorm, he takes comfort in a remembered story of a young girl, frightened during the night, slipping into bed with her parents for a sense of safety and comfort. He imagines her parents' welcoming her as a tangible, even ultimate, declaration of their love for her, "though they never let her sleep between them," which would undercut the supremacy of the marital bond.[12] From this remembered story, the speaker turns to an examination of his own current status:

> I am not a father, but I think about the love of fathers,
> the sheet thrown back for the daughter, the rough hand
> rejoining the hand of the mother.
> And because of her story
> I know more about the love a man can feel for a woman,
> love not born of the self
> or what the self gives the world [AH 123].

Near the end of *Armored Hearts* and throughout *Vagrant Grace*, Bottoms at last speaks as a father, completing the circle of his relationship with his own father and the values regarding family and the masculine role that his father represents. "Sleepless Nights" contrasts the middle-aged shame of drunkenly lurking outside his ex-wife's home (and his former home, of course) without any effective sense of place or identity with the mature hindsight that allows him to understand that earlier self:

> another night, pacing another darkness
> ringed with geese and black sheep
> and swans, singing again,
> laughing, shouldering the complaints
> of a newborn daughter [AH 136].

In "A Daughter's Fever," the speaker-father spends a night with his feverish infant daughter, telling her stories "to guide her home." In doing so, he cannot avoid memories of his own past and the false paths that kept him from home for so many years. But those memories have an entirely different context now: "So many ways / to enter the forest and never return. / But happily that's another ending" (137). In another poem, "Bronchitis" (VG 5), the father-speaker again watches over a sick child, "All the loose uncertainties of fatherhood [grating] / in the joints of [his] chair" (VG 5). His concerns for his daughter transform him as a reader, reorient his concerns from traditional masculine conceptions of military history toward what we might call a more feminine concern with the effects of war and violence on domesticity and parenting. The emblem of this reorientation in "Bronchitis" is the young girl, a three-year-old, who is the first victim of Sherman's assault on Atlanta, according to the history the speaker reads while his daughter struggles for breath in an adjoining room. The girl's presence in the narrative makes the speaker question whose story history actually is, if he doesn't even know this girl's name, and

> Neither, it seems
> does the man who wrote the history,
> who mentions her only as a footnote in the abstract
> strategies of war [7].

In "On Methodist Hill" (VG 8–10), the speaker and his daughter tour a cemetery where she continually pulls him toward the graves. He wants to shield her from darkness, death, and suffering of all kinds, but she has a natural curiosity that resists his protection. The church setting, with its stained-glass representations of Christ and his suffering, prods the narrator to imagine the last supper as a meal to which Christ "had not invited his women, / or his family," because he anticipated "some violence." In realizing that all efforts to protect, even the divine, ultimately fail, the speaker finds himself weeping as his "four-year-old climbs a vandalized angel" (VG 10). The adverb that the speaker applies to his tears—"unaccountably"—becomes ironic if we consider this speaker as an older, more mature version of the speaker in "Wrestling Angels," the first poem in *Armored Hearts*. Just as his father was lost to his family for fifteen months during World War 11, the speaker has been lost to himself and his family for far longer—an absence that is characterized by the self of "Wrestling Angels." In watching his child climb on a totem of his own lost years, he cannot escape the possibility that perhaps someday she will be similarly lost to him, an insight that makes his weeping entirely accountable, in fact.[13]

"Night Strategies" moves Bottoms' exploration of fatherhood beyond the personal to something more akin to the universal. As the speaker bathes his young daughter, an activity that he figures as a sacrament by making the soap he uses a "wafer" (VG 27), he remembers the story of a young woman raped by soldiers in Sarajevo. The gentleness with which he approaches his female child becomes, then, his answer, his explanation, to her question that he imagines she will necessarily some day articulate to him as the primary male figure in her life:

> the only answer I have
> is this nervous
> exaggeration of tenderness,
> and that every ministry of my hand, clumsy
> and apologetic, asks her
> to practice such a radical faith [28],

In becoming a father, the speaker has practiced his own radical faith, has taken the leap that carries him across the chasm that he once believed to separate him from his own father and from the qualities of fatherhood. On the other side, he finds that additional radicalism is required, both of him and of the child he has brought into a world still marked by the destructive forces of the masculine. His nervous, exaggerated tenderness is all he has to offer by way of explanation. It is simultaneously not nearly enough and everything.[14]

In his foreword to Perry Garfinkel's *In a Man's World: Father, Son, Brother, Friend, and Other Roles Men Play*, Daniel Coleman uses a term taken from Harvard Medical School psychologist Sam Osherson, "shroud of silence," to describe the phenomenon that "enfolds vast areas of men's experience, their emotional lives in particular" (xii). In "Country Store and Moment of Grace" (VG 37–55), Bottoms frames a key question in relation to this shroud of silence: "And what more frightening / than a room of quiet men?" (VG 48).[15] This typical male trait characterizes the exact nature of his uncle's and father's reticence about their war experiences in "A Sunday Dinner" (VG 84–87). Although he understands and respects their need for silence, he also indicates that, because they are males who will not or cannot talk, we, their descendants and loved ones, must wait "until the end" (86) to understand what they understand of this life and perhaps the next. These father figures know parts of the story of us, the human story, that we cannot know. But, in assuming his role as purveyor of what he himself knows and what he intuits of their knowledge through his hard-won sympathetic identification with these men and their values, Bottoms approaches Larry May's notion of a moral male who understands "moral responsibility as a matter of what individuals in groups owe their communities" (1).

Bottoms has returned from his own war — a war with self — victorious against that silent shroud. In raising his voice, he makes his poetry a vehicle for rendering "gender visible to men," which is, according to Kimmel, a necessary step in the revisionary process contemporary feminism has necessitated in American culture (3). I do not want to suggest that this rendering of gender as visible to men is the only or even the primary accomplishment of Bottoms' work; I only wish to stress this valuable byproduct of his career. Nor do I believe that the effect of his work is to make gender visible only to men. Rather, I believe that he is also making masculinity visible to women as well as men. Kimmel says, "We need a new definition of masculinity for a new century, a definition that is more about the character of men's hearts and souls than about the size of their biceps or wallets" (333). Ronald F. Levant concurs, arguing that "the only course left was to forge a new middle path between traditional masculinity and the sensitive man ideal-one that allows every man to decide for himself what combination of old and new traits he wants to incorporate into his reconstructed masculine code" (4).

As our culture continues to negotiate the complexities of the paradigm shift in gender roles and expectations that characterized the last quarter of the twentieth century and that continue to complicate our lives today, we could, to paraphrase Robert Frost's "Birches," do worse than read the poetry of David Bottoms. In reading it through the lens of gender, I believe, we free Bottoms from the stereotypes that have sometimes unfairly limited critical response to his work; concurrently, we free ourselves from the distorting binary oppositions that similarly limit our thinking about masculinity.

Notes

1. In their headnote on Ann Beattie, another writer whose career has often been evaluated in terms of her generational identity, the editors of the *Norton Anthology of American Literature* acknowledge the unfairness of so limiting one's assessment of a writer's body of work. Of Beattie they say:
> to stress Beattie's importance as portraitist of a generation may be to do her a disservice, since she is above all else a writer, and one with an unrepresentative, even idiosyncratic, style. Her stories and novels should not be taken merely as vehicles for displaying social attitudes and manners, but as mannerist compositions that need to be not only looked at but listened to. Her style is too pronounced, too carefully contrived, to be treated as a transparent medium through which "reality" is given us directly [2529].

I want to attach this disclaimer to my own efforts to link Bottoms to his generation, acknowledging that to do so is to skew his work in a specific way. But I undertake that task partly as a corrective measure designed to point out qualities that have been previously overlooked, and partly as an opening into other aspects of the work that have been equally neglected or misrepresented.

2. This essay is not the place to enter into the debate about what universals there might be that are not somehow socially constructed. Suffice it to say here that Suarez is right in naming Bottoms as a poet interested primarily in the individual as it reveals the universal. Bottoms clearly accepts the concept of the universal as it has been traditionally conceived. In fact, he acknowledges that the chief source of his poetry is his "Southern Baptist education ... shaped out of a tradition and family model that asks one to believe things that are quite obviously unconfirmable" ("Turn Your Radio On" 86). We can note, however, that even in affirming his traditional conception of the universal Bottoms cites tradition and family, which are both products of the ways we organize ourselves as a society.

3. In his book *The Company We Keep: An Ethics of Fiction*, Wayne C. Booth calls for a return to ethical criticism, a practice that he defines, in part, by a call to revive an ancient metaphor for our relationship with written texts. He suggests that we think of those works as friends, of their authors' gifts to us as friendship offerings. He says, "Perhaps most obviously, this metaphor spontaneously revives a kind of talk, once almost universal, about the types of friendship or companionship a book provides as it is read" (170). He then goes on to acknowledge the reader's role in this metaphorical exchange: "We judge ourselves as we judge the offer. Here is circularity with a vengeance. But we need not fear it as a vicious circle, so long as we do not pursue hard final judgments of 'wicked' or 'blessed' but rather ways of testing and improving our re-creations" (178). For Booth, and for me as I approach the emerging representation of masculinity in Bottoms' work, "ethical criticism [is] any effort to show how the virtues of narratives relate to the virtues of selves and societies, or how the ethos of any story affects or is affected by the ethos-the collection of virtues-of any given reader" (11). I believe Bottoms offers his readers, through his account of his personal evolution as a man, a chance to reconsider masculinity in the late twentieth century, to test and improve our initial re-creations of his poems (and perhaps the poems of other males who take on similar elements of the gender-charged ethos of our time). In this specific way, then, mine is an effort at ethical criticism in Boothian terms.

4. My argument will depend on examples from only two of Bottoms' collections, *Armored Hearts* and *Vagrant Grace* (1999). Because *Armored Hearts* contains the poet's own selections from

his three previous books, I believe it represents the best evidence of those poems on which Bottoms wishes his reputation to stand and, thus, also the best evidence of his evolving persona as it relates to my own thesis. In subsequent references, *Armored Hearts* and *Vagrant Grace* will be abbreviated as AH and VG, respectively.

5. When interviewers Alice Friman and Marshall Bruce Gentry asked Bottoms about this epigraph and what it asks of the reader, he responded by saying that it asks nothing of the reader, that only God can do the remaking suggested by the epigraph from Saint Augustine (104). While theologically Bottoms is correct, I want to suggest that metaphorically it is impossible to ignore the epigraph's invitation for the reader to inhabit the poems as if they were a house and that house itself a metaphor for the poet's soul. Thus, like Friman and Gentry, I have to believe that the poet is, perhaps unconsciously, asking me via metaphor to assist in the act of remaking named here. For Bottoms' sense of the relationship between metaphor and poetry in general and his in particular, see "Turn Your Radio On."

Also, to place my sense of Bottoms' speaker as one who undergoes an evolution in the context of the poet's broader world view, see Don Russ's essay "Up toward Light: Resurrection, Transfiguration, Metamorphosis, and Evolution in David Bottoms' *Armored Hearts*." Russ makes a convincing argument for a classic post-structural dilemma in the poetry: "Indeed, [Bottoms] draws again and again upon the time-honored Judeo-Christian and classical sources for his imagery, at first ironically, playing up the failure of the older systems of belief, but then increasingly suggesting new hopes and possibilities. And side by side with such biblically cast imagery as that of resurrection and transfiguration and the classical imagery of metamorphosis, the imagery of Darwinian evolution — for many, one would assume, the very antithesis of traditional Western sacred meaning — also comes to suggest something positive, allowing finally some consoling recognition of kinship with all evolved life and thus some sort of salvation from modern isolation, darkness, and despair" (66).

6. Within his portrait that emphasizes the latter-day Fugitive-Agrarian strain of lament in Bottoms and his work, Skube also details the poet's straightforward acknowledgment that he couldn't live in East Cobb were his wife not a lawyer and if not for his devotion to his ten-year-old daughter — a departure from the backward-looking, nostalgic tone of much else in this journalistic profile. These elements of the present-day Bottoms persona are, for me, even more salient than the more heavily emphasized elements of Skube's characterization because they suggest precisely the evolutionary stage to which Bottoms has come at this point in his career and in his life.

7. Although my point of departure has been a sociological and cultural-historical examination of the masculine, it seems imperative to note here that the dynamic I am describing lends itself quite naturally to a psychological reading as well. One might depart from Freud, Lacan, and/or others and produce an equally or more coherent reading. Bottoms' own professed interest in Jung (see the Friman and Gentry interview, for example) also invites that particular psychological approach. More than a sociological or cultural-historical reading even, mine is a method best described by Michael Dunne in *Hawthorne's Narrative Strategies*. Dunne acknowledges that he is, in fact, doing his best to describe what he sees happening on the page (19).

8. Although the level of crime recounted in Bottoms' poetry doesn't come close to murder, the philosophy that emerges in this poem recalls the thinking of Flannery O'Connor's most famous criminal, the Misfit of "A Good Man Is Hard to Find." That character says to the terrified grandmother he is about to kill that "[Jesus] thrown everything off balance [by raising the dead]" and goes on to say that, because of that imbalance, one is left with no option other than "[enjoying] the few minutes you got left the best way you can-by killing somebody or burning down his house or doing some other meanness to him. No pleasure but meanness" (132).

9. "One might, in fact, do a profitable reading of all of Bottoms' fishing poems in terms of their intertextual links to Eliot's "Fisher King."

10. Here is perhaps the best place to note that Bottoms also uses other familial male figures to work toward his reconciliation with the adult male role. Among the most significant examples are poems about his father-in-law (see especially, "Last Supper in Montana," AH 128–29; "The Pentecostal," AH 130; "Their Father's Tattoo," VG 33–34; and "Occurrence in the Big Sky," VG 88–90); an uncle (see especially "My Uncle Sowing Beatitudes," VG 81–83, and "A Sunday Dinner," VG 84–87); and his grandfather, who appears in several poems in *Armored Hearts* as well

as being central to "Country Store and Moment of Grace," the long poem that is the centerpiece of *Vagrant Grace* (37–55). The uncle sticks in the speaker's memory as much for his refusing to engage in a violent exchange with a drunken, angry cousin and for his choosing not to shoot an available deer as for his World War II heroics. The father-in-law, in his unexpected death, becomes an emblem of the imperfectability of one's maleness, the inevitability of one's exiting this life with any number of his male tasks unfinished.

11. In many ways, "Armored Hearts" seems an inversion or a deconstruction of Robert Frost's "Mending Wall," which also features two neighbors with divergent points of view on an aspect of their properties that ironically connects as well as separates them. Here, Bottoms' speaker, like Frost's, is the more imaginative, the more poetic of the two, and he is able to seize the advantage largely through his being the bearer of the tale. Just as Frost's speaker believes that nature reveals the universe's proper order, this speaker puts himself forward as a proponent of letting the ducks and turtles settle their varied claims on the pond "naturally." Frost blames the neighbor in "Mending Wall" for being afraid to question his father's teachings, which provide the basis for his firm belief in the rightness of walls between neighbors. One of the inversions within Bottoms' treatment of similar subject matter and dramatic situation is the implication that this speaker is acting out of reverence for a certain version of masculinity that we, having read his other poems, can attribute to his newfound reconciliation with the father. The neighbor also represents a version of masculinity, one inherited from a more traditional and/or less pondered and grasped father figure. The dilemma here is not, as Frost might suggest, to get beyond the father, but to understand and choose the better father or the better aspects of the father.

12. This poem too might be read through an intertextual relationship with "Mending Wall," here complicating even further the issues of separation and connection that interest Frost.

13. Two poems from *Vagrant Grace*—"Our Presbyterian Christmas" (31) and "My Daughter at the Gymnastics Party" (32)—link the speaker's experience as a parent more directly to his own mother than to his father. In the first of these, Bottoms evokes "The Boy Shepherds' Simile" with its links to his mother's role in his life, and in the second he actually assumes the maternal position, sitting on the sidelines watching his child at an athletic event: "I remembered my sweet exasperated mother." In coming as a father to a fuller understanding of both the male and female roles in parenting, Bottoms indicates one key aspect of the new version of masculinity that he is embracing.

14. In this poem, Bottoms does much to counter or place in context perhaps his most disturbing poem regarding male dominance of the female, "The Farmers" (AH 12–13). A rape poem, perhaps influenced by Dickey's "May Day Sermon" and "Cherrylog Road," "The Farmers" employs an uncharacteristic third-person narration notable for its narrator's aesthetic detachment. The assault on the female, like the assaults on graveyard angels and dump rats in poems from the same phase in the poet's career, is a communal experience, a gang rape, marked by an inhuman disregard for the woman's humanity. After the men satisfy themselves, the woman watches them return to their "reaping" in the fields. Thus, Bottoms linguistically links their work life as male farmers and their approach to this woman: raping and reaping are two sides of the same coin, just as the Sarajevo soldiers who rape the woman in "Night Strategies" see her as one of the many spoils due a warrior. The use of his characteristic first-person and, more importantly, his ability to see his personal connection to the abstraction of masculinity represented in the actions of the soldiers in the later poem, even as he is personally at his most gentle and loving with the daughter, suggest an ideological maturity to match his personal growth.

15. This long poem, by far the longest Bottoms has published to date, deserves its own extensive examination—a task that space does not permit here. However, it is central to my argument in that the speaker reflects on both present-day experience and childhood memories, coming to terms with the South's racial history, among other things, through his reexamination of the integration of his grandfather's store, with a group of men as silent witnesses to the grandfather's exchange with a black woman buying a soft drink. The boy speaker too is a silent witness; but, as an adult, he voices like a refrain the word "Amen" in the poem's final section (53–55). In its more literal meaning of "so be it" as well as in the colloquial sense of "I agree" common to southern use of the word, "Amen" indicates the speaker's (re)affirmation of traditional values as learned from his male relatives, even in light of his subsequent lived experience and that of his region

and nation. Through his inscription to three male contemporaries, Bottoms also suggests that the "Amen" he speaks is not his alone but that of any number of males who have shared his experience of time and place.

I anticipate that future critics will turn their attention to the full analysis that this major work deserves.

Works Cited

"Ann Beattie." In Baym, 2529–30.
Barnes, Roy. "Introduction of David Bottoms." Poet Laureate Inauguration Ceremony. Atlanta, 31 May 2000.
Baym, Nina, gen. ed. *The Norton Anthology of American Literature*. Shorter 5th ed. New York: Norton, 1989.
Booth, Wayne C. *The Company We Keep: An Ethics of Fiction*. Berkeley: University of California Press, 1988.
Bottoms, David. *Armored Hearts*. Port Townsend, WA: Copper Canyon Press, 1995.
———. "Turn Your Radio On: The Spirits of Influence." *Southern Quarterly* 37.3–4 (1999): 85–92.
———. *Vagrant Grace*. Port Townsend, WA: Copper Canyon Press, 1999.
Bryant, William Cullen. "Thanatopsis." In Baym, 471–73.
Dubbert, Joe L. *A Man's Place: Masculinity in Transition*. Englewood Cliffs, NJ: Prentice-Hall, 1979.
Dunne, Michael. *Hawthorne's Narrative Strategies*. Jackson: University Press of Mississippi, 1995.
Eliot, T. S. *The Waste Land*. In Baym, 2048–60.
Friman, Alice, and Bruce Gentry. "Fishing from the Poetry Boat: A Conversation with David Bottoms." *Southern Quarterly* 37.3–4 (1999): 93–105.
Frost, Robert. "Birches." In Baym, 1867–68.
———. "Mending Wall." In Baym, 1859–60.
Gerzon, Mark. *A Choice of Heroes: The Changing Faces of American Manhood*. New York: Houghton-Mifflin, 1982.
Goldberg, Herb. *The New Male: From Macho to Sensitive But Still All Male*. New York: NAL, 1979.
Goleman, Daniel. Foreword. *In a Man's World: Father Son, Brother Friend, and Other Roles Men Play*, by Perry Garfinkel. New York: NAL, 1985.
Hill, Robert W. "Warbling with TV in the Background: David Bottoms in the Suburbs." *Southern Quarterly* 37.3–4 (1999): 80–84.
Kimmel, Michael. *Manhood in America: A Cultural History*. New York: Free Press, 1996.
Levant, Dr. Ronald E. *Masculinity Reconstructed: Changing the Rules of Manhood—At Work, in Relationships, and in Family Life*. New York: Plume, 1995.
May, Larry. *Masculinity and Morality*. Ithaca: Cornell University Press, 1998.
O'Connor, Flannery. "A Good Man Is Hard to Find." *The Complete Stories*. New York: Noonday, 1971. 117–33.
Russ, Don. "'Up Toward Light': Resurrection, Transfiguration, Metamorphosis, and Evolution in David Bottoms' Armored Hearts." *Southern Quarterly* 37.3–4 (1999): 66–72.

Skube, Michael. "Simply Grounded: Georgia's New Poet Laureate." *Atlanta Journal Constitution* 31 May 2000: Fl-2.
Suarez, Ernest. "A Deceptive Simplicity: The Poetry of David Bottoms." *Southern Quarterly* 37.3-4 (1999): 73-79.
Thoreau, Henry David. *Walden*. In Baym, 868-967.

Grueling Miracle: Faith in Middle Age
Laurence Lieberman

Part I: "Easter Shoes Epistle"

When a poet discovers a new form that is a radical departure from his usual practice and plunges into a technical gamble that gives him surprising access to a register of voice that had — until now — seemed far beyond his range, he may feel that everything is beginning again in his life as an artist. His zeal in exploring new subjects becomes a fearful embarkation. In David Bottoms' recent book, *Waltzing Through the Endtime*, he is such a pioneer, once again. This book's opening passage is a showcase of Bottoms' new style:

Yesterday morning five plumbers from Sundance
dug up the pipes in our front yard —
                                           twelve feet down and roots
through a joint, a total blockage.
Now mounds of sour mud sag beside a canvas tarp, while the last rain
        dripping
like wax through the Bradford pears, glistens
on the boxwoods.
                Stench and flowers, and an urgent glaze
over the neighborhood, the dogwoods already mustering an incredible
    witness,
and the jungles of hydrangea,
                            the Japanese cherries, the azaleas deviling
the roses, and oddly, in the street,
even an old work boot, like a shriveled potato,
rain-curled, corroded,

Grueling Miracle (Laurence Lieberman)

>   shooting its little feelers toward the curb.
> Every leaf an oracle, sure,
>   and in the local phone book
> not one listing under *mystagogue*.
>   [from "Easter Shoes Epistle"]

The first in this poem's multiplicity of shoes emerges from the excavated yard sludge like random contents of a shark's stomach. The human castoff seems reincarnated as kindred to all the flowers, the organic mulch of dugup "sour mud" converting the shoe to its weedy floral mire, while the shoelaces become shoots — "little feelers" — of a rotting "shriveled potato." In this season, Spring, nature conjures messages from the spirit world with every petal, every leaf; each is an "oracle" carrying missives of divinity, each an "incredible witness" to revelations of the spirit that are exploding all around us. An "urgent glaze" because nature is in siege of little miracles! And the old shoe, a "work boot," has been absorbed into sludge-like mix, which establishes the shoe at the poem's outset as the one item of our attire that both tugs us down into a familial linkage with nature's muck (since our soles trod earth daily), and partakes of the otherworldly essence. Like the fallen leaves and petals the shoe nestles among, it becomes a witness, an oracle in its own right. Shoes are inherently magical, and it's a seamless transition for an old shoe to become a symbol of neglected "faith" in the homespun mythology of the poet's mother on the second page. She's about to polish his "penny loafers," to divest them of "filth of pasture,/polluted creek."

Consider the quiet irony of "not one listing under *mystagogue*," while the writer, himself, is performing the role of would-be mystagogue, a professional guide who instructs us readers in the countless embodiments of revelation that flash all about us in Spring. Bottoms' new style in this book, coupled with his evident breakthrough in form, is already bountifully mustered in the first passage of the opening poem which — to my ear — is more redolent of Hopkins' devotional poems (like "Pied Beauty," say) than works of Dickey or Warren, his more obvious precursors.

So many thousands of nature's tiny floral bits are trying to "shame us into faith" as they "shake off in the wind, flicker and drift," but the narrator, who finds himself in a middle-aged funk, is mostly blinded to the constant barrage of vehicles of revelation, tidbits that keep flashing all about him, since he suffers from a spiritual malaise:

All morning the tiny petals of these pears
shake off in the wind, flicker and drift, as though their own small
    witness
is to shame us into faith...
                                                   In middle age, truly,
it's all a grueling miracle, the spirit sagging like a bag of cut grass,
or curling on itself like an old boot...

    The speaker's faith, which comes and goes like some "old boot," eludes him for now. His powers of belief are frozen, and he can't move forward in his life. Doubt keeps an upper hand over faith. He senses the beauties are all still out there — that "grueling miracle" — but when he reaches out to touch them, he cannot make contact.

* * *

    The poem's opening sketch may also be viewed as a remarkable extended metaphor that mirrors the queasy state of the narrator's spirit, his inner disgruntlement. In my reading of the initial lines, the metaphor gains power by working at two removes from the crisis of faith that it veils:

Yesterday morning five plumbers from Sundance
dug up the pipes in our front yard —
                                            twelve feet down and roots
through a joint, a total blockage.
Now mounds of sour mud sag beside a canvas tarp, while the last rain
    dripping
like wax through the Bradford pears, glistens
on the boxwoods.
                    Stench and flowers...

    The key words, here, are "total blockage." Strong overtones of that phrase instantly likens the outdoor plumbing nightmare of the speaker's "front yard" to a dreaded malfunction of the human digestive tract, while the "dug up pipes" the five plumbers hope to repair may be taken to resemble faulty intestines and colon. Both levels of the trope are stylistically enhanced by the network of interwoven lines and spaces, twisting from side to side. Moreover, the pungently sensuous music evokes both the peculiar mixture of yard odors and a human body's discharge of fecal matter, bile, and other fumey contents: "Now mounds of sour mud sag beside a canvas tarp... Stench and flowers."

But the speaker's soul-sickness is the condition of "blockage" finally mirrored by both readings of the plumbing narrative, and he finds himself jealous of his bird and animal companions, who busy themselves with more primal worries. Only the "grouchy tabby" is likened to us at all, but its "skulking about in its own eternal moment" is merely a farcical imitation of our dilemma:

> Only we have to travel on faith,
>   struggling not to notice the absence,
> the stray shoe in the street, the fugitive foot...

Thus concludes the long first section of the poem with a return to the anonymous lost shoe, which plays neatly into the mother's shoe adage in the anecdotal flashback of the speaker's boyhood in section two. And the portrait that follows of his own much-weathered "penny loafers" on a kitchen chair, prior to his mother's applying her polish, is the first in a litany of personal and family shoes that sweeps though the remaining three sections of the work.

Each family member comes to be associated with special shoes they have worn at key moments in the narrator's treasured memory flux. The shoes all seem to incarnate some prized aspect of each character's life at a particular time of their work or play, his mother's "hospital shoes," his father's "wing tips" employed in "kicking up a coaching box," his wife's "Spanish boots" the day he evidently first saw her (and fell in love on the spot?) dancing in a "cowgirl bar in Great Falls, Montana." He was hypnotized by those "silver heels and toes." And his daughter "on her toes," shaking low branches of their pear trees, while "petals like soggy pearls" clung to her shoe soles. And these all add up to a mental scrapbook of pictures that the speaker would "lay aboard," so to say, to brace himself to be prepared for the coming apocalypse ("stocking up like Noah for that darkest flood").

In the *Epistle*'s unfolding philosophy, the middle-aged man's Faith is one of the few most essential necessities he must store, or stock up on, to get ready for the darkest hour, even though at times our Faith becomes diminished to the brittle fragility of a "stale cracker." However, those family portraits may rival Faith in their indispensable value, since they are treasures that our "memory smuggles into the afterlife," and when our belief system fails us for a time, they may run Faith a close second in seeing us through the crisis. Those memories — as salvaged and transfigured in poems — may become our most soul-saving "pocket charms against oblivion." And indeed, in this poem which superbly implements and enacts its message, the family pictures — which range from cameos to full-blown vignettes — lift the reader's heart with their stunning clarity and fervid nostalgias.

Three generations of the author's dearest womenfolk sparkle across this meditative *Epistle*— his mother, daughter, and wife — as the angst-harried man slogs through the mental quagmire of middle age. Any vestige of the "mounds of sour mud' with which this verse chronicle began is surely washed away by the radiant portrait at the finish, in which Bottoms handsomely envisages a fable of shoes drawn from one Easter of his wife's childhood in Southern California. Clearly, the healing fountain that carries him to ablution and cleansing through his season of doubt is the gift of family joys and recollections. None is more touching than the little surprise apotheosis of whole glittering walls of shoes viewed by the once-indigent child in the Palm Springs shopping mall of the emblematic closing lines, one of David Bottoms' strongest endings:

> Sure, some children have less, but put yourself in that child's mind
> and picture the Cadillac pulling
> into your graveled drive.
>   Surely you'd remember the crunch
> of those tires, your Sunday-school teacher's teal and gold sandals
> tracking the sandy grass,
> and certainly for the rest of your life
> the huge double doors of that Palm Springs mall revolving
> into a city of light —
>   fountains of brass cherubs,
> chandeliers, skylights, and that one fragile storefront of glass
> where every wall sparkles with shoes.

The voice surges to an orchestral vibrance in this allegory of a "city of light."

Part II: "Kenny Roebuck's Knuckle-Curve"

In reading "Kenny Roebuck's Knuckle-Curve," we may discover how well David Bottoms' newly-attuned verse instrument can deliver a rare twang in the short poem, too. Like Robert Penn Warren's masterful Grandfather Clock poem, this work steps out of Time into no-Time, a greatly expanded single moment, and that timeless prolonged pause of the linear flow of free association in the mind of the batter as he waits out and studies the pitched ball is duplicated by the wiry syntax of the one long sentence that comprises this compact lyric:

> Slow and goofy as the kid himself, it rises out of crowd-noise and
>   memory,
> wobbles off the mound in a long jerky float
>   like the face of a drunk
> coming out of a bar, luminous under streetlights,
> rising, dipping, weaving,
>   hovering over sidewalk and oily streets,
> closer, closer, until gradually you see it's a face
> you know, a face
> you've mourned in the mirror —
>   stitched, battered, scarred —
> the very mug of failure, but floating now in hard-won abandon,
> lost to the world, recklessly at peace,
> easy to swat as a saint,
>   and you rock back, swing,
> and it hops, weaves, jerks,
> rockets at your crotch, and once again the world isn't what you think,
> and the memory, already wobbling, knuckles off
> into voices, laughter, jeers,
>   that sobering pop of the catcher's mitt.

Both the flow of the hitter's reverie and the syntactical weave of the lines suggest the illusion of limitless duration. This amazing subject is perfectly suited to Bottoms' new aerations of form. The tighter constriction of his former close-knit stanzas and columns of verse might have felt too rhythmically cramped. I suspect that this theme would seem unwieldy, or intractable, to Bottom's habitual prosodic units of that earlier period in his work, and perhaps he would have abandoned the effort. This is all purely hypothetical speculation about decisions in the private chapel of the author's craft, but as a reader I like to presume that I can intuit the special excitement an artist feels as he happens upon a subject that is an uncanny match for the strophes of a newly initiated openness of form. The breath pauses inherent in this structure, the many phrases hanging suspended as the verse block unfolds, leads to a new momentum of pacing, such that the work may seem to write itself, effortlessly. Form and content are so magically wedded to each other, an alternative form becomes unthinkable. Indeed, that is the way this poem's 19 lines sweep me up in their electric transport.

The opening phrase—"Slow and goofy as the kid himself"—validates the need for the boy's name in the title. This "knuckle-curve," unlike any other, is the one pitcher's personal invention, much as the poem is one artist's unique creation. The sparky lines are peppered with moments of Bottoms' signature comic panache—"it hops, weaves, jerks,/ rockets at your crotch" and "easy to swat as a saint"—but though humorous, we must take note that this event is also a mystical conundrum, no less *spiritual* for the mundane happenstance of a pitched baseball. We are apprised that any one such pitch comes to have a cyclic life of its own. It's birthed out of dream and memory, then dies back into memory even as it's still happening:

> ...and the memory, already wobbling, knuckles off
> into voices, laughter, jeers,
>   that sobering pop of the catcher's mitt.

What a play upon the mystery of time flux, which mirrors the magical turns of the ball's movement across space.

In John Berryman's poem "Olympus," the speaker is elated to have come across a definition of the "art of poetry" in a book review that approaches his own ideal: "language/ so twisted & posed in a form/ that it not only expresses the matter in hand/ but adds to the stock of available reality." Perhaps Bottoms' knuckle-ball poem handily illustrates this formula. What other medium could rival the poem in deciphering the enigmas of the baseball myth? A series of still photos, or a movie, perhaps. But we need to be reminded that there are secrets lurking behind our most robust and palpable daily experiences that can best be illuminated only by the magic of a poem, by language wound about itself like vines on a page. Non-readers, beware! Even reading aloud won't afford this singular wakening. There is no substitute for the pleasure we can get from that mastery of poetic form. You must see and get in visual step with the crisscrossing dance of lines across the page. This lyric is a creditable word mimesis for the wildly twirling ball itself.

Part III: "Little Drop of Wickedness"

David Bottoms' virtuosity with his new form is perhaps shown to best advantage in the opening pages of his dazzling snake poem, "Little Drop of Wickedness." The great challenge of working with this prosody, I believe, is that the wide-open spacing of the lines makes it nearly impossible to hide any soft spots. The constant shifting of space breaks in the line, from side to side, leaves all key words and phrases hyper-exposed. This style risks a naked baring of all joints and seams, such that any flaws in language or rhythm won't escape notice. A few readers have observed a semblance to Charles Wright's special crosscurrents of lineation in Bottoms' recent practice, but the younger man's language and imagery is so much more pitched to an extrovert tracing of the world's palpable surfaces, the vivid contours of things, any likeliness to Wright's verse shaping comes to seem no more than cosmetic. Wright's from, so to say, was a safe model for Bottoms to have chosen for leads, since the senior poet's meditative fantasias clearly take on the everyday details at a far more abstract remove.

But looming over this work, more crucially, is the example of D.H. Lawrence's classic serpent poem, which becomes most evident when Bottoms pays him singular tribute as early as the second page:

> *A lord of the underworld,*
>   says Lawrence of the creature drinking
>   at his water trough.

Indeed, Lawrence's encounter with his snake was clearly the harbinger for the hypnotic trance that ensues between man and creature in *Little Drop*. A powerful undercurrent that simmers through both poems is the gradual dominance of the spirit world over the vividly rendered details of scene and setting. Whereas the persona in the earlier work ascribes his impulse to kill the snake to the internalized "voice of my education," he quickly suppresses the hostile urge and gives himself over to the spirit of reverence. Then, toward the last, the social voices momentarily get the better of him, and he flings a log at his "guest" writhing into a hole, only to revert to the stronger will to pay homage to "one of the lords of life":

> For he seemed to me again like a king,
> Like a king in exile, uncrowned in the underworld,
> Now due to be crowned again...

> And I have something to expiate.
> A pettiness.
>
> [from "Snake"]

Finally, the speaker vows to atone for his "pettiness," but oddly to our ears, he robs the word "expiate" of most of its accustomed religious savor. "Pettiness," after all, is not one of the deadly sins. More a social blunder... A far cry from truly invoking the bastion of Christian guilt, he confesses to a lapse into bad manners. A sin against civilization, not the High Church. But we know, too, that Lawrence reprimands himself for a more serious violation of the integrity of the animal's spirit. Its being is sacred to him, a scruple much close to pantheism than churchly deism.

Conversely, the speaker in *Little Drop* would take Lawrence to task for attributing lordliness, or any measure of untainted Godhead, to a snake. He accordingly takes the serpent's rank down a peg—"*Agkistrodon Contortrix* ... could be the name of some minor Greek god." Though his tone, here, is lightly satiric, Bottoms won't stand for what he takes to be idolatry of the snake that would compromise the staunch Christian axioms that underpin his new poem. The lower case "g," here, is underscored by the reference to the "sound of the Lord God" in the next section of the poem. Thus, he respectfully throws down the gauntlet in his quest to rival Lawrence's vision in this ambitious work. The speaker in *Little Drop*, though allured and bewitched by the snake's charms on the first page, soon girds his loins for a battle of spirits with the "guest" who has slithered, unnoticed, into his garden. If briefly thrown off his guard, he draws on the lesson he'd learned in childhood from his grandpa, his mentor and gunslinger of the chicken farm, to distrust the "wiley ... serpent's smile." While Lawrence struggled against the inner "voices" of caution, Bottoms faithfully espouses the bequeathal of his patrimony. A code of vigilance.

I postulate two duels that ripple across this work's expansive format: the contest between man and reptile, an inwardly tumultuous bout; and the rivalry between two poets with opposed views of the world of the spirits, which remains covert, except for the explicit passage I quoted in the third section. Bottom's strict monotheism is posited against Lawrence's polytheistic leanings. The spiritual center of gravity of the poem's collage-like structure is the briefest unit, section four, which is truly profound in its concision and resonance:

> Have you heard above the wind
> *the sound of the Lord God*
> > *walking in the garden in the cool of the day?*
>
> Have you heard a distant rumble and a sigh like rain in the trees?
>
> *In the war,* says my pal Steve Belew,
> *you could hear that rumble for miles rolling trough the jungle…*

To my ear, the brilliance of the repeated phrase "Have you heard" recalls the equivalent shuddering majesty of the phrase "Have you not heard" in line 5 of Hart Crane's final masterpiece, "The Broken Tower." In both poems, this is the rhetorical question that commands the reader to listen to the great voice of the spirit world (it is also, in Hayden Carruth's phrase, "the voice that is great within us"), which unmistakably comes to us on the wings of the wind, thunder and rain:

> Have you heard a distant rumble and a sigh like rain in the trees?

If that line, placed in its strategic moment of a sprung rhythm, doesn't shake us readers into keen alertness to harken to the epiphanies of that other world, maybe nothing will. That single line, daring to be set off to stand by itself, evokes all the power of revelation lurking behind Nature's every move in the acoustic surges of this poems' music. We become persuaded that so much power waiting to spring upon the reader, the *listener,* must be either the war (pal Steve Belew's Vietnam War) or God's impending touch. We hear forebodings of Apocalypse.

In this larger scheme of things, the snake's threat — the danger of its poison — must be perceived to pale to a "little drop." Its stature as a satanic agent for inflicting "wickedness" may seems to plummet, at this phase in the poem's discourse. But our snake leaps back to full eminence as a viable antagonist to the human persona when he is named at the start of the fifth section, "Copperhead." Again, the duel that dominated the work's foreground from the start is the warring between man and snake. In D.H. Lawrence's poem, the persona defers to the snake's quiet dignity and soulful presence. But in *Little Drop*, man and snake become, at last, equally matched sparring partners.

* * *

A technician's handling of form immediately declares itself with a delicate webwork of lines and shuffled spacing, as in the opening passage:

Ruckus around the bird feeder — two greedy mockingbirds mugging a
    cardinal —
and a small wind whirling
                      up from the creek beyond the cul-de-sac,
but no other disturbance, no ado,
no alarm but my heart going off at the presence of my guest.

This morning, yes, a visitor under my pear tree and cherries,

when I walked out to read my novel under my canopy of blossoms and
    leaves,
a visitor beside my table, a stranger,
                      unexpected, unnerving, coiled
like a wreath on a root-knee.

I edged under the canopy
and sidled toward my chair, and his spoon head bobbed into my shadow.

Odd to say how benevolent he looked and languid
with his fat jaw
            draped over the hourglass ridge of his back,
and how gently he offered his gaze,
                  how congenial his greeting,
as though all my fears were fallacy,
and the history of evil,
        some pathetic bamboozle.

    The first of many images that depict the snake with exquisite precision — "coiled/ like a wreath on a root-knee" — may inadvertently also suggest the coiling of lines into a word wreath. A fine metaphor for this poet's newly forged line matrix. As the artist struggles to find the language that perfectly renders the creature's unique appearance before him, he may simultaneously be seeking clues to help him discover the new turns of style that his open verse paragraph is taking. In my reading, the two mysteries are interlocked. Certainly, there is a great advance of style exhibited here, and a more obvious mimetic relation between line movement and details of animal portraiture is conveyed by the last visual image:

> Odd to say how benevolent he looked and languid
> with his fat jaw
>   draped over the hour-glass ridge of his back...

    The positioning of "fat jaw," spaced over the next line, clearly imitates the snake's anatomy, and while too much of this kind of minute reciprocity between details of style and subject would seem forced, or stilted, here it works like a natural unfolding of design on the page.

    A still more effective example of Bottoms' flair for stylistic mimesis would be a single line, spaced out as an independent unit, in the second section of the poem, "Muscled and thicker than a boy's fist." Line and serpent become wedded, as child Bottoms vividly recalls the image of a falling snake his grandpa had gunned down from a pine branch. A number of single lines are similarly isolated, or set off, in this anecdotal flashback to grandpa's encounter with the snake-thief of chicken eggs:

> *Ah, how wily the serpent's smile!* quipped my grandpa
> as he raised his double-barrel to the pine branch
>   and blasted the coachwhip
> onto the roof of our chicken house.
>
> He found a dead branch and raked the snake down.
>
> Muscled and thicker than a boy's fist,
>
>   shiny black
> as if coated in motor oil, it gleamed as he turned it in the sun.
> Not poisonous, he said, but a snake —
>   the serpent, the deceiver —
> and certainly the eater of chicken eggs.
>
> He held it up, let me look, then flung it into a briar patch.

    The slow pacing of spare units seems especially well-suited to this lustrous shimmer of dream-like memory images from earliest childhood. The improvisatory risk and naked openness of form strikes me as an ideal line dance for entering parts of the author's psyche that might have been inaccessible to more restrictive verse patterns. How stunningly alive this prosody becomes when it mates with a subject that revels in the new possibilities of stanzaic measure. And moreover, we may come to feel that no other form could have led to such a full exploration of this subject's labyrinth of self-discovery.

* * *

A minor humdrum squabble in the first line of the poem charmingly prepares for the extended vying for dominance between man and snake that soon follows. The "greedy mockingbirds" are battling against the cardinal at the bird feeder, competing for territorial rights over the food source. Meanwhile, the speaker takes for granted the calm and peacefulness of his backyard garden, a haven of solitude and safety in his life as a writer and reader, "no other disturbance, no ado." But the abrupt shift in tone to the next line reveals that he is stung to the quick by that sudden notice of his visitor, "No alarm but my heart going off at the presence of my guest." Evidently, his first shock is the snake's threat to his exclusive territorial rights, which allies him to the cardinal under attack in the opening lines. The fearful poet hates to give up sole possession of his sacred work space, his sanctuary.

Hence the stage is set for the power struggle to come. The "canopy of blossoms and leaves" utterly belongs to him, he feels, and no other being in the universe has the right to infringe on that pure ownership. The repeating phrase "canopy of blossoms," at intervals in the long poem, comes to symbolize this claim. The work's deepest mystery becomes inherent in this image, and that secret is held in suspension until the final lines.

I continue to be astonished by the successful nine repeats of the word "my" in the twenty lines of the first section — as applied to "heart," "guest," "pear tree and cherries," "novel," "canopy," "table," "chair," "shadow," and lastly, "fears." Virtually all of the adjectival possessives until the final "my" chant a litany of private belongings, but the culminating image widens the poem's perspective to the public arena of "the history of evil." And soon we learn that the problem of evil in the context of the speaker's aspiring vision of Christianity is central to the poem's quest, with special attention drawn to calculating the magnitude of Satan's role in the human world's worst ills. When the persona challenges the snake's stature, he is struggling to deflate the monstrous version of Satan beheld in the chatter of our day, a taking down of the Devil to proper size, much as the snake of the poem "studies *me*, sizes *me*/ ponders with his small tongue *my* human/ folly" (italics mine). The gaze that would diminish each opponent's size and intensity of sting is a mutual tactic in this bout between the two embattled species.

Grueling Miracle (Laurence Lieberman)

* * *

In due course, this elaborate work identifies three distinct incarnations of Satan: the Copperhead, the smack peddler in Saigon, and the womanizing gold digger who seduces the innocent paralegal lady. The Middle Eastern con artist is dispatched swiftly in the poem's impressive collage-like structure. Until the penultimate section, in which the two main Satanic beings are closely juxtaposed in the verses, two separate narratives are explored in alternating sections that mirror and counterpoint each other very effectively like the plot and subplot of a play. Bottoms' rather considerable talent as a novelist works much to his advantage in assembling the fluctuant two stories. Also, section two, the anecdote about the child Bottoms and his grandpa who shoots a snake, is handled succinctly as a flashback. The grandpa is a stunningly vivid character, far more memorably rendered than the couple portrayed in the main subplot. The love betrayal motif is initially burdened by the obvious cliché of viewing the cad as a snake, but the author's grace and ingenuity of verse shaping lift the story into an original tack, while interlocking themes in the various episodes provide still another rich dimension.

The other major advance of style in this author's best new poems is the heightened incisiveness of language and imagery, particularly revealed, here, in the precision of words literally depicting the snake. Bottoms' range of imagery would merit close study, in itself. His vivid pictorial exactitude recalls Lawrence or Roethke. No less impressively, surreal images exhibit the snake's power to camouflage itself in Nature's interplay of colors, its quick swerves between light and shade, which adds a fourth dimension to the scene portrayed. Midway in the poem, he half-jokily refers to the blossoms as "psychedelic." And given the two-way action of hypnosis performed by each antagonist upon the other, in turn, psychedelic hallucination is the quality of transport skillfully evoked. The snake induces trance with his stare and the wave-like moves of his body, while the persona employs his boot like a swinging pendulum:

> ...the serpent, the deceiver —
> whose split tongue seems to know me, whose slit eyes seem to know...

His head bobs right,
            then back, as it follows the toe of my boot.
He will not take his eyes off my boot.

After the speaker had taken some pains to puncture the snake's charisma, thereby deflating its power, its threat, in sections two and three, he briefly lets his guard down in section five. In this compelling unit, Bottoms displays the fullest range of versatility of images, from graphic concreteness to surreal dream flashes. In the deft shifts between pictorial levels, he lays the groundwork for the transcendent vision that will erupt in the poem's amazing finish. At the start of this pivotal rich passage, he restores the snake's dignity by declaring its scientific and popular names:

Agkistrodon contortrix, copperhead,
                                        lover of brush piles and fallen logs,
stone heaps, old tires, flat rocks beside cool water,

lover of field mice and fat lizards,
frogs, gophers, skinks, lover of my naked heel in nightmares of fishing...

His split tongue tastes my blood in the air. His spade head finds
a shaft of wormy light,
                        the psychedelic blossoms shiver.
I ease between the arms of my chair. If I leaned down only slightly,
I could touch the tip of his tongue.

The two Whitmanesque catalogues that follow, listing the snake's accustomed roosts and hideaways, then its carnivore-favorite foods, are linked by the chanted phrase "lover of." The persona has drifted into reverie, a meditative detached survey of the snake's habitual haunts and appetites. He seems, for this carefree moment of idling, to share the snake's ardors — the tone is affectionate, even praiseful, until the third turn of the litany shocks him into the reminder that his personal safety is at risk here, and he may be poised to join the troop of victims, "...lover of my naked heel in nightmares of fishing...." But he's still utterly immersed in trance, both the snake's hypnotic power over his psyche and the passive lilting of his own addictive play of verse litanies: "His split tongue tastes... His spade-head finds," followed by "I ease... If I leaned down... I could touch." He is so locked into absorption of this daze of syllables, the daze of snake-mystique, he cannot go into retreat. Indeed, just this once, he feels tempted to "touch the tip of his tongue."

The poem's music reaches its apogee in this rare blend of symmetries, the lovely intertwining of multiple lists without strain of syntax. The reader, so to say, may well partake of the persona's helpless trance.

***

Anticipating the work's final climactic moment, I find in this unit of the poem the key to unraveling how the persona convincingly negotiates the single abrupt shift from *my canopy of blossoms* to *our* canopy in the last three lines. With far less leaning to discursive or rhetorical asides than in some other long poems of this recent cycle, the author is now ready to risk his images to fully embody his message. Perhaps the first clue that our serpent may not be strictly a corporeal entity, trapped in its fleshly casing, is the middle line in section three — following the speaker's comic reduction of the snake's celestial rank from "lord" to "minor Greek god":

> leaf-stir and quivering light

This line, the only one of thirteen that is set apart, may seem to flutter with its mystery. At this moment in the unfolding of images, his first glance at the hovering snake almost mistakes it for the leaves blowing in the wind and flickers of sunlight on its body, which serve to camouflage the creature. It hides in these optical sleights. A reader takes the pitch of the lines as no more than this masking aspect, for now. But some shimmer of magic still clings to the images and carries forward.

Much earlier, we noted in section one that the snake is given to sudden moves into shade or light — it plays with these elements, as in "his spoonhead bobbed into my shadow," and this move is complemented by the counter-move in section five, "his spade-head finds / a shaft of wormy light." But clearly, something more than tricks of camouflage is resonating in the later passage, as suggested by the evocative next phrase, "the psychedelic blossoms shiver." In this new context, the actual living snake has returned to the garden setting from its temporary withdrawal into the cerebral precinct of the narrator's meditation. But the palpable snake comes back to him with a startle, as if reborn from his own dream-life: "lover of my naked heel in nightmares of fishing."

This more cryptic version of the reptile seems to become somehow entwined with the "wormy light" and the shivering "blossoms." No longer just camouflage, perhaps light and flowers are now becoming irreducible elements of the snake's organic make-up.

The last two segments of the poem carry this transmutation of the snake by the alchemy of images to brilliant completion:

> So easy to misread the world's mixed messages —

> these blossoms going electric in the shivering light, the red tongue
> bobbing
> on the scaly stem...

Again, readers should welcome the author's greater willingness to trust his images to reveal the essence of his vision in the best new poems. The snake, itself, appears to be trading identities with the flowers, one the mirror-image of the other. How can we know which blossoms are snake-mouths in disguise? Perhaps all the blossoms are potentially wicked, poisonous, kindred to the snake. Complicit, they may all partake of the serpent's purchase of the world's evil. Secret co-conspirators. They're "going electric in the shivering light," since they may hatch into snake months, snake tongues, in the dream-life.

To engage in combat with the uprisen hovering body of the snake is one test of the man's wits, but a still greater challenge it is for him to grapple with a phantom snake that arises from his own unguarded dreams, a snake which finally becomes the perfect embodiment of the "world's mixed messages." How, indeed, can you successfully do battle with an opponent that appears to recede and become transfigured, step by step, into the nearest flora of the garden?

Somehow, we are still taken by surprise when the final lines of the work carry to completion the enigmatic merging of snake and flora:

> Then wind in our canopy—
>
>   blossom and quivering light, hiss
> and mouth-flower blooming, so easily misread...

Prior to this moment of culmination, the naïve human protagonist believes he is at last winning the contest, for his boot, rocking "back and forth," seems to have full command over that "fanged rusty teaspoon," and he even supposes that he has disgraced his opponent into the cowardly pose of "bluffing some bravado." But the giveaway clue that he has lost the struggle for sole possession of his idyllic work space is one word—the conversion from *my* canopy to *our* canopy. And the last image, "hiss/ and mouth-flower blooming," confirms the snake's victory in transcendence.

The strength of Bottom's poetry is as poignant, here, as in any other poems of this collection. I believe that no amount of discursive writing could have approached the power and concision of these images to convey the upshot of *Little Drop's* vision. Though the Devil may appear in various guises, it is perhaps futile to simply whip the agent of Satan "a little harder" with a "knobby stick." Perhaps the speaker took exception with his old pal Steve Belew for missing an opportunity to flout, or otherwise punish, the Middle Eastern smack peddler in that Saigon bar. Passive Belew went soft on evil that day.

But *Little Drop's* cohesive passion resists any simplistic equating of the Devil with animals *or* humans, who happen to harbor portions of the world's evil in their own corpus. Hence the persona's wish to vanquish the snake, or eject it from his garden, is to radically "misread the world's mixed messages," since the nucleus of our world's great evil is spread out over all of Nature, though at any give moment it may inhabit one living receptacle or another. The speaker, then, finds that he would be better served by sharing his "canopy of blossoms" with the vessel that contains a "Little Drop of Wickedness." He would keep the agents of evil near at hand as a reminder — so as to bolster vigilance of spirit, the best weapon against the immanent evil that lurks everywhere. For the snake's venom is finally rooted in the pervasive integument of all living organic life. His "mouth-flower" is "blooming," since it is indissolubly woven into the tapestry of plant life that gives it concealment. Camouflage, yes. But the hideaway merges with the hider. They are one.

Part IV: "Homage to Buck Cline"

Probing readers of my long narrative poems have asked me, from time to time, why I don't try my hand at writing novels. Perhaps mistakenly, I assume their proposal implies that my modest knack as a story-maker would come to nobler fruition if I were to channel it into the *higher calling* of prose fiction. My answer is that it's still a challenge — not to say a true adventure — for me to search for a form of the poem that would leave no doubt that the genre of verse is the indispensable mode for my passion of tale-spinning. Perhaps more than any other long poem I've read in years, David Bottoms' "Homage to Buck Cline" once again persuades me that the art of poesy can still hold its own against any rivals in fostering a remarkable story.

However, on first reading, the rather slack pulse of the opening page may lead a reader to speculate that the many elements of setting and action might have come together more cohesively in a paragraph than in the relaxed meander of lines. The frequent space breaks in the line, leaving short phrases afloat, may seem diffuse like needlessly chopped-up prose.

But the rich music of naming does seem to gain buoyancy from the layering of clauses, even in the opening lines:

> At the edge of town,
> past Landers' Rexall Drugstore, the road whipped right then hard
>   downhill
> over the tracks of the L&N Railroad,
>   and one night in '65,
> stoned on a glass of Mateus rosé, with spaghetti
> homemade by my girlfriend's mother,
>   I gunned it for the thrill of the dip,
> and peeled a little rubber coming back to the road…
>
> Up ahead the river, the Etowah,
>   and the buttery glaze the moon spread
> across the concrete railing of the bridge,
> then the traffic light at the corner of the North Canton Store,
> where sour Buck Cline
>   sat in the dark patrol car with the gold badge
> of the Canton Police stenciled on his door…

Music *is* the key issue here, and a reader gradually discerns the very special rhythm and pacing that allows the many authentic names to breathe and resonate. Even so, the line may seem to ramble overmuch until the texture of language starts to crackle, as in the comic simulation of the good cop's reverie:

>   …waiting for some Romeo,
> Don Juan, some small-town Lothario, to run the light
> in his father's Impala…

But the fuller justification of such porous line play in Bottoms' recent shift to open form emerges in the nostalgic flashback to his childhood dallying around his grandfather's horse barn. Surely the compact portrait of the farm yard deploys the many surprise turns of lineation in this verse tapestry:

> Take the polished memory of my grandfather's horse barn
> with its hayloft full of jewels,

> or the pasture and the riding ring, the
> dog lots
> full of beagles, the swayback chicken houses crawling
> with mice,
> with cockroaches, slugs, with maggots of the dream-life...

At last, the crisscrossing network of little word chains is hitting on all eight cylinders. The intricate looping of the form does both visual and aural justice to the seemingly discordant mix of sensory images and their dream doubles. How else to reconcile the amazing contrarieties yoked by the phrase "maggots of the dream-life"?

This passage is the first of several key digressions from the main storyline, the encounter between the persona and the cop who threatens to arrest him for reckless speeding. All five of the digressive units may come to be recognized, finally, as tableaux that illustrate the author's message throughout. There must be "something divine in the memory." And again, it is the poem's innovatory form that most persuades the reader that the genre of verse greatly exceeds prose fiction in its power to implement the complex design of this work's metaphysical vision. The five distinct tableaux of the poem's middle segments become linked into a second storyline or subplot, in their own right. These speaking pictures, if you will, are interlaced by an extraordinary series of metaphors. The various settings portrayed draw on the speaker's memory of events scattered across his past. They leap over all hurdles of time and space. One scene, clearly antedating his birth by a few years, proclaims his father's legendary prowess as a star football player in "Canton High, 1941,/ the fall before the war." The five tableaux are all suffused with an intense nostalgic savor, and each, in its way, contributes to the creed that our life of memory is strongly tinged by divinity.

The first scene is the portrait of his grandfather's farmyard, which naturally spills over into the related memory of Mr. Cantrell — yet another of the speaker's endeared mentors of childhood days — who teaches him "on the floor of his South Canton greenhouse" about the mysteries of nurturing flowers, "the good rose requires good filth." This metaphoric adage quickly finds its subtle application to the persona's baser impulses (those Poe would call "perverse"), which overpowered his good judgment when he suddenly "floored" his gas pedal and went ballistic for limitless speed. Could this "perverse" wildness be the tipsy youth's human equivalent to the "glazed filth" that fortified the rose? Hence the first metaphor forecasts the teen persona's redemption to come in middle age. The whole Buck Cline interlude recalls the dissolute vagaries of Shakespeare's Prince Hal.

As in other poems of this cycle in Bottoms' work, the handy nuggets of wisdom that surge into his creative reverie emanate from a refreshingly human — if unlikely — mix of lowly and exalted sources, ranging from Poe and Homer, at one extreme, to neighbor Cantrell and the homemade exhibit of the High School Science Fair at the other. In the second tableau, the satiric tone of "*Glimpse Into Eternity*" at the student's booth in the Fair lulls a reader into a falsely dim expectation. But the jokey simplistic diorama opens a surprise gateway into lasting truth:

Something divine in the memory:

all those dusty little windows of the brain opening inward,
a mirror inside a mirror
      inside a mirror. *Glimpse Into Eternity*, read the sign
at the Cherokee High School Science Fair,
and when you leaned into the peephole of the big black box
taller than your head,
      somehow your eyes kept going and going...

This briefest unit of the poem is truly pivotal, since it lays the groundwork for the visionary lyric's original telescoping structure. Each of the succession of three memory vignettes that follows in the rich midsection of the poem functions like one of those "windows of the brain opening inward," carrying us ever deeper and deeper into the vision of the naked soul of the speaker journeying through a hall of mirrors to a life-transfiguring collision with his father's spirit. In each vignette, the "eyes" of memory transport keep "going and going" — there is no stopping them until the exhaustive vision is complete.

All three tableaux lead, incrementally, to the speaker's full revelatory awaking to the might and scope of his father's spirit. The first memory is culled from the years of his young manhood ("Sunday evening, early nineties"), and the undoubted power of the flashback is verified by the piercing look in the eyes of "the old saw from my hometown," who shares with him a telling glimpse of his father's football glory and high school stardom, years before his own birth. The validation of the sacredness of this slice of memory is affirmed by both the "old hymn" chimed by the "bells of the First Baptist" church that triggered the man's spiel, and the "gleam of deep reverie" in his eyes as he divulged the words of his father's renown. While the persona must surely have known about his father's local athletic fame prior to this exchange, the legendary or mythic ring now hits his ears with a special new epiphany:

> Something about his eyes I've remembered,
> pale, but sharp,
>   the streetlight under the bleached stars catching them
> in that gleam of deep reverie — like the eyes of a scientist,
> or a saint,
>   when the clouds finally open...
> "Your old man," he said, "you should've seen him play football,"
> meaning Canton High, 1941,
>   the fall before the war.

The speaker may as well have included *the eyes of a poet* in this short list of awakeners to transcendent life, since those Yeatsian "clouds" in his own vision do "finally open" at this moment in the work's discourse. Indeed, we now come to recognize that the true great journey of this verse elegy to lost youth was hidden in the opening pages, concealed by the strong overt cop story, the linear narrative that frames the poem at both ends, start and finish. It is the lone soul's irrevocable voyaging, which boldly skips across the barriers of time and space. Perhaps this long ambitious work, more than any other piece in *Endtime*, resonates with the epigraphs from Whitman and Flannery O'Connor at the book's outset ("Darest thou now O soul...").

The divine leaps of memory catapult the persona's soul, as exhibited by the shift in form, here, to a non-linear flow of events. The soul's escape from Time's horizontal boundaries is portrayed as a journey that moves vertically down, layer by layer, passing through the portals of each of those "dusty little windows of the brain opening inward." The naked spirit travels under the stars and communes with the stars' magically wavering lights, which keep shifting and altering in Bottoms' remarkably transformative imagery. The comic overtones of some of the star tropes may fool the reader into taking them too lightly as mere ornaments, a flourish of the author's playfulness of style ("dizzy stars," "bleached stars," "nervous stars," "charming stars," etc.), but when the opening star motif culminates — at the poem's finish — in the one star that the persona consigns to Buck Cline's "crown," an emblem of his being anointed into sainthood, we find that the chain of stellar images, though whimsical, was forging a metaphor of grave and weighty consequence. And we may discover, on repeated readings, that throughout the poem, the life of the speaker's soul is treated as coolly non-sequential. It goes on and off like a light bulb. Or shimmers and dims like a pulsating star's life. Consider the early passage about the cop/teen encounter:

> ...the stars flared and calmed and flared again
> as he glanced from the license to my face and back,
> breathing my name twice, or my father's...

Perhaps guided by the star images, we may best learn to read the work's middle passages. Following the brief unit recalling the High School Science Fair, the divinity of memory takes over the poem's zigzag orbit, its long vertical digressions from the base narrative's horizontal flow. These salient memories become the fabric and life blood of our dark secret being. In the last tableau, the persona's father taps into that deep subliminal life when he quietly chants his way into the secret reservoir of the "whipped" and "weeping" man, whom he defeats and subsequently comforts.... But those memories may come together in a blessed conjunction—one "we used to credit to the stars"—that anneals the psychic underpinnings of the speaker's soul. Only the firm network of these memories can *toughen* the spirit to be ready for the "tumble and drift of eternity":

> And so much hangs on it,
>   the way memory toughens us up for that tumble
> and drift of eternity, for the unpatrolled landscape
> of the psychic unfurling,
>   and so much, certainly,
> on those unknown connections, far back, we used to credit to the stars...

Our great self-healing task, then, is to ferret out those key sacred memories and restore the "unknown connections, far back" between them. In his art, Bottoms would build a web of permanent unassailable memories which may bulwark the last "psychic unfurling" needed to face death and the hereafter.

* * *

When the persona briefly revisits "the polished memory" of his grandfather's farm early in the work, he largely anticipates the metaphoric passage that will launch the poem's closing unit — the abrupt return to the Buck Cline saga following five forays into memory zones that have crucially shaped the speaker's heart:

> *Like the generation of leaves,*
> Homer says, *the lives of mortal men.* Or something close, and that night whole generations trembled
> under the nervous stars as Buck Cline,
> like a slightly stunted Ajax, leaned down
> and speared me in the eyeball with the beam of his flashlight.

Thus, one of the creditable strengths of this work is its grasp of the carryover of genetic traits across three generations of males in the author's family — grandfather, father and himself — a companion trio to the vision of three generations of his filial women in "Easter Shoes Epistle." Why did "whole generations" *tremble*, while Buck Cline was slowly sorting out his options for penalizing the wild young lawbreaker in his charge? If he opted to impose the full just wrath of the Law, jail time and a not-to-be-expunged felony on the boy's record, that would disgrace the much-honored family name; and the overtones of "trembled" suggest that the taint would sweep back across many generations. Such is the close-knit grip of community in this small Southern town. But most particularly, the lines shudder with the threat to bring down his father's good name. And I find that the risk to survival of the persona's loving father-son bond is the central underlying motif of this entire poem, though that relationship is covert and never revealed explicitly. As in *Hamlet*, the vision of Bottoms' compassion for his father's near-constant physical pain, coupled with his heroic verbal restraint in the face of suffering, is the one theme that most endows this work with tragic reverberations. Though the speaker never encounters the father directly, the oblique remembering of his father's personal struggle with pain gives these lines immense poignancy:

> And stayed tough enough
> even after the war
> when the shrapnel gnawed into the small of his back
> with every step he took
> up or down the service ramp at Holcomb Chevrolet, every step
> he took across the concrete garage
> on that splinter of a bone
> the Japanese navy left in his leg…

Whatever may have transpired between father and son remains off-stage, but strong mutual regard hinted between them gains power from indirection. Wayward side glances. The father's pain, much as his inner wounds suffered in silence, partakes of the divine essence. As does the persona's memory. But in this work's calculus of divine inklings, when acute pain and memory are fused — coming together — Divinity seems most to abound, a doubling of effects:

> ...that memory always alive and violent, though never spoken,
> having in its pain too much of the divine,
>
> the unapproachable...

* * *

In my reading of *Buck Cline*, the most essential links between father and son are authorial, hidden in the language arts and style of Bottoms' evolving craft. In the first of three father tableaux, the "old saw from my hometown" in the "early nineties" concludes his honorific testimonial to the father by condensing the man's virtues in one exactly right word, "as if he'd tasted its weight/ on his tongue for years, careful for the perfect usage,/ that true word that said it all — 'Tough.'" He divulges the one palpable word with an oddly keen savor of discovery. And we, too, are struck by the surprisingly fresh ring of this word in the special new context, since various forms of *tough* had been casually uttered in the opening pages. We heard about the renegade or delinquent "rowdies, the would-be toughs," and next, Buck Cline's chief mission in middle age had shrunk to "making/ his poor living/ out-toughing the tough." Finally, near the poem's finish, we learn that our fate at the *Endtime* of life will be measured by how well "memory toughens us up for that tumble and drift of eternity." But the clear center of gravity for the many repeats of the word *tough* is the incarnation of the father's human essence in that one valiant trait. All other variations of the word take their cue from that baseline "perfect usage."

To belabor the obvious parallel to this writer's new turns of verbal nuance, he clearly aspires to something of his father's discipline in a toughening of style. Senior Bottoms had learned to cope with constant bone aches by suppressing the impulse to vent his hurts with spoken outbursts of any kind, whether from anger or self-pity. He perfectly adopted the pose of lip-biting silent angst:

> ...when the shrapnel gnawed into the small of his back
> with every step he took...
>
> ...every step...

> on that splinter of a bone
>
>   the Japanese navy left in his leg,
> that memory always alive and violent, though never spoken...

In these measures, Junior Bottoms, too, has learned to hone the dormant power of the unspoken, since too much saying will undoubtedly diminish the force of speech — only words *tough* enough can slip through this censor.... After the relaxed near-prosy opening page, or so, the way these passages in mid-poem build taut phrasing and compression may sneak up on the readers, catching us unawares. The repeated phrase "every step," especially, asserts a rhythm of chanting that mirrors the father's stoic, embattled vision. Every line, every word, follows suit, emulates the mentor's example. These lines may seem to mimic the blunt incisiveness of "that splinter of a bone." Like those unwavery heroes, or anti-heroes, in Faulkner's novels, the father acts out a passion of indomitability. And the verse technique, here, echoes that passion.

The last of five tableaux carries Bottoms' art of the speaking picture to a new high water mark of strength. The passage resembles some enigmatic collisions between agonizingly mismatched humans in the stories of Flannery O'Connor. The similitude is mostly a matter of tone. A horrific violent grappling of two unlikely opponents — such as the father and the "big man in overalls" — peaks in a totally improbable moment of deep communion. The sparks of revelation fly wildly about, and a reader is left bewildered by the outcome. What source did the following vision spring from?:

> ...the umpire, Doyle Fowler, threw off his mask and charged around the backstop,
>   the man, though, the mouth, had picked up a shovel,
> and caught him with the blade
> square in the face,
>   and my father, out of the dugout, fallen suddenly
> on him, the mouth, the drunk,
>   arms around him in a wrenching hug,
> not out of anger, but something else,
> and them on the ground,
>   the one man weeping,
> and my father talking, not shouting, but talking quietly
> and hugging the whipped man harder and harder,

> as though he'd known all along
> > a secret the man thought no one knew...

Somehow, the father's mysterious power to grant the beaten man consolation, even a kind of merciful grace, is totally credible. Whatever the father "quietly" says to him is probably less relevant than the tenderness that is evoked by the cadence of the lines of verse. Moreover, the father's power of verbal restraint must give him access to a language which illumines the secret life: words that radiate light which opens the vision of a "scientist or saint"—not to say verse technician—on the very brink of big discoveries.

This unit, as much as any sweep of lines in the work, demands the palpitant articulation of Bottoms' side-to-side shifts of caesuras within the line, since the diagonal latticework of phrasing visually simulates the flying shovel and entanglement of limbs. That line grid so handily exemplifies the apt correspondence between style and content, it should lay to rest any question about the clear necessity for this work's story to be rendered in Bottoms' expressive new form of verse rather than prose fiction.

The opening lines of the passage reveal yet another vindication for the firming up—"toughening" so to say—of concise language in this author's recent art. And I'm always grateful to find covert clues in the images of the poem, itself, for any important breakthrough in its style or form:

> Tough also one night
> at Little League when a drunk behind the backstop kept deviling the
> > umpire—
> big man in overalls, a mill worker, hard, poor, angry,
> all the desperate adjectives,
> > > and the words frothing out merciless and ugly,
> and the man's own boy at the plate
> trying to see the baseball through that rain of curses...

First, I'm struck by the natural verve of "big man in overalls, a mill worker, hard, poor, angry," which approaches the flat straight monosyllabic style of much good fiction, a possible import from Bottoms' own work in two novels. But when I consider the refreshing ease of delivery of this language in the tempo of the line, I'm reminded of Robert Penn Warren's telling me in his letters of the early eighties—when he'd just launched the last matchless phase of his own poetry—that he vowed never again to waste his best energies on writing fiction, for fear of the poems he might let slip away.... And I'm still puzzling over the beguiling ambiguity of the next floating phrase, "all the desperate adjectives," which hovers — to my ear — between two curiously opposed readings. Does the speaker rebuke himself for the over-the-top list of words describing the "mill worker," or is he already berating "the mouth" of the drunken man whose invective of "curses" reveals his sloppy morals as an index of his puerile habits with language — "the words frothing out merciless and ugly." I'd like to suppose that the pejorative "desperate adjectives" cuts both ways. Regardless, the language esthetic lauded, here, which strongly refers to Bottoms' evident aspirations for his own art, would favor a lean restrained vocabulary, rather than effusive "frothing." The father's superior ethical values, implied by the restraint of "talking quietly," is touted here, and the carryover to many passages in the poem's spare beauty of style is evoked, as well.

Finally, the whole vivid setting recalls the incisive portraiture of Medieval exemplums, and it makes us harken for the lost tangible extrovert virtues of old-time allegory.

* * *

Many poems of *homage* seem routinely easy to bring off, but a full coming to terms with your father, that's a soul-wrenching event. That's a once-and-forevermore rite of passage. Bottoms clearly has a fondness for both of his wife's parents, and his portraits of his in-laws in the poem "Vigilance" are endearing and serve his art's message well enough, but very likely at little cost to his psychic buoyancy or deliverance. Indeed, his mother-in-law appears to have provided the key word for his last book's title, *Endtime*. However, he must have known, instinctively, that to approach his actual father's raw spirit too directly in his art would be like staring into the noonday sun without any protective shades.

Not that the semi-comical tribute to the traffic cop who spared him from the early ignominy of jail time for reckless driving wasn't a worthy and befitting subject for this largest canvas in his recent book. But the devastating plunge into the secret depths of his father's soul, a psychic excavation that must inevitably threaten — and perhaps transfigure — the seat of his own identity, that's the hidden subject which invests this work with profound consequence. Certainly, the tale of Buck Cline is rendered with undoubted charm and panache, yet the drama of exposing the raw nerve of his father's indomitable being soars beyond the cop story with unforeseen intensity. That is the dimension which gives this poem its true stature.

My best guess is that the author merely set out to write a portrait of tribute to the good cop, and then the father anecdotes grew, tangentially, out of the aura of bravado that clung to the Bottoms family name ("breathing my name twice, or my father's"). And curiously, when I ponder the various characters that inhabit this work, the man Buck Cline seems to fade into a mythic prototype, whereas the flesh-and-blood father gains a searing hyper-reality in retrospect. But I have no quarrel with this apparent disproportion, since the overall vision strikes the right balance. Bottoms' lightness of touch in the humorous dialogue and comic nuances of imagery help to lift the story-line into an enchanted dream trajectory of fable or parable:

> Saint Buck, I kept saying all the way home, and lit in an uncluttered
>   niche
> of my memory
>   a little shrine ... Saint Buck
> of the handy blackjack,
> Saint Buck of the billy, of the speed trap, of the dark patrol car lurking
>   in the shadows,
>   troubled patron of would-be toughs,
> of war heroes and weeping boys,
>
> street cop, surely, of the City to come...

But as in Flannery O'Connor's great parables, it's the excruciating details of tortured humans that come to be most dizzying and unforgettable.

Works Cited

Bottoms, David. *Waltzing Through the Endtime*. Port Townsend, WA: Copper Canyon Press, 2004.

Contributors

DAVID BAKER is the author or editor of more than a dozen books, most recently a book of poems, *Never-Ending Birds* (2009), and *Radiant Lyre: Essays on Lyric Poetry* (2007). He holds the Thomas B. Fordham Chair of Creative Writing at Denison University and also teaches regularly in the MFA program for writers at Warren Wilson College. He is poetry editor of *The Kenyon Review*.

EDWARD BYRNE is the author of six collections of poetry, most recently *Seeded Light* (2009). His literary criticism has appeared in various collections, including *Mark Strand* (2002), edited by Harold Bloom, and *A Condition of the Spirit: The Life and Work of Larry Levis* (2004), edited by Christopher Buckley and Alexander Long. He is a professor in the English department at Valparaiso University, where he edits the *Valparaiso Poetry Review*.

FRED CHAPPELL is the author of 15 collections of poetry (*Shadow Box*, 2009, is his fifteenth), eight novels, and three collections of short fiction. He is an eight-time recipient of the Roanoke-Chowan Award for Poetry, as well as the Sir Walter Raleigh Award for Fiction, the Bollingen Prize for Poetry, the T.S. Eliot Prize, the Thomas Wolfe Prize, the Aiken Taylor Award in Modern American Poetry, and the Prix du Meilleur Livre Étranger (Best Foreign Book Prize). He received his B.A. and M.A. from Duke University and taught for 40 years at the University of North Carolina at Greensboro.

ALICE FRIMAN has published eight collections of poetry — her ninth, *Vinculum*, is forthcoming from the Louisiana State University Press. Previous books include *Book of the Rotten Daughter* (2006) and *Inverted Fire* (both from 1997) and *Zoo* (1999), which won the Ezra Pound Poetry Prize and the Sheila Margaret Motton Prize. She has received fellowships from the Indiana Arts Commission, the Arts Council of Indianapolis and the Bernheim Foundation, and she won the 2001 James Boatwright III Prize for Poetry. She was a professor of English at the University of Indianapolis from 1973 to 1993. She is poet-in-residence at Georgia College and State University, Milledgeville.

MARSHALL BRUCE GENTRY is a professor of English at Georgia College and State University in Milledgeville and editor of the *Flannery O'Connor Review*. The author of *Flannery O'Connor's Religion of the Grotesque* (1986), he has published articles on O'Connor's work in a variety of journals and collections. He co-edited *Conversations with Raymond Carver* and has published articles about American writers in a variety of journals and edited collections.

JANE HILL is the author of *Gail Godwin* and *Cobb County: At the Heart of Change* and the editor of four anthologies of contemporary literature. She has published articles on Ann Beattie, James Dickey, Mary Lee Settle, Bobbie Ann Mason, and other contemporary authors. She received her Ph.D. from the University of Illinois at Urbana-Champaign in twentieth century American literature and is the chair of the English department at Marshall University.

ROBERT W. HILL is an emeritus professor of English at Kennesaw State University, where he was the chair of the English Department from 1985 to 1996. He earned degrees in English at the University of North Carolina, Chapel Hill, and in 1972 his Ph.D. from the University of Illinois at Urbana-Champaign, with a dissertation on the poetry of James Dickey and Theodore Roethke. A former co-editor of the *South Carolina Review* and current co-editor, with Robert Barrier, of the online literary journal *Kennesaw Review*, Hill has published articles and poetry. He co-authored with Richard J. Calhoun *James Dickey* (Twayne, 1983).

LAURENCE LIEBERMAN is the author of 17 books of poetry and criticism, including *The Osprey Suicides; New and Selected Poems, 1962–92*; *Compass of the Dying*; *Flight from the Mother Stone*; *Hour of the Mango Black Moon*; *Beyond the Muse of Memory: Essays on Contemporary American Poets*; *Dark Songs: Slave House and Synagogue*; *The Regatta in the Skies: Selected Long Poems*, and most recently, *Carib's Leap: Selected and New Poems of the Caribbean* (2005). He is an emeritus professor of English at the University of Illinois at Urbana-Champaign.

DON RUSS is a Florida-born poet who has taught writing, literature, and film at Louisiana State University, the Georgia Institute of Technology, and Kennesaw State University. His poems have appeared in periodicals and anthologies throughout the United States, Canada, and England, and his book of poems, *Dream Driving*, was published in 2007 by Kennesaw State University Press. He lives and writes in Atlanta.

W. A. SESSIONS is Regents' emeritus professor of English at Georgia State University. He received his A.B. from the University of North Carolina at Chapel Hill and his M.A. and Ph.D. in English and comparative literature from Columbia University. He is a poet, a playwright, a critic, and a lecturer, and has written extensively on Francis Bacon, Edmund Spencer, John Milton, William Shakespeare, and Flannery O'Connor. The author of *Henry Howard, The Poet Earl of Surrey* (1999), he is currently writing the official biography of Flannery O'Connor.

DAVE SMITH is the chairman of the writing seminars department at Johns Hopkins University and the Elliot Coleman Professor of Poetry. He is the author of 31 books, most recently *Hunting Men: Reflections on a Life in American Poetry* (2006); *Little Boats, Unsalvaged* (2005), and *The Wick of Memory: New and Selected Poems 1970–2000* (2000). He recently edited, with Robert Demott, a collection of essays called *Afield: American Writers on Bird Dogs* (2010).

Contributors

MICHAEL SOWDER is a former student (MFA 1994) of David Bottoms and teaches poetry writing and literature at Utah State University, where he is the poetry editor of *Isotope*. He is the author of the award-winning poetry collection *The Empty Boat* (2004 T.S. Eliot Prize), *A Calendar of Crows* (2001, New Michigan Press Award), and, with Margaret Aho, the chapbook *Café Midnight* (2003). He is also the author of *Whitman's Ecstatic Union* (2005) and his poetry and essays appear in journals and magazines throughout the country.

ERNEST SUAREZ is the Ordinary Professor of English and chairs the English Department at the Catholic University of America. His books include *James Dickey and the Politics of Canon: Assessing the Savage Ideal* (1993) and, with T.W. Stanford III and Amy Verner, *Southbound: Interviews with Southern Poets* (1999). He has written on Ezra Pound, Robert Penn Warren, the New Criticism, the New Left, the politics of canon formation, and Southern rock and blues, especially the Allman Brothers. In 1999, he was selected as the District of Columbia Professor of the Year.

WILLIAM WALSH is the author of *The Conscience of My Other Being* (2005), *The Ordinary Life of a Sculptor* (1993), *Speak So I Shall Know Thee: Interviews with Southern Writers*, and *Under the Rock Umbrella: Contemporary American Poets from 1951–1977* (2006). His work has appeared in the *Michigan Quarterly Review*, *The Kenyon Review*, *North American Review* and numerous other journals. He is also an internationally recognized photographer. His latest collection of poems, *Wild Wreckage*, is forthcoming in 2011.

Index

"Adios, Horses" 24
"After the Dinner Party" 203
"All Landscape Is Abstract, and Tends to Repeat Itself" 115
"All Systems Break Down" 158, 161–162, 164, 187
"All Systems Tower and Collapse" 161, 163–164
"All the Animal Inside Us" 195–196
"Allatoona Evening" 63, 68, 70, 186, 202, 230
"Allatoona Storm" 42, 49, 172
Allman, Duane 151–152, 213
"Amazing Grace: The Aesthetics of a Spiritual Quest" 45–56
"American Mystic" 35
Ammons, A.R. 27
"Andalusia Visit" 41, 43
angels 10, 16, 35, 102, 113, 117, 139, 147, 156, 159, 162, 172–173, 184, 194, 213, 237
"The Anniversary" 59, 85, 226–228
Any Cold Jordan 4, 8, 66–67
Appalachia 115
"Appearances" 137, 146, 185
"Arcana Mundi" 30
archetypes (archetypal) 46, 52, 58–59, 66, 68–69, 106, 162–164, 192–193, 204
"Armored Hearts" (poem) 35, 61–62, 87, 156, 168, 182, 228–231
Armored Hearts: New and Selected Poems (collection of poems) 29–30, 35–38, 45, 48, 56, 57, 58–59, 61, 69–70, 85, 88, 140, 142–144, 157, 162, 167–169, 176–179, 182–186, 196, 198, 201–202, 205, 212, 216, 218–221, 233, 235–237
"The Artificial Nigger" 24
"As I Walked Out One Evening" 3
"At the Grave of Martha Ellis" 150, 152, 231
"At the Still Point" 7–10
Auden, W.H., "As I Walked Out One Evening" 3
"Audubon" 128–129
"Awake" 225

Baker, David 48, 106
baptism 66, 138, 166, 183
"Barriers" 231
baseball 9, 18–20, 47, 65, 114, 131, 193–194, 218–219, 246, 266
Becker, Ernest 63, 198
"Below Freezing on Pinewood Mountain" 30, 168, 177, 210
Berry, Wendell 16
Berryman, John 246
"Birches" 234–235
Bishop, Elizabeth 4, 91, 133, 202
"Black Hawk Rag" 41, 151
"The Blue Mountain" 36, 38, 201
Bly, Robert 27, 122
Bottoms, Rachel 52, 142, 145–146, 148
"The Boy Shepherd's Simile" 9–10, 164, 181, 200, 207, 237
The Branch Will Not Break 133, 190
Brock, Van 190–191
"The Broken Tower" 249
"Bronchitis" 144, 146, 170, 232
Brothers Karamazov 125
Bryant, William Cullen 209
"Buckdancer's Choice" 190
"Burnt Norton" 7
Byrne, Edward 136

"Calling Across Water at Lion Country Safari" 34, 184
"A Canoe" 38, 224–225
Carvainis, Maria 66–67
"The Catfish" 29, 83, 184, 216
Cavafy, C.P. 200
"Cemetery Wings" 139, 141, 180
Chappell, Fred 2, 12, 24, 45, 85, 129, 190
Christ (Christianity) 37, 41–44, 47–48, 50–51, 69–70, 79, 90, 113–117, 120–125, 139–140, 156–159, 164, 169–173, 176, 183, 198–202, 207–209, 227, 233, 248, 252
"The Christmas Rifle" 30, 206–207, 218
Civil Rights 52, 79, 210

Index

"Coasting Toward Midnight at the Southeastern Fair" 15, 161, 213–214
"Cockfight in a Loxahatachee Grove" 212
"The Copperhead" 29, 59, 110–111, 161, 185, 188, 195–196, 249, 253
"Country and Western" 161
country music 31–32, 190
"Country Store and Moment of Grace" 4, 20, 51–56, 73, 77, 83, 86, 113, 118, 121, 133, 143, 147–150, 168, 171, 234, 237
Crane, Hart 249
"Crawling Out at Parties" 390, 59, 184, 196, 215

"The Darkling Thrush" 22
"A Daughter's Fever" 142, 154, 232
Deep Hidden Meaning ("DHM") 3, 66, 191
Deliverance 127
The Denial of Death 63, 198
"Design" 17
"The Desk" 59, 66–67, 85, 134–136, 226
Dickey, James 2–3, 8, 12–16, 20–21, 27–28, 31, 38–39, 45–51, 60, 68, 85, 87, 89–92, 109–112, 115–116, 121–122, 126–128, 131–133, 139, 173, 189–191, 195–196, 212–214, 224, 237, 241
Dr. Faustus 125
"Dragons of Eden" 58, 122, 195
"The Drowned" 17, 107
"The Drunk Hunter" 30, 107, 137, 159–160, 163, 112
"Drunk in the Bass Boat" 30
Dubbert, Joe L. 86, 210–211, 218–219

"Easter Shoe Epistle" 21, 41, 42, 152, 157, 173, 240–245, 263
Easter Weekend 3–4, 9, 58, 67, 69, 94–95, 98, 101, 104
"Elegy for a Trapper" 30, 36
Eliot, T.S. 7–8, 11, 13, 25, 28, 95, 159, 225, 236
Emerson, Ralph Waldo 23, 91, 153
"Entering Scott's Night" 8
"The Evolution of the GOB Aesthetic" 27–44

"Face Jugs: Homage to Lanier Meadows" 223–224
"Faith Healer Comes to Rabun County" 47
"A Family Parade" 38, 112, 136, 145, 227
The Far Field 133
"The Farmers" 136, 146, 237
Faulkner, William 7–8, 11, 13, 23, 85, 265
"Feeling Into Words" 193
"Fiddle Time" 224
"The First Step" 200
"Fisher King" 126
"Fishing from the Poetry Boat: A Conversation" 57–70

Flagon and Apples 27
"For the Last Wolverine" 46
"Free Grace at Rose Hill" 36, 38, 84, 169, 181, 209
Friman, Alice 57, 211, 236
Frost, Robert 17, 234, 237

"Gar" 29
Gentry, Bruce 3, 57, 94, 211, 236
Gerzon, Mark 205–206, 218
"Gigging on Allatoona" 30
Goldberg, Herb 205
Gone with the Wind 72, 76
"A Good Man Is Hard to Find" 23
Good Old Boy 27
"Gospel Banjo: Homage to Little Roy Lewis" 179, 224
"Grueling Miracle: Faith in Middle Age" 240–268

Hannah, Barry 22–23, 44, 124, 174
Hardy, Thomas 22
Harmonium 27, 91
Hayden, Robert 19–20
Heaney, Seamus 11, 15, 61, 64, 193
"The Heaven of Animals" 173, 190
hero 24, 32, 57–58, 62, 72, 76, 81, 86, 160–161, 166–169, 205, 218–231, 237, 263–268
"Heron Blues" 39, 113
"Heron on the Oconee" 25
"Hiking Toward Laughing Gull Point" 108, 163, 184, 217, 219
Hill, Jane 71, 94, 204
Hill, Robert (Bob) 68, 87, 212, 214
Hirsch, Ed 129, 199
Holtzclaw, Connell (Connie) 68, 94–104
"Homage to Buck Cline" 41, 84, 86, 122–123, 150–151, 173, 257–268
"Homage to Lester Flatt" 179, 223
"A Home Buyer Watches the Moon" 92, 108, 114, 140–141, 164, 177, 215–216, 219
"Home Maintenance" 36, 92, 222
Hopkins, Gerald Manley 91, 240, 270
"How Death Isolates" 158
Hugo, Richard 1, 4, 27–28, 39, 65, 103
"Hunting on Sweetwater Creek" 29, 112
"Hurricane" 165, 179

"Ice" 57, 166
identity 11–13, 15–16, 18, 25, 69, 71, 73, 77–78, 82, 85, 109, 115, 143, 205–206, 215, 218, 220–221, 226, 229–230, 232, 235, 267
"'If It Touches Us, It Touches Us': The White Southern Male Struggle with Race" 71–86
illumination 89–90, 137; *see also* seeker; yearner

Index

"In a Jon Boat During a Florida Dawn" 29, 137, 164
"In a Kitchen, Late" 29, 35, 60, 196
"In a Pasture Under the Cradled Moon" 32, 137, 165, 182, 219–220
"In a U-haul North of Damascus" (poem) 32, 110, 137, 162, 165, 181, 190, 219–220
In a U-haul North of Damascus (poetry collection) 29, 48, 59, 107, 134, 140, 147, 168, 178, 214, 218
"In Heritage Farms, Settled" 92, 182, 216
"In Jimmy's Grill" 30, 210, 215–216
"In Louisiana" 59, 226
"In the Big House of the Allman Brothers My Hearts Gets Tuned" 41, 152
"In the Black Camaro" 66, 136, 114, 216
"In the Ice Pasture" 33–34, 57, 166, 183, 221
"In the Wilderness" 38, 113
"Into the Darkness We're Headed For" 159

Jamming with the Band at the VFW 27, 31, 210
Jeffers, Robinson 27
Jung, Carl 61, 66, 125, 153, 192, 195, 197, 199, 236

"Kenny Roebuck's Knuckle-Curve" 151, 244–246
Kimmell, Michael 86, 206, 211, 223, 234
Kinnell, Galway 47
"Kinship" 30

"The Lame" 47, 137
"Last Nickel Ranch: Plains, Montana" 36–37, 93, 206
"Last Supper in Montana" 36, 37, 139, 169, 178, 236
Lawrence, D.H. 35, 134, 195, 247, 249
Leaping Poetry 122
"Learning to Let the Water Heal" 47, 162
Let Not Your Hart 132
Lieberman, Laurence 1, 240
"The Light of the Sacred Heart" 18, 66, 164, 178–179, 217–218
"Little Drop of Wickedness" 29, 125, 247–257
"Local Quarrels" 215
"The Logic of the Original Dream" 120–135
"The Lost Hunter" 158
"Love at the Sunshine Club" 24
lyric 8–10, 16, 20–21, 24, 33, 40–41, 107, 136–138, 141, 143–147, 150–152, 154, 189–191, 260
lyric narrative 33, 136, 138

Manhood in America: A Cultural History 206
"The Meadow Mouse" 190, 196
"Melville in the Bass Boat" 121, 153, 155, 173

memory 1, 4, 8–9, 11, 20, 29, 40–45, 51–56, 58–59, 78–79, 81–83, 85, 89, 112–114, 118, 124–125, 134, 136–154, 159–161, 168, 170–174, 184, 193–195, 208–209, 224, 237, 243–245, 265
metaphor 10–12, 15–16, 34, 40, 50–51, 61–66, 77, 84–85, 108, 120–125, 137–152, 155–157, 173–174, 179–180, 182, 192, 197–198, 202, 213, 217–220, 224–227, 235–236, 242, 250, 259–260, 261–262
Moby Dick 121, 153, 173
Morgan, Robert 92
"A Morning from the Gospel of St. John" 38, 150, 230–231
"My Father's Garbage Can" 24
"My Old Man Loves My Truck" 24–25
"My Perfect Night" 89, 185
"My Uncle Sowing Beatitudes" 85, 128, 150, 236

narrative 1, 2, 4, 7, 12–13, 17, 21, 33, 40, 43, 45, 49–51, 53, 60, 64, 66, 73, 75, 77, 79, 85, 94, 87, 89, 106–107, 110, 112, 114–115, 129, 132, 136, 138, 151–154, 166, 171, 189–194, 203, 208, 218, 222, 225, 232, 235, 243, 253, 257, 261, 262
"Naval Photograph: 25 October 1942" 85, 226
negative capability 60
"Neighbors, Throwing Knives" 215
New Testament 44, 178
"A Night, Near Berkeley Springs" 180
"Night Strategies" 83, 116, 146, 170, 233, 237
"The North American Sequence" 190

"O Mandolin, O Magnum Mysterium" 41–42, 154
"Occurrence in the Big Sky" 38, 39–40, 90–91, 93, 113, 236
O'Connor, Flannery 8–9, 23–24, 42, 153, 202, 236, 261, 265, 268
"An Old Hymn for Ian Jenkins" 179
Old Testament 59, 66, 172, 177, 192
"Olympus" 246
Ommateum 27
"On Methodist Hill" 38, 114, 144, 156, 170, 232–233
"On the Willow Branch" 29, 35
"The Onion's Dark Core" 187–203
"The Orchid" 47
The Other Side of the River 21
"Our Presbyterian Christmas" 38, 113, 237

"Paper Route, Northwest Montana" 137
Parker, Billy 4, 67–68, 214, 216
pastoral 13–16, 18, 21, 23, 89
"The Pentecostal" 36–38, 41, 169, 181, 236
"The Performance" 190
"The Pike" 190

Poe, Edgar Allan 16
"The Poisoned Man" 109–110
prayer 25, 32, 36–38, 55, 69–70, 76, 111, 159, 162–165, 167, 181, 206

Ransom, John Crowe 31
"Rats at Allatoona" 29, 167, 185
"A Real Mix: Rebirth and Gender in *Easter Weekend*" 94–105
rebellion 67, 76, 159, 162–163, 205, 210–221, 225–226
"Recording the Spirit Voices" 164, 178
"Red Swan" 57, 182–183
"Rendezvous: Belle Glade" 66, 216–217
"Rest at the Mercy House" 163, 167, 185
"The Resurrection" 166
Roethke, Theodore 1, 4, 90, 93, 122, 133, 190, 196, 253, 270
"The Rolling Circle: Memory and Maturity" 136–154
"A Room on Washington Avenue" 150
Rose Hill Cemetery 9, 36, 38, 84, 87, 94, 99–102, 152, 169–170, 181, 209, 222
"Rubbing the Faces of Angels" 47
Russ, Don 156, 176, 213, 236

Sagan, Carl 54, 58, 122, 195
"Scavengers at the Palm Beach County Landfill" 160
"*Searching for the Kingdom of Heaven*: A Spiritual Journey" 155–175
Seay, James 2, 28, 109, 132
"The Second Coming" 114
second coming 124, 165, 174, 179, 183
seeker 89, 91, 124–126, 155–175, 209
"Sermon of the Fallen" 164, 177, 182, 209
Sessions, W.A. 7
Shall We Gather at the River 133
Shapiro, Karl 130
"The Sheep Child" 60, 195
"Shelves on the Clark Fork" 169–170
"Shingling the New Roof" 223–224
"Shooting Rats at the Bibb County Dump" (poem) 42–43, 46–47, 160, 177, 196, 212, 229
Shooting Rats at the Bibb County Dump (poetry collection) 27, 45, 47, 72, 89, 106–107, 112, 136, 144, 151, 158, 188, 212
"Shooting Rats in the After Life" 41–43, 124, 152, 172
"Sierra Bear" 35–36, 185
"Sign for My Father, Who Stressed the Bunt" 18, 50–41, 65, 120, 131, 193, 218, 226
"Sign from My Fathers" 106–119
Silence in the Snowy Fields 27
"Sitting at Dusk in the Backyard After the Mondrain Retrospective" 12
"Sleeping in the Jon Boat" 29, 110

"Sleepless Nights" 30, 142, 232
"The Slug" 122
Smith, Dave 2, 11, 13, 27, 45, 63, 109, 128, 139, 189, 197
"Smoking in an Open Grave" 30, 47, 136, 160, 177, 212
"Snake on the Etowah" 29, 35
"Sounding Harvey Creek" 164, 185, 221
Southern writers (writing) 2, 7–8, 11–13, 21, 30–32, 45, 52, 71–74, 81, 83, 106, 109, 115, 132, 140, 133, 139, 190–191, 204, 212
Sowder, Michael 155
"Speaking into Darkness" 47, 162
"Steve Belew Plays the National Steel" 30, 38, 117
Stevens, Wallace 27, 91
"Still Life on a Matchbox Lid" 24
storytelling 7, 52
Strecker, Edward 211
"Stumptown Attends the Picture Show" 72, 74
Suarez, Ernest 45, 87, 187, 204, 213, 235
"A Sunday Dinner" 83, 85, 234, 236

Tate, Allen 11–12, 15–16, 31
"The Tent Astronomer" 164, 186
"A Tent Beside a River" 179, 182, 208
"Thanatopsis" 209
"Those Winter Sundays" 19–20
"Three-quarter Moon and Moment of Grace" 40–41, 153, 174
"To Own My Father's Name: Not Hiding the Masculine" 204–235
"Tradition and the Individual Talent" 11
transcendence 34–35, 44–46, 50, 93, 109, 111, 115, 120, 122–124, 156–158, 160, 203, 208, 253–254, 256, 261
"A Trucker Breaks Down" 177
"A Trucker Drives Through His Lost Youth" 137
"Turn Your Radio On" 207–208, 212–213, 235–236
"Turning the Double Play" 110–111

"Under a Cradled Moon" 32, 137, 165, 182, 219
"Under the Boathouse" 16, 65–66, 110, 138–140, 165, 188, 192
Under the Vulture-Tree (collection of poems) 29, 33, 35, 48, 57–59, 166, 179, 221
"Under the Vulture-Tree" (poem) 120, 137, 167, 180, 184, 190–191, 193–194
"'Up Toward Light': Resurrection, Transfiguration, Metamorphosis, and Evolution in *Armored Hearts*" 176–186

Vagrant Grace 4, 20, 30, 38, 45, 48, 51, 56, 71–73, 83, 85, 107, 112, 115–118, 123, 143–

144, 146–147, 150, 152, 156, 159, 167, 170, 172, 204, 227, 231, 235–237
Vanderbilt Fugitives and Agrarians 12, 14–18, 20–21, 89, 236
vengeance 85, 159–160, 235
"vigilance" 41, 44, 154, 174, 248, 257, 267
"The Vigilant Words of David Bottoms" 11–26
violence 7–8, 11, 29, 36, 52, 83, 92, 97, 147–149, 159–164, 171, 195, 199, 201, 232–233
"The Voices of Wives Dreaming" 57–58, 156, 166, 222

"A Walk to Carter's Lake" 38, 116, 147
"Walking the Floor Over You" 24
"Walkulla: Chasing the Gator's Eye" 29
Walsh, William 120
Waltzing Through the Endtime 1, 3, 15, 20–22, 25, 30, 39–41, 48–49, 56, 84, 116, 123–124, 128, 134, 150, 152–154, 156–157, 159, 171–172, 174–175, 240, 261, 264, 267
"Warbler at Howell's Drive-In" 229
"Warbling with TV in the Background" 87–93
Warren, Robert Penn 2, 4, 15, 45, 48, 68, 89, 91, 109, 121, 124, 126, 128–129, 132–133, 136, 139, 143, 153, 155, 157, 163168, 187–189, 191, 196, 203–204, 241, 245, 266–267

The Waste Land 93, 225
"Watching Gators at Ray Boone's Reptile Farm" 27, 28–29, 48, 184, 196
Welty, Eudora 8, 11
"What Is Not Poetry" 130
"White Shrouds" 57, 166, 190, 221–222
Whitman, Walt Award 45, 89, 136, 155, 187
Wilson, A.N. *Jesus: A Life* 69
"The Window" 212–213
Wordsworth, William ("spontaneous overflow") 9
Working the Heavy Bag 24–25
The World of the Ten Thousand Things 49
World War II 13, 31, 54, 76, 86, 114, 127, 151, 210, 218, 223, 233, 237
"Wrestling Angels" 47, 66, 87, 136, 139, 144, 156, 159, 177, 181, 212–213, 217, 233
Wright, Charles 2, 12–16, 21–22, 24, 48–51, 115–116, 129, 39, 143–144, 147, 247
Wright, James 133, 190, 195–196
"Writing on Napkins at the Sunshine Club" 30

yearner (spiritual) 126, 155

"Zion Hill" 36, 38, 169, 181, 209
The Zodiac 90, 190, 214

www.ingramcontent.com/pod-product-compliance
Ingram Content Group UK Ltd.
Pitfield, Milton Keynes, MK11 3LW, UK
UKHW041929140426
5217IPUK00014B/388